D0031928

NO LONGER PROPERTY OF
SEATTLE PUBLIC LIBRARY

THE MONEY PITCH

THE MONEY PITCH

BASEBALL

FREE AGENCY

AND SALARY

ARBITRATION

Roger I. Abrams

 Temple University Press
PHILADELPHIA

Temple University Press, Philadelphia 19122
Copyright © 2000 by Temple University
All rights reserved
Published 2000
Printed in the United States of America

♾ The paper used in this publication meets the require-
ments of American National Standard for Information
Sciences—Permanence of Paper for Printed Library
Materials, ANSI Z39.48-1984

Library of Congress Cataloging-in-Publication Data

Abrams, Roger I., 1945–
    The money pitch: baseball free agency and salary
arbitration / Roger I. Abrams.
        p. cm.
    Includes index.
    ISBN 1-56639-774-X (cloth : alk. paper)
    Baseball players—Salaries, etc.—United States.
    1. Title.
GV880.A27   2000
                                    99-087922

To my mother,
Myrna Posner Abrams,

and my late father,
Avel Silverman Abrams

Preface

I have always been fascinated by the game of baseball. Growing up in New Jersey, a few miles from where the national game was first played in Hoboken, I rooted for the Yankees of Mickey Mantle, Yogi Berra, and Phil Rizzuto. My mother was (and is) an avid Yankees fan. My childhood was a time when most games were played during the day. I would return home after school, and, without asking, would know the Yankees' fate that afternoon, because the ceramic figurine of the Yankee pitcher normally standing upright on the television set would be turned face down on its side if the Yankees had lost. A three-game losing streak—admittedly a rare occurrence for the Yankees in the 1950s—would find the pitcher submerged in our fish tank. (Perhaps that is the origin of the phrase "to go in the tank"?)

This book continues the story of the baseball business I began in *Legal Bases: Baseball and the Law*, published in 1998, where I explored the legal terrain of the game by combining two of my life interests—baseball and law. The story was incomplete, of course. I needed to do more work in disciplines related to law, drawing from the fields of economics, strategic analysis, and game theory that lawyers too often ignore, to better understand the business enterprise that has grown up around the game we first played as children.

Baseball provides a very suitable playing field for discussing the economic marketplace and the tactics of negotiations. It is a microcosm of the economic and interpersonal bargaining that go on throughout life. Baseball is also fun to think about, write about, and read about. If you want to learn something about economics and game theory, baseball provides the full tablespoon of sugar that can sweeten that process. At the same time, if you want to learn how baseball salaries are established, economics and game theory offer valuable tools of analysis.

For the academic, writing a book for a popular audience presents serious challenges. Much of the sophisticated economic literature on baseball is simply unintelligible to the average fan, but this body of work does contain insights worth sharing. There has been very little research directly applying the comparatively new techniques of game theory and strategic analysis to baseball salary negotiations, but after the necessary transliteration of these disciplines into plain English, they provide a systematic way to understand the methods used by clubs, players, and owners to reach agreement on pay levels. I have tried to write a book that is both firmly grounded in the research literature and accessible to the serious sports enthusiast. My study of the baseball enterprise remains a work in progress, for there will always be new sets of questions to answer.

At the same time, the book is filled with stories about the personalities of the game. In preparing this text, I have had the pleasure of revisiting the history of the national pastime, searching for useful illustrations of the salary negotiation process in operation. Reading the biographies of the greats of the game—Babe Ruth, Ty Cobb, Honus Wagner, Rogers Hornsby, John J. McGraw, and Albert Spalding—is nice work if you can get it. For my discussions of the salary arbitration process, I draw upon my own experiences as a baseball salary arbitrator, using publicly available data accompanied by some personal accounts.

The business of baseball faces extraordinary challenges as we enter the twenty-first century, just as it did a century ago when there was only a single twelve-team major league and increasing fan restlessness with the quality of play on the field. And today, as then, the economics of baseball remains at the top of the list of concerns. The financial disparity between the have and have-not clubs appears more marked then ever. There are also now entirely new issues, unimaginable a hundred years ago, that await resolution: Will the complex construct of luxury taxes and revenue sharing included in the 1996 collective bargaining agreement narrow the financial gap between teams? Will the potential financial bonanza of the internationalization of the sport resuscitate the economic health of a business enterprise that perpetually claims to be on the verge of bankruptcy? Will baseball again suffer from the throes of labor unrest when the current collective bargaining agreement expires? Obviously, there is more research to do on the business of baseball. For now it is enough to focus on baseball's money pitch—the fundamentals of the game's salary system.

I owe thanks to many friends and colleagues who read the various versions of my manuscript and offered their suggestions, including Paul Weiler, George Thomas, Marie Melito, Donald Welsch, and Steve Klein. My partner for life, Frances Elise Abrams, not only contributed her important editorial insights but has also shown enormous patience with a grown man's obsession with a child's game. Branch Rickey, the University of Michigan lawyer who revolutionized the modern game, wrote: "I wonder why a man trained for the law devotes his life to something so cosmically unimportant as a game." My involvement with this subject may in fact not be "cosmically important," but it sure is fun.

I dedicate this book to my mother, Myrna Posner Abrams, and my late father, Avel Silverman Abrams. It was they who introduced me to the game and made possible the education that has helped me understand it.

Introduction

Thank you, baseball. The fun is back.
ROGER ANGELL

In his valedictory remarks for the *New Yorker* magazine upon the close of the 1998 "bang-up summer" of baseball, Roger Angell, the game's scribe laureate, reminded those who had written off the national pastime after the labor wars of the 1990s that this sport remains a pleasure to watch. It has remarkable regenerative powers. A contemporaneous New York Times/CBS News poll confirmed Angell's insight: The public's interest in baseball had increased 50 percent since the depths of baseball's manic depression, the near fatal strike of 1994–95.

For a century and a half, Americans have enjoyed the game of baseball, played with nine players on a team, a bat and a ball, and ninety feet between the safety of the bases. Talented young athletes, heroes to millions, play the game for pay. Almost from the moment of baseball's creation as a sport, money has been as much a part of the game as peanuts, popcorn, and Cracker Jack. This book is about the money side of the baseball business and in particular its "money pitch," which sets player salaries and club profits.

All of us have a "money pitch," a surefire strategy we use to see us through a time of trial. It might be a student's study method that aces a big exam, a businesswoman's cultivated touch that clinches a sale, or a craftsman's technique that refines the *objet d'art*. For a major league hurler, the "money pitch" might be his nasty slider or cutter that causes the batter to swat air and not cowhide.

For baseball general managers and the players' agents, the "money pitch" is the presentation in negotiations that makes the deal. In every baseball player's salary negotiation, there comes the moment when the bargaining parties weigh the advantages of an agreement against its costs. Throw the wrong pitch and the deal heads south.

For club owners and baseball players, the last quarter century has seen a revolution in the economics of the professional game. For the best players, free agency and salary arbitration have produced riches once beyond imagination. For the best club owners, the emergence of the modern megabusiness of baseball under free agency has enhanced public recognition and increased private wealth. But not everyone wins all the time, of course. Remember that even the most successful club loses one game out of three and that even the best batters rarely hit safely more than once in every three trips to the plate. On balance, however, free agency has been great for the game.

Deception is an essential part of the national pastime, as Branch Rickey explained:

> In pitching we want to produce delusions, make a man misjudge. We fool him—that's the whole purpose of the game. The ethics of baseball would be violated if man did not practice to become proficient in deception. In other words, you can't go to heaven if you don't try to fool the batter.

Just as pitchers disguise their offerings, batters choke up and punch the ball the opposite way, and runners steal a base when they catch a pitcher off guard, the economic players of the baseball enterprise have practiced deception from its inception. Players threaten to stay home and leave the game unless their demands are met. Owners bemoan their fate and claim they lose money each season, while prospective purchasers line up to acquire their franchises.

Tricks, dodges, bluffs, and clever play are part of the game of salary negotiations as well, where the rule is that you don't tip off your money pitches, but that you must understand the limits of pretense. If you demand too much, offer too little, move too soon or too late, you may end up empty-handed. Reputation is everything. If you are regarded as an unreliable and disingenuous negotiator, you might as well hang up your wing tips. If you are recognized, even feared, as a tough bargainer, you will be respected. Be patient but decisive, open to suggestions, and true to your word, and you might pull off a double steal with both the player and the club happy with the outcome of the negotiations.

For decades, America's sports fans have watched with astonishment as baseball player salaries skyrocketed. Although salaries in basketball, football, and hockey also soared, those in baseball have attracted the greatest public attention, perhaps because the game is the one most people played as children. It looks so easy, at least the way these splendid athletes play it. How could this seasonal work be worth what these men are paid? For most of the 1990s, the average major league ballplayer's annual salary exceeded a million dollars. Why are baseball players paid so much money?

Baseball is more than just another profitable business, of course. It remains the national pastime, and, because of that unique status, it attracts the attention of millions of fans during both the season and the off-season. It is part of the American civilization, an increasingly expensive part. Fans think they end up paying the cost of the increased player salaries through the price of game tickets, although research has shown that increases in admission prices precede, rather than follow, the rise in player salaries. While fans used to focus on a player's batting average, now they pay as much attention to his signing bonus.

The public's consternation has been compounded by the periodic labor disputes that have interrupted the game eight times in the past twenty-five years, by some players' scandalous use of illegal drugs, by the notorious gambling of the sport's most prolific hitter, and by the general, churlish attitude of some of these fortunate young men who seem to have no loyalty for the home team. Ballplayers used to be role models, but no more. Cardinals Hall of Fame pitcher Bob Gibson could say with conviction: "Why do I have to be a model for your kid? *You* be a model for your kid."

Baseball players have always been well paid. In 1869, when Harry Wright assembled the first all-professional team, Cincinnati's Red Stockings, he paid them about seven times what an average worker earned at that time. More than a hundred years later, before free agency became effective in 1976, ballplayers earned about eight times the average worker's salary. By the mid-1990s, however, the multiple had increased dramatically. Now, major league ballplayers, on average, earn more than fifty times the average worker's salary.

This book will tell the story of how these few thousand very talented young men obtain their extraordinary riches. It will explain how agents negotiate player compensation, how salary arbitration works, and how the free agency "auction" operates.

Historical examples are always instructive. Ty Cobb was the game's toughest competitor on the base paths, but he also flashed his spikes when negotiating his salary. He was successful at both endeavors. Babe Ruth, the game's greatest attraction, was its highest paid player during the 1920s and 1930s. Defensive about his level of pay, the Babe insisted the Yankees paid him only what he was worth:

> It isn't right to call me or any ballplayer an ingrate because we ask for more money. Sure I want more, all I'm entitled to. The time of a ballplayer is short. He must get his money in a few years or lose out. Listen, a man who works for another man is not going to be paid any more than he's worth. You can bet on that. A man ought to get all he can earn. A man who knows he's making money for other people ought to get some of the profit he brings in. Don't make any difference if it's baseball or a bank or a vaudeville show. It's business, I tell you. There ain't no sentiment to it. Forget that stuff.

Babe, of course, was correct, but how much *was* he worth? No one has ever forced an owner to pay his players outrageous salaries, but the dynamics of the baseball salary system have caused otherwise sensible businessmen to make some irrational decisions. Using the stories of the stars of the past and some basic principles of economics, negotiation analysis, and game theory, I will analyze the business of baseball, focusing particularly on this salary-creation process. I will try to follow the advice Albert Goodwill Spalding repeatedly gave the editors of his annual *Official Baseball Guide:* "Keep the book free of statistics as much as possible."

Salary negotiations set the price a club must pay for a player's services. This individual bargaining operates under the "private law" of the collective bargaining agreement negotiated by the club owners and the players association, which represents all players at the major league level. The competitive market of interested clubs and available players determines the salaries of players eligible for free agency. The salaries of comparable ballplayers determine the pay of players eligible for salary arbitration. For the remainder, the most junior ballplayers, management and the players' agents negotiate salary terms under a reserve system, with the floor of minimum salaries and benefits established by the collective bargaining agreement. With one potential purchaser for a player's services, the parties do not enjoy equal bargaining power. Novices straight from high school or college normally sign modest minor league contracts, but, as we will see, a few select "bonus babies" can command significant money up front.

The distribution of quality players among all the major league teams is an important issue. If all the best players played for the wealthiest big-market franchises, the outcome of games would be foreseeable and boring. The uncertainty of each game's result is critical to the fans' interests and the sport's entertainment value. Club owners have created procedures, such as the amateur draft, to help equalize the relative playing strength of the thirty clubs. However, other major league rules and practices, such as exclusive territorial franchise rights and minimal revenue sharing, undermine any effort at parity. I will examine how the magnates of the game have wrestled with these economic disparities.

To help in analyzing baseball's money machine—free agency and salary arbitration—I will tell the stories of some colorful characters from the history of the game who played a role in the development of the modern business of baseball. I will first discuss the history of pay for professional athletes. The figure of Albert Spalding—star pitcher, club owner, league strongman, and sporting goods tycoon—looms large over the formative years of organized, professional baseball. His story will guide us through the remarkable transformation of a summertime pastime into the nation's foremost commercial amusement. He helped make baseball a steady, solid business enterprise.

To set the ground rules for the discussion of the salary determination process, I shall explore the major league wage system and the current distribution of salary income among players. After a brief introduction to the basics of the market and fundamental principles of supply and demand that determine player "prices," or salaries, I turn to consider the participants in this salary treasure hunt: Who are these club owners, ballplayers, and agents? What role does the players association have in setting salaries?

I analyze the negotiation process by using as a case study the hypothetical salary negotiations between Roy Hobbs (the character played by Robert Redford in *The Natural)* and the New York Knights. You might remember Hobbs's epochal home run at the end of the 1984 film. How would his performance convert into an increase in his salary were he negotiating today?

Turning from the mythical to the historical reality, I analyze Ty Cobb's successful 1913 salary holdout against the Detroit Tigers. Cobb's attitude about the game—he intimidated opponents by flashing his sharpened spikes—translated into a very successful salary negotiation strategy.

I then explore in depth the operation of baseball's unique system for determining the salary of players with three years of major league service: binding, final-offer, salary arbitration. Although the collective bargaining agreement lists the factors arbitrators must consider and those they cannot consider, the process is designed to encourage voluntary settlements rather than rulings imposed by salary arbitrators. In 1986, 1998, 1999, and 2000, I served as one of these arbitrators, and I tell the stories of some of the cases I heard.

To bring the discussion up to the present day, I next review the rules and practice of the free agent auction, the source of riches for elite ballplayers. I conclude the book with a discussion of those ballplayer characteristics that most bother the fans—ingratitude, lack of courtesy, and disloyalty. Because my friends and colleagues know I have written about the business of baseball and have heard cases in salary arbitration, they ask whether I personally think ballplayers are paid too much. Frankly, the question stumps me. I guess the answer depends on what each person considers "too much." Club owners would certainly prefer paying players less, but that does not mean they are paid "too much." Many players mouth the expected platitudes about their salaries. Pete Rose, for example, offered, "Playing baseball for a living is like having a license to steal." Yet few (including Rose) have ever declined salary increases, proving that players, like owners, are motivated by self-interest. In fact, most would prefer to be paid even more for their services—although in 1960 Ted Williams asked the Boston club to decrease his $125,000 salary because he thought he had had such a lousy season in 1959. (He had batted only .254 in 103 games, with ten homers and forty-five RBIs, far below his career .344 batting average, with thirty homers and more than a hundred RBIs a season in a career spanning eighteen years.)

Nevertheless, is it "fair" for an athlete to earn more than $10,000,000 a year? That seems to be more a moral question than a legal or economic one. The collective bargaining agreement resolves the legal issues, and thus the salaries are perfectly lawful. The free market determines the economic issues, and the factors of supply and demand command these salaries. I do not think that baseball players contribute as much to the national welfare as others in American society, yet few people are harmed by the salary levels of this very small cadre of high-priced talent.

It does us good as a society to have the diversion of baseball entertainment. Baseball remains the most affordable of the major spectator sports. If we see baseball players for what they are—entertainers and not just young men playing a child's game—and recognize the value we receive from their performances, then overall they probably are paid what they are worth. When they are paid too much, the market will correct itself. Baseball club owners compete with other forms of entertainment for a limited resource, the public's disposable income for entertainment. A Broadway musical costs about $75 a ticket, much more than a baseball game and even more than a football game. Admission to a hit movie costs between $5 and $10 a ticket: Is that price too high or too low? Customers exercise their choices based on price and preferences. If people did not like baseball or do not want to pay what it costs to attend a game, they would switch to another activity. Thus by the measures of law and economics, baseball salaries are just right— neither too high or too low.

The 1998 baseball season was a turning point in the history of our national pastime. It was a year of triumph for two remarkable gentlemen ballplayers, Mark McGwire and Sammy Sosa, both of whom broke baseball's longstanding home run record and did so with class and grace. The New York Yankees, no longer a cauldron of temperamental prima donnas, won more games in 1998 than any other team in history, sweeping to a World Series victory. The 1998 season also saw the end to Cal Ripken, Jr.'s consecutive game streak. David Wells, the Yankees' disheveled star hurler, pitched a rare perfect game and then was traded to Toronto for Roger Clemens. Game attendance rose dramatically to above 70,500,000, tangible evidence that the fans had returned to the sport after the 1994–95 labor debacle. As the 1998 season drew to a close, for the first time in over a decade more than six out of ten poll respondents said they were interested in major league baseball, an almost 50 percent increase compared with five years earlier. Baseball anointed a permanent commissioner for the first time since the owners ousted Fay Vincent from that position in anticipation of the 1994–95 labor dispute. Bud Selig, the former owner of the Milwaukee Brewers, brought to the commissioner's office the potential for stability and long-term labor peace. Only time will tell whether Commissioner Selig can reverse baseball's well-earned disputatious business reputation.

Baseball's money pitch to the public is that it captures an idealized version of the American spirit. Like the country it reflects, the game is not without flaws, but it has persevered and, at least for the moment, triumphed over its self-inflicted wounds. Each new generation of players and fans is touched by the endearing and enduring qualities of this game. They do not need to be convinced of baseball's valued place in the pantheon of American life.

THE MONEY PITCH

ONE

Play it as a business.
A. G. SPALDING

A. G. Spalding and the Development of Baseball Professionalism

A. G. Spalding established professional baseball as a
stable commercial enterprise—what he termed a
"systematic business"—and earned a fortune
providing sports paraphernalia to the American
public. (National Baseball Hall of Fame Library,
Cooperstown, N.Y.)

Albert Goodwill Spalding's mother had misgivings when, 150 years ago, her precocious teenager left their Rockford, Illinois, home to be paid to pitch for Chicago's Excelsiors Club. Under the prevailing rules of the national amateur association, the Excelsiors, a "gentlemen's athletic club," was not allowed to pay players to perform. To circumvent this situation, the team offered Spalding a position as a grocery clerk for $40 a week, although his primary duty in his new job was to pitch for the Excelsiors. Mrs. Spalding criticized her son for accepting anything of pecuniary value to play a game. Spalding felt differently: "I was not able to understand how it could be right to pay an actor, or a singer, or an instrumentalist for entertaining the public, and wrong to pay a ballplayer for doing exactly the same thing in his way." Although his first visit to Chicago proved short-lived—the Excelsiors folded in a month—it marked his initiation into a world where men made their living playing the game of baseball, an enterprise that would consume his attention for the next half-century.

The life of Albert Goodwill Spalding exemplifies the evolving business and financial side of the game of baseball. He recognized the need to firmly establish the amusement venture as a stable enterprise, and he fiercely promoted the sport. Spalding understood better than most that this game, this pastoral pastime, was an American gold mine, which he would develop as an entrepreneur without peer for almost a half century from the late 1860s until 1908.

Perhaps more than any other figure in the game, Spalding was responsible for establishing professional baseball as a respectable and profitable commercial undertaking, which, although not in the same financial league as coal, steel, or railroads, was of far more daily importance to the public. He fostered the myth of a Cooperstown genesis for the sport in order to construct an American origin for a game actually derived from the British game of rounders. Spalding staunchly promoted the right of club owners to direct the baseball enterprise as a "systematic business." And his Chicago-based sporting goods business, which would supply the balls and bats needed to play the game all over the country, would make him a wealthy man.

The Origins of Professional Sports

Sports have their origins in the basic human instincts for self-protection, religious observance, entertainment, and amusement. In order to survive, primeval humans practiced their fighting abilities, building endurance and skill that would provide food and self-defense. Physical play evolved into ritual hunts, stylized battles, displays of status, and religious ceremonies.

All civilizations have enjoyed organized sport competitions. Sponsors paid Greek athletes for winning athletic events, most importantly in the Olympiad. The word *athletics* itself derives from the Greek word *athon*, meaning "prize." Ancient athletes brought glory to their home cities and, as a result, received honors, triumphant recognition, and payments (including tax exemption for life). Organized sports began as a simple diversion for its participants, much as baseball did in American cities in the 1840s. Following the death of Alexander the Great in 323 B.C., however, sports in Greece became an entertainment for spectators who would pay entrance fees to watch the contests. Athletes won prizes that differed according to the popularity of each event.

Professional sports became an employment opportunity for poor athletes when wealthy patrons began to support their training. Aristotle is said to have paid the training expenses of a boxer named Philammon. Roman athletes formed a *xystus*, a professional organization that ran the contests, distributed the prizes, and made certain its members were duly honored. This ancient guild attempted to protect the rights of its members, representing athletes before the emperor Trajan when he decreased their special allowance. In this representation, however, the *xystus* was not as successful as the Major League Baseball Players Association would prove to be in the 1970s.

Nineteenth-Century Sports Entertainment

Organized sports became a fixture of European and American entertainment during the nineteenth century, and participants were compensated for their performances. Professional cricket was played in England starting in mid-century and was transported to the United

States, where it remained more popular than baseball until the Civil War. However, cricket proved too slow for the strong-willed, fast-paced Americans. Matches would take days to complete. Cricket also required manicured lawns for the bowler, playing conditions that were not readily available in the United States.

Individual, as opposed to team, sports also flourished in nineteenth-century America. Although boxing matches were generally outlawed, bare-knuckled pugilists fought for prizes in matches lasting hours under the blazing sun. In 1849, Yankee Sullivan and Tom Hyer fought a well-publicized $10,000 championship prizefight. County fairs featured foot-racing (called *pedestrianism)* and horse-racing events staged by promoters. Gamblers flocked to cockfighting, a common pastime dating back seven hundred years in England and normally staged at local pubs.

Baseball began as an outdoor diversion in America's growing East Coast cities in the 1840s. On late weekday afternoons and weekends, young men from the newly urbanized, white-collar workforce began to play a variation of the bat-and-ball games that had been common in America for centuries. The game of baseball first took root in Manhattan, where participants formed social and athletic clubs, with the first, the Knickerbocker Base Ball Club, founded on September 23, 1845. A club maintained strict internal rules to insure appropriate behavior. Rather than being paid for their athletic exhibitions, members paid an initiation fee of $2 and annual dues of $5 to participate in the contests, which were always followed by a sumptuous dinner.

The Knickerbockers was an exclusive gentlemen's social organization limited to forty members. It leased a room in New York's Fijux's Hotel to conduct regular business meetings. If members breached the rule against swearing or similar verbal impropriety, the club assessed a fine. Arguing with the decision of the umpire during a match, for example, would cost a player twenty-five cents.

These inaugural participants in what was to become the national pastime were amateurs in name and in fact. They enjoyed playing the game because outdoor recreation promoted good health and because participation in the club contributed to good fellowship. Sportsmanship and fair play stood at the core of the upper-middle-class values of these early baseball competitors.

When the Knickerbockers had difficulty finding a field to play their games at Madison Square in the crowded southern end of Manhattan, they crossed the Hudson River by ferry to Hoboken, New Jersey, where they leased the cricket pitch at the Elysian Fields picnic grove for weekend play. After many intraclub contests, on June 19, 1846, they played the rival New York Base Ball Club in what may have been the first real baseball game. The Knickerbockers lost by a score of 23–1, but they did not use their "first nine," and even supplied some players to the opposition.

By the 1850s, young men on the East Coast had created a sport we would recognize as baseball, played on a diamond-shaped field by two teams of nine players each. Bases were set ninety feet apart. Sixty amateur clubs formed the National Association of Base Ball Players in 1858, and changed an important scoring rule. Previously, under the Knickerbockers' rules, a team needed twenty-one aces (later renamed *runs)* to prevail. Now, the team with the most runs after seven or nine innings was declared the winner. This speeded up the game, which, like cricket, sometimes had required more than one day to complete. The new shorter game made baseball commercially viable as a spectator sport. The initial rules of the National Association, however, flatly prohibited all player compensation.

From a Game to a Business

As the United States emerged from the Civil War with a new entrepreneurial spirit, it was foreseeable that some enterprising ballplayers would recognize the game's potential for profit as entertainment for spectators. Americans were drawn to the game not only to play but to watch it played as well. As Mark Twain said, baseball suited America with perfection: It was "the very symbol, the outward and visible expression of the drive and push and rush and struggle of the raging, tearing, booming nineteenth century." While young men would continue to play baseball on the amateur level, as they do today, the best players of the game soon would soon be compensated for their athletic performance as professionals. Profit, not principles, drove the nation's economic machine, and baseball became a business.

There was a direct relationship between the development of baseball as a profit-making enterprise and the advent of salaries for ballplayers. When entrepreneurs discovered that spectators would pay to watch the games, ballplayers demanded part of the gate receipts. When an all-star team of Manhattan players scheduled a series of challenge matches against a similar assemblage of Brooklyn players in contests held on the Fashion Race Course on Long Island in 1858, the owner of the enclosed playing field charged the four thousand spectators fifty cents each to watch the proceedings. Soon after that, clubs would pay players for the entertainment they provided to paying spectators.

It is likely the first paid baseball player was the "speed-balling" pitcher James Creighton, a "ringer" who first played for various Brooklyn clubs in 1859. He spun the ball toward the plate, leaving batters helpless against his offerings. Creighton's professional career was short-lived, however. On October 14, 1862, he ruptured his bladder while striking a home run and died four days later at the age twenty-one of internal bleeding, a tragic end to the first professional's playing career.

Taking the next step, as clubs moved from having only a few paid players to employing an entirely professional roster, required enormous entrepreneurial skill. In 1869, Harry Wright, the son of an English professional cricket player and a fine cricket player and baseball outfielder in his own right, assembled the best American ballplayers for a club to represent the city of Cincinnati. Aaron Chapman, a young Cincinnati lawyer, had first organized the local amateur Red Stockings club in 1867, and he now raised the capital needed to transform the organization into a professional nine that would boost the identity of the Queen City. But it was Wright who would make it a successful enterprise. As the playing manager, he earned $1,200 for the season, and he paid his younger brother George, the star shortstop, $1,400. Other than the pitcher, Asa Brainard, who earned $1,100, and the third baseman, Fred Waterman, who earned $1,000, the remaining members of the squad were paid $800 each.

In the Red Stockings' maiden season, the club completed a nationwide barnstorming tour with fifty-six wins, one tie, and no defeats. It outscored opponents 2,395 to 574. George Wright batted .519, thus earning his generous salary. Spectators from Massachusetts to California paid fifty cents each to watch Wright's star-studded team defeat their local heroes. The Red Stockings even turned a profit, although a marginal one of $1.39.

Harry Wright had shown that young men could earn a living playing baseball if they were excellent performers whom spectators wished to see play what had become the national game. Young Albert Spalding's scrapbook contained a newspaper clipping about Wright's successful experiment in professionalism. The column also noted that the Wright brothers had opened a sports equipment store in New York, an example Spalding was to follow as well.

It was a small leap from a single all-professional club to an all-professional league with clubs attached to the nation's major cities. On the evening of March 17, 1871, representatives of ball clubs from across the country met in a Manhattan restaurant, Collier's Cafe, on the corner of Broadway and Thirteenth Street, to form the National Association of Professional Base Ball Players, a ten-club circuit. Wright had moved the Red Stockings to Boston, and his team would dominate the league for the next five seasons. Spectators were charged ten cents to watch each National Association contest, at least when they were held as scheduled.

Holding to the schedule would prove rather difficult, for the National Association lacked stability. Any club could join by paying a $10 entrance fee. Some participating clubs did not finish the full season or pay their players on time. The best National Association players would "revolve" from club to club, seeking better and more reliable pay. Only the more prosperous teams could afford to purchase the services of the most talented players. The weaker teams simply folded. Although baseball had become a business, it lacked the league-enforced structure and permanence it needed to be a stable business enterprise.

Driven to dominate this new league, Harry Wright traveled to Rockford, Illinois, to recruit the Forest City's star hurler, Albert Spalding, to pitch for his club. Spalding signed a contract at an annual salary of $1,500. By 1874, Wright had increased Spalding's salary to $2,000, the highest on his club and in the game. Although he later would make his mark as an entrepreneur, Spalding first came to national attention as the best pitcher in baseball at a time when pitchers pitched every day. He won 206 games in only five years, including 24 straight wins in 1875. A. G., as he liked being called, learned more than baseball skills from Harry Wright: He learned how to run a business. By the mid-1870s, Spalding knew he wanted to manage a baseball franchise, and he would soon get his chance.

The National Association of Professional Base Ball Players struggled along for five years. Wright's Boston squad captured four of the five pennants, winning 225 games and losing 60, including a remarkable 71–8 record in 1875. That year, with an annual club budget of $35,000, Wright's Boston team had a net worth calculated at $3,261.07. He had established an all-professional club as an ongoing business enterprise, a worthy ancestor of today's baseball teams. The National Association, however, had not yet developed a reliable business structure for presenting entertainment to the public.

The National League

A Chicago coal baron, William Hulbert, the owner of that city's White Stockings baseball club, recognized that the chaotic instability of the National Association presented a valuable business opportunity for a rival circuit. A stable league with a limited number of clubs joined in a closed cartel could prove very profitable. Hulbert was also peeved at the National Association's leadership, whose Judiciary Committee had awarded his star shortstop, Davy Force, to the Philadelphia club. (Force had signed contracts with both Chicago and Philadelphia, a common phenomenon at the time.)

During the summer of 1875, in preparation for his new business venture, Hulbert assembled a stellar cast of baseball all-stars who signed contracts to play for his Chicago club the following season. He even enticed A. G. Spalding away from Boston for $2,000 a year plus 25 percent of the home gate. Spalding would manage Hulbert's team as well as pitch. A. G. also convinced three of his Boston teammates to join him in Chicago. Hulbert then snatched Cap Anson from the Philadelphia club to anchor the Chicago infield at first base, thereby avenging the loss of Davy Force in the process. Anson was to become the best ballplayer of his era, spending the next twenty-two years in a Chicago uniform as player and later as the club's manager.

Hulbert carried out his scheme to create a new business for baseball on February 2, 1876, at the Grand Central Hotel in Manhattan, where he and seven other handpicked club owners from Boston, Cincinnati, Hartford, Louisville, New York, Philadelphia, and St. Louis formed the National League, a joint venture that has lasted almost a century and a quarter. The "magnates," as they called themselves, would run the league, not the players, as had been the case in the National Association. The circuit would be limited to eight clubs in cities with at least 75,000 inhabitants. (There were only a few dozen American cities that met this requirement at the time.)

Adam Smith observed in *The Wealth of Nations* that "people of the same trade seldom meet together, even for merriment and diversion, but the conversation ends in a conspiracy against the public, or in some contrivance to raise prices." As though to prove Smith's point, as their first order of business the National League club owners fixed the prices they would charge the public. They mandated a leaguewide admission price of fifty cents, at least twice the standard rate in other leagues and five times the price of admission to National Association contests in the early 1870s. (Admission to a baseball match was still only half the cost of attending a Broadway theatrical performance, however.) Each club secured a territorial monopoly, maintaining the prerogative to keep other National League clubs out of its geographic region. Many years would pass before there would be any major league professional rivals in baseball or any other sport to compete for the public's entertainment dollar: It would be fifty years before professional football entered the scene (with Red Grange), and seventy years before professional basketball reached major league status (with George Mikan).

But organized baseball still had to contend with the enterprising spirit of individual ballplayers who had shown the ability to "revolve" from club to club seeking higher salaries. The league owners first prohibited players from changing clubs during a season, which had been a common practice before the advent of the National League. This still left open the possibility of player movement after the expiration of a player's contract at the close of the season. The magnates knew that club competition for players drove up salaries. During the first four years of the National League, player salaries constituted almost two-thirds of the cost of running a ball club, as clubs bid against each other for the services of the best players. To halt this market-driven escalation of prices for players who were freed from their contractual obligations, the owners soon established a leaguewide player reservation system first proposed by Boston's Arthur Soden after the 1879 season. Under this arrangement, clubs could "reserve" five of their players, about half a team's roster. No other club could contract with these reserved players even after their individual contracts had expired. Players considered it an honor to be among those reserved, but across the league salaries immediately dropped by 20 percent.

At first, the reserve system was maintained as a secret agreement among the magnates. Strict adherence to its terms became a condition of continued participation in the league. By 1883, the magnates extended the reservation system to eleven players per club, which in effect was each team's entire roster. They also reached agreement with a newly created professional league, the American Association, not to tamper with each other's reserved players. The reserve system was now fully implemented, and its existence became public knowledge. It would remain the backbone of baseball's labor relations structure for almost a century.

Although criticized by many economists as an artificial constraint to hold down player salaries, the reserve system in fact served the vital needs of the fledgling baseball enterprise. Each team, while independently owned, was dependent on the ability of all other clubs in the league to field competitive squads. To present attractive contests, each club in the league had to be capable of winning contests, since no one would pay to see one-sided matches between teams with vastly different player talents. (While the Red Stockings' 71–8 record in 1875 was remarkable, it was not good for business to have any club so powerful.) Without a measure of competitive balance, the National League would have been doomed.

More importantly, the reserve system insured the financial stability of the business enterprise during its formative years. Player reservation allowed clubs to maintain control over player resources and to depress the prices paid for the services of ballplayers. Economically viable clubs could field competitive teams that could present attractive commercial amusements. The clubs apportioned gate receipts, with a visiting club receiving a 30 percent share, enough to keep clubs in weaker markets solvent if they could keep player salaries low enough.

A. G. Spalding pitched for Hulbert's Chicago White Stockings during the National League's inaugural season in 1876, winning forty-seven games, the seventh-highest season total in baseball history. Injuries curtailed his on-field participation in 1877, but he continued his involvement in the club's business as team secretary, while Cap Anson took over the managerial chores. In 1882, at Hulbert's death, the club's stockholders made Spalding the team's president.

The Business Spirit

Post–Civil War America exploded in commercial innovation. Manufacturing flourished as a flood of immigrants brought cheap labor to our shores. The railroads revolutionized the transportation of persons and products. But America's boisterous marketplace needed order, and industrial leaders accordingly formed giant trusts to control competition and systematize the exchange of goods and services.

A. G. Spalding's entrepreneurial spirit flourished in this atmosphere, and it was as successful as his fastball. He recognized that participants in the new national game required equipment—balls, bats, and later gloves. In March 1876, a month before the opening of the first year of the National League, Spalding opened his emporium for the sale of sporting goods at 118 Randolph Street in Chicago. He also filled the growing demand for information about the national game by procuring, through Hulbert's influence, the exclusive right to publish the *Official League Book*, which he supplemented with his own publication, *Spalding's Official Baseball Guide*. These annual publications touted the successes of the National League and promoted Spalding as the premier commercializer of the sport.

Spalding recognized the market value of selling his baseball products as the only "official" and "authorized" commodities. He paid the National League $1 for every dozen balls it used in exchange for its designation of the Spalding baseball as its exclusive ball. Americans now played baseball with A. G. Spalding's equipment. (A young John J. McGraw saved up a dollar to purchase a Spalding baseball through his catalogue.) Although other ballplayers, most importantly Al Reach, realized the financial potential of such auxiliary sporting goods businesses, Spalding was preeminent, capitalizing on his on-field reputation as the game's best pitcher to became the game's most successful nineteenth-century entrepreneur. He thereby established the model of combining baseball with outside businesses, which continues today as club owners marry the national game to their other commercial interests, such as television and beer.

Spalding's management of the White Stockings and later of the entire National League stabilized the professional enterprise and secured its acceptance as a proper commercial amusement for Victorian America. He always recognized the publicity value of his personal participation in league activities. His greatest stunt by far was the 1888–89 world tour of baseball all-stars.

At a time when the United States was stretching its economic influence around the world, Spalding saw a potential global market for his goods, if only he could create interest in America's national game. The world tour began with games on the West Coast and then moved on to an extended visit to Australia, where large crowds attended the exhibitions. The road show also traveled to Cairo, where the all-stars played baseball on a sandy diamond in front of the pyramids. Games in Italy and Paris did not create much interest, however. The tour played twelve games in the United Kingdom, where A. G. attempted to prove the American sport's superiority to cricket, but without much success. The world tour is often remembered for its grand homecoming banquet, served in "nine innings" at Manhattan's Delmonico's, with remarks offered by Mark Twain. Attendees reveled in a nationalist euphoria, denounced those who would find foreign origins for America's game, and elevated A. G. Spalding to the pantheon of American heroes.

The Marketplace for Players

While president of the White Stockings, Spalding recognized that the reserve system, which bound a player to his club for his entire professional baseball life, both created a marketable asset for management and provided leverage in salary negotiations. If the White Stockings owned the exclusive right to negotiate with a player (which was, in effect, an option), then the club could sell that right the same way as Spalding sold his sporting goods. In an important early example of such a player transaction, Spalding sold Chicago's exclusive right to contract with its right fielder, Michael J. "King" Kelly, to the Boston club after the 1886 season; for this privilege Boston paid Chicago the unprecedented price of $10,000. Kelly was one of the game's greatest "artistes," as the stars of the game were then called, as well as a strikingly handsome marquee idol. He exploited his baseball fame in the off-season, touring on the vaudeville stage, telling baseball stories and reciting "Casey at the Bat." Although he received no portion of the money Spalding received for the reassignment of his contract, Kelly contracted with Boston at $2,000 a season and authorized the club to use his picture for an additional $3,000 a season.

Pure cash sales of players, a common practice in the major leagues until Commissioner Bowie Kuhn aborted Charlie Finley's fire sale of Oakland A's stars in the 1970s, undermined the league's competitive balance. Clubs short on cash would sell their primary assets—their best ballplayers—regardless of the on-field consequences. Although Spalding was not hurting for cash when he sold Kelly, with the transaction he had popularized a financial ploy that would become an essential part of the baseball business. Financially weaker clubs would transfer their stars to richer clubs, much as, before the advent of the farm system, minor league clubs would sell their best prospects to the highest-bidding major league team. The reserve system, initiated as a means to achieve competitive balance and league stability, thus proved to be a successful way to enrich club owners.

Even with the restrictive reserve system effectively reducing player bargaining power, the magnates continued to worry about player salaries. In 1885, the owners fortified their control over the expenses of their player resources by agreeing to an absolute player salary ceiling of $2,000, which was increased to $2,500 in 1889. At the same time, they agreed they would now rent the players their uniforms. What had started as a joint venture designed to bring financial stability to the sport had become a cartel committed to high admission prices, exclusive territories, low player salaries, and blacklisting for anyone who would not submit to league edicts.

With stability and control over player resources, the National League became a significant financial success. Crowds of five thousand per game were common. By the 1880s, annual gate receipts for the entire league topped $10,000,000. The players, however, were not satisfied with their circumstances. In response to restrictive labor practices and collusive salary limits, in 1886 they formed the first union in professional team sports, the National Brotherhood of Professional Baseball Players.

Led by John Montgomery Ward, the stellar pitcher for the New York Giants, the Brotherhood issued public calls for reform. In response to the union's attack, in 1888 the magnates devised an even more restrictive wage system, not unlike that used in industry, which paid players in accordance with their personal conduct and performance. Under the so-called Brush Classification Plan, named for John T. Brush, the owner of the Cincinnati franchise, managers and owners would classify their players according to their "habits, earnestness, and special qualifications," using the prior season's performance as a measure. Under this arrangement, the league's Class A players were to be paid $2,500 a year; Class B, $2,250; Class C, $2,000; Class D, $1,750; and Class E, $1,500. Although some club owners objected, the league put the plan into effect.

Ward's Brotherhood was treated with scorn by the magnates, in particular by Spalding, who by this point had solidified his place as the league's strongman. Finally, in 1890 the players, led by Ward, declared an open revolt against the club owners and created their own league, the Players League. Spalding declared that he would wage war without quarter against this rival in "the irrepressible conflict between Labor and Capital." This "battle royal for the control of professional baseball," as Spalding described it, was fought daily in the press, and Spalding proved a master in using his twin weapons: "printer's ink and the bluff."

The Players League had its greatest success in New York, where the Ward-led club, staffed by the game's biggest stars, pummeled his former team, the National League Giants, at the turnstiles. As that National League club approached bankruptcy, Spalding arranged a financial bailout, joining with three other club owners, each of whom

put up $20,000, to keep the Giants afloat. The National League strug-
gled through the season and then bought out the Player League's dis-
heartened financial backers, who had "unconditionally surrendered."
Spalding announced triumphantly, "When the spring comes and the
grass is green upon the last resting place of anarchy, the national agreement [among National League owners] will rise again in all its weight
and restore to America in all its purity its national pastime."

The Decline of Professional Baseball in the 1890s

In 1891, A. G. Spalding officially retired as president of the Chicago
club, although he continued to exercise control through his handpicked
successor, Jim Hart. The 1890s brought the nation's economy into a
severe depression, the first since the advent of the National League.
Fan attendance at baseball games fell precipitously. For example, the
Baltimore Orioles' attendance at Union Park in 1892 totaled only 93,580
for seventy games. Club owners cut deeply into player salaries, a pat-
tern they would follow in all later economic downturns. The decline in
attendance spurred some commercial innovations, however. One
owner, Chris Von der Ahe of the St. Louis Browns, recognized the additional profit-making potential of concessions at his ballpark by selling
souvenirs to the fans. Von der Ahe also was the first to equip his ballpark with a ladies' restroom, although few women attended the games.

Concerned about the financial health of some of the league's clubs in
the late 1890s, the more prosperous owners began to buy into the financially weaker clubs. The Baltimore Orioles' owners, Ned Hanlon and
Harry von der Horst, bought half the stock of the Brooklyn Bridegrooms,
and the Brooklyn owners, Frederick Abell and Charles Ebbets, purchased half the Baltimore club. Hanlon and von der Horst renamed the
Brooklyn club the Superbas, although the fans sometimes called them
the "Trolley Dodgers," which was later shortened to the "Dodgers." Baltimore shipped their finest stars north to take advantage of the larger
New York market. When John McGraw refused to leave his adopted
hometown of Baltimore, Hanlon asked the twenty-five-year-old to manage what was left of the Orioles. It was the beginning of McGraw's
remarkable managerial career that would span thirty-three years.

In 1899, Frank and Stanley Robison, owners of the Cleveland Spiders, purchased the St. Louis Browns and changed that club's name to the Perfectos. They moved their offices and all of their players of major league caliber, including the great Cy Young, to St. Louis. The decimated Spiders finished the 1899 season at 20–134, the worst record in baseball history. Of course, since the 1890 bailout, Spalding, John Brush of Cincinnati, and Arthur Soden of Boston continued to own stock in the New York Giants.

"Syndicated baseball," the label given to this intertwined ownership, stimulated fan distrust in the legitimacy of the contests. If a single person owned competing teams, fans reasoned, how could the spectators be assured that unrestrained effort at victory was made on the field? Although he had engineered cross-ownership himself during the Players League war, Spalding was appalled at this development and would reenter baseball management in 1901 to put an end to what he defined as syndicalism.

In a sign of things to come, the first player holdout over a salary dispute occurred in 1896. Amos Rusie, "the Hoosier Thunderbolt," had won twenty-three games for the New York Giants in 1895, but he also lost twenty-three while leading the league with 201 strikeouts. The Giants' wealthy new owner, Andrew Freedman, by all accounts a bombastic autocrat associated with Richard Croker and the Tammany Hall machine, docked $200 from Rusie's final paycheck, claiming the right-hander had not tried hard enough. Rusie vowed to sit out the next season, furious at his mistreatment by the club owner. Freedman would not budge, and Rusie held out the entire 1896 season. The other National League owners, who appreciated the fan-drawing power of Rusie's fastball, put up $3,000, and the pitcher reported for the 1897 season and continued his Hall of Fame career with a 28–10 record and a league-leading 2.54 era. Rusie's holdout would not be baseball's last, however.

Competition Between Leagues

A leaguewide ceiling on player salaries is effective only if baseball players have no alternative purchasers for their services. Throughout the dismal decade of the 1890s, player salaries remained low, but that alone did not insure economic prosperity for the clubs. In 1900, facing increased financial jeopardy—two-thirds of the twelve league clubs were unprofitable—the National League eliminated its four weakest franchises—in Baltimore, Louisville, Washington, and Cleveland—dropping to a league of eight teams. This was an open invitation for the creation of a rival enterprise. In 1901, president Ban Johnson renamed his Western League the "American League" and expanded into the cities the National League had abandoned, declaring his eight-club circuit a new major league. It would compete successfully for the public's patronage and the ballplayers' services.

A total of 111 experienced National League players jumped to the rival league, attracted by the offer of an extra $500 in salary. Some were offered quite a bit more. Honus Wagner, the best hitter, fielder, and base runner in the National League, reportedly was offered $20,000 in cash by Washington owner Clark Griffith to move to the new league. Wagner declined, however, and remained loyal to his hometown Pittsburgh Pirates, who increased his salary from $2,100 to $2,700.

At the same time it was facing competition from a rival circuit with greater financial staying power than the ill-fated Players League a decade earlier, the National League experienced an internal schism that threatened the economic model Spalding had nurtured through the 1880s—a league of clubs owned by independent entrepreneurs. Coming out of retirement, he reappeared on the baseball scene in 1901 to lead the opposition to the effort by Giants owner Andrew Freedman to convert the business organization of baseball from a joint venture of independent capitalists to a jointly owned trust known as the National League Baseball Trust. Conceived as a syndicate run by a five-man Board of Regents, the Baseball Trust would own and operate all the games, allocate franchises, and reassign players annually. It would thus maximize profits from the professional game as similar trusts had done throughout the American economy.

Spalding saw Freedman's scheme as a fundamental threat to the national game. Although he did not oppose increasing owners' profits, Spalding recognized that the public's interest in the game depended upon its belief that each club stood on its own, and would prosper by winning and fail by losing. Spalding sought the National League presidency to replace Nick Young, the incumbent who supported Freedman's trust venture. The eight league clubs split evenly, with the western clubs supporting Spalding, and the eastern clubs Freedman. The Freedman forces walked out, and the remaining owners illegally declared a quorum and elected Spalding as league president. While his election was later voided in court, Spalding had succeeded in killing the trust scheme and preserving the business structure of baseball, his life's work.

Spalding's National League sought an end to its competition from Ban Johnson's American League, reaching a peace treaty in 1903. Under the National Agreement, the leagues pledged to "perpetuate baseball as the national game of America." The leagues remained separate entities, but were governed jointly by a three-member National Commission. By assuring that the leagues would no longer compete on the economic playing field, the National Agreement restored the owners' monopoly power in the players market.

Spalding saw as his final duty for the national game to firmly establish the myth of baseball's American origin. Acting on his own in 1905, he appointed a group of baseball experts to determine when and where the game was first played. He then supplied this "Board of Baseball Commissioners," as it was known, with all the evidence it would need—a letter from one Abner Graves, who claimed that "the present game of Baseball was designed and named by Abner Doubleday of Cooperstown, New York, in 1839." On that fateful day, as Graves remembered it sixty-six years later, the creator had halted a game of marbles behind the village tailor store to draw a diagram of the diamond. Doubleday then explained his new game to his young friends and anointed it "base ball." In March 1908, Spalding's commission issued its verdict, affirming the game's Cooperstown conception. It was a quintessential A. G. Spalding exploit; the board's judgment was announced in the pages of his own annual best-selling baseball guide.

The Threat of the Federal League

Organized baseball would not have Spalding's help in contesting its last significant business rival, the Federal League of Baseball. By that time, Spalding had retired to southern California, where he would pass away in late 1915, eulogized as the "Father of Baseball." Baseball had become a successful enterprise for which many could claim paternity, Spalding among them. He had recognized early on that the commercial sport needed a stable foundation and strong leadership if it were to survive and flourish, and he provided both the economic structure and the operational direction needed to reach those goals.

Recognizing that the American public was hungry for more baseball entertainment, the Federal League owners prepared to repeat the American League's successful assault on the established order little more than a decade earlier. Their appeal to major leaguers to jump to their new circuit drove up player salaries, which had been restrained under the major leagues' strict reserve system. As a direct result of the Federal League challenge, the salaries of players who did move to the new association, such as future Hall of Fame pitcher Mordecai "Three Fingered" Brown, increased, as did the salaries of those who stayed with their major league clubs. The Tigers, for example, raised Ty Cobb's salary from $12,000 to $20,000 to keep him in the Detroit outfield. Harry Sinclair, the owner of the Federal League's Newark franchise, relocated from Indianapolis for the 1915 season, offered the Giants' John McGraw $100,000 to manage the team, but he declined to throw in his lot with the Feds. As he explained to the press, "If I had my way, those fellows would be left to die a natural death."

The death of the Federal League did come after two seasons, when the major leagues bought out their rivals after the 1915 campaign. Thus freed from economic competition, major league clubs offered most ballplayers a job, including those who had remained loyal to the National and American Leagues, but at significant cuts in salary. Red Sox center fielder Tris Speaker, for example, was "offered" a 60 percent pay cut, although he had been the only .300 hitter in the Boston lineup for the 1914 and 1915 seasons and was the club's primary gate attraction. Speaker declined the offer. When he would not sign for the 1916 season, Red Sox club owner Joseph J. Lannin sold his contract to Cleveland for $50,000, the highest amount ever paid for a player's contract to that time.

The Pirates were ready to reduce Honus Wagner's salary from $10,000 to $5,700, but he held out, announcing his retirement. The woe-begotten Pirates, in dire need of the "Flying Dutchman" to entice patrons to the park, resigned Wagner at his previous salary. The clubs reduced player salaries even further during World War I, when, buckling to government pressure, the owners cut the length of the season from 154 to 128 games.

Controlling the Supply of Players

A critical aspect of the business of baseball is control over the sources of new talent for the game. As part of the peace treaty of 1903 that ended the economic rivalry between the American and National Leagues, the owners had banned the practice of "farming," which meant that major league clubs could not own the contracts of players in the minor leagues. Clubs circumvented this restriction by selling a player's rights to a minor league club with an "option" to repurchase, but this ploy was banned in 1907. Still, there were no restrictions on the size of a club's roster, and to protect their talent, clubs expanded their rosters. Brooklyn, for example, had sixty-one players in 1909. In 1912, the clubs agreed to an overall limit of thirty-five reserved players, with an in-season limit of twenty-five.

Following the transformation of the governance of baseball to the single commissioner system in the 1920s, the revised National Agreement among the owners did not include the previous restrictions on ownership of minor league players. Resuscitating the moribund St. Louis Cardinals franchise, Branch Rickey developed the farm system approach to stocking major league clubs, which would assure that wealthy clubs and franchises with savvy business leadership would continue to dominate the market for quality baseball players.

Twentieth-Century Salaries

Historically, baseball salaries have been more sensitive to economic downturns than to economic prosperity. The salaries of baseball players in the days of prosperity after World War I remained modest even though baseball profits increased dramatically during this period. Chicago White Sox owner Charles Comiskey was legendary for his parsimonious player salaries. In fact, he would not even pay to clean the team's uniforms, leading his players in 1919 to dub their team the "Black Sox" based on their on-field appearance. Little did they appreciate that this moniker would become their historical nickname, but for very different reasons. Some of the White Sox, undoubtedly induced by their low salaries, were susceptible to the lure of gamblers, who stood ready to pay them for fixing the World Series. When the 1919 White Sox threw the Series, the taint on the game was catastrophic. Judge Kenesaw Mountain Landis, the owner's commissioner, saw to it that none of those players ever earned a major league salary again.

With Babe Ruth's mighty bat leading the way, baseball flourished in the 1920s. The salaries of its greatest stars kept pace, but day-to-day players did not share in the largesse. One day in Philadelphia, it is said, Casey Stengel stood dazed and motionless in center field. When his manager ran out to inquire what was wrong, Casey responded that he was too weak to move because the Dodgers did not pay him enough to buy food.

Spalding's Legacy

A. G. Spalding deserves much credit for making baseball a business. At his death in September 1915, he was remembered by the *Sporting News* for having provided "entertainment for the masses." He was a consummate businessman, seeking profits with stealth and steadfast determination, the same characteristics he showed as an ace pitcher. Aggressive, dominant, manipulative, and ruthless—Spalding stood as a symbol of entrepreneurial America. His legacy was an organized game "played," he said, "as a business," with stable clubs and professional players, the best in the land. Theodore Roosevelt once remarked, "When money comes in at the gate, sport flies out at the window." But Spalding and his partners in the baseball enterprise proved that money and sport can coexist. In fact, money was the engine that drove the baseball enterprise and that brought America its first national sports amusement.

Spalding gave the business of baseball the strong hand and direction it needed when confronted by external rivals and internal dissension. Never doubting his own rectitude, he took control. A remarkable amalgam of populism, self-promotion, and vision, A. G. Spalding accepted the nation's universal acclaim, which, in the end, he undoubtedly deserved.

TWO

We're not playing for marbles.

ROSS YOUNGS, 1920s Giants outfielder, after he crashed into Cincinnati's Babe Pinelli

Baseball's Salary System

After escaping from Cuba through the treacherous waters of the Florida Straits, Orlando "El Duque" Hernandez quickly achieved prominence at the negotiation table with a four-year contract valued at $6,600,000 and on the mound with a 12–4 season for the record-breaking 1998 Yankees. (Scott Halleran/Allsport)

As children growing up in New Jersey, we collected marbles, the brightly colored spheres of glass used at times for a game of skill in the school yard but even more often prized for their beauty. Marbles were for collecting and for trading. I knew I would always be better off if my trading partners *really* wanted what I had. Competition among potential buyers enhanced a marble's market value and thus increased its price. Normally, these transactions involved the trade of one or more of these treasures. Marbles thus became the currency of the neighborhood.

The currency major league baseball club owners use to purchase the labor of ballplayers is more than children's baubles, for they pay these talented young men millions of dollars. Much like my hometown marble exchange, however, the bargaining power of participants in baseball salary negotiations depends, in part, on how much a club owner wants to reach an agreement with these jewels of the baseball diamond. Competition between purchasers elevates price, which is a function of what purchasers want (that is, the demand). The more buyers there are and the more they are willing to pay, the better off the sellers will be.

The most common method clubs and players use to set player salaries is direct negotiations between the representatives of the parties involved. Negotiating a salary may not be as much fun as hitting a home run, but it is as much a part of the game. The outcomes of salary negotiations turn on a variety of factors, including the nature of the market forces applicable to particular players, the relevant structure of rules applied to individual players under the collective bargaining agreement, and the negotiating abilities of a player's agent and the club's representative. Like a shortstop handling a tricky hop, a negotiator must charge the ball and adjust during bargaining. Bobble the ball, and you might lose your chance to complete a play.

Orlando "El Duque" Hernandez

The fabulous 1998 major league season had many surprises and stars—Mark McGwire, Sammy Sosa, Kerry Wood, and David Wells, among others. No one could have predicted a home run race to the finish, with two players surpassing Roger Maris's record set thirty-seven years earlier. Who could have foretold Wood's twenty-strikeout performance or Wells's perfect game? Under baseball's salary system, each of these stars in baseball's galaxy will be well paid for his efforts.

One of the most interesting stories of the year involved a veteran pitcher who escaped from Cuba, where he had achieved fame as the premier pitcher on the national amateur team. Orlando Hernandez had amassed the best win-loss record in Cuban history, 129–47, and was the most popular pitcher in Havana. His father, Arnaldo Hernandez, had played fourteen years in Cuban baseball. He had been called "El Duque" (the Duke) for his generous and gracious behavior in the club-house. His elder son would inherit the moniker.

Orlando's younger half-brother Livan had preceded him out of Cuba. With the help of Cuban American sports agent Joe Cubas, Livan defected when the Cuban national team played in Monterrey, Mexico, on September 27, 1995. Livan went on to become the youngest pitcher to start a World Series game, and as the Series' Most Valuable Player (MVP), led the expansion Florida Marlins to the 1997 championship. After Livan's escape, Orlando was banned for life from playing for the Cuban team in international tournaments out of fear that he too would defect. But he would not be deterred from his dream of playing base-ball in the major leagues.

On December 26, 1997, Orlando Hernandez and seven others left Cuba in a small craft, originally described as a raft, although some doubt that description. Crossing the shark-infested Straits of Florida, they landed on the Caribbean island of Anguilla. The U.S. Coast Guard rescued the eight men and brought them to the Bahamas. There his brother's agent, Joe Cubas, advised Hernandez not to accept a visa to enter the United States directly from the Bahamas, because that would mean he would have to enter the major leagues through baseball's amateur draft. Instead, Her-nandez established residency in Costa Rica and was granted free agency by mid-January. The New York Yankees signed him to a four-year con-tract on March 7, 1998, with $1,000,000 signing bonus and guaranteed salaries of $500,000 for 1998, $1,600,000 for 1999, $1,700,000 for 2000, and $1,800,000 for 2001. El Duque's perilous journey had proven lucrative.

Hernandez's 1998 maiden season was a spectacular success. He started and won his first game in the majors on June 3, and completed the season at 12–4 for the Yankees. He won the pivotal game in the American League Championship Series against Cleveland. Few ballplayers have traveled to professional baseball through such treacherous waters.

The Salary Pyramid

Market forces of supply and demand, which we describe in Chapter 3, set the general level of player salaries. In this chapter, we shall discuss baseball's wage system in the aggregate, much as each club must assess its total salary structure each season. Baseball players are well paid by any measure, but they are not all paid at the same level. Many more ballplayers earn salaries down near the bottom end of the pyramid than at the superstar level.

Baseball's salary pyramid reflects in part the distribution of talent among major league players. It also reflects the fact that players have different statuses under the collective bargaining agreement. Some negotiate in a free agent market; others are left with little bargaining power to negotiate with the club that holds their exclusive rights.

Although fans normally fixate on the salaries of individual star players, major league baseball rosters include twenty-five men. Each club has some highly paid players and many lower paid players. Normally, a club will carry ten pitchers, leaving fifteen men to play the field, eight of them playing every day (nine in the American League, which uses the designated hitter). Some field players platoon on a regular basis, depending on whether the opposing pitcher is a righty or a lefty. Half the pitchers will be starters and the remainder relievers, with one or two specializing in working the late innings and in closing games. Management must be able to pay all of these players at competitive major league salaries if it is to field a successful team. For a club to be successful in negotiations, it must sign its stars, its journeymen, its junior players, and its rookies at salaries it can afford.

Some players move between salary levels during their major league careers based on particularly good (or particularly bad) seasons. Someone who achieves superstar acclaim can live off that status for a number of years and still draw crowds to the ballpark. At some point, however, fans and the club owners react to a reduction in player performance. Indeed, the average ballplayer spends only about five years at the major league level, although established players can have careers spanning two decades or more. But at some point, even the best players must hang up their spikes. It is inevitable.

A Revolution in Baseball Salaries

A player's salary is the product of the structure of the applicable negotiating rules set by the terms of the collective bargaining agreement between the clubs and the players association. These rules have changed over time. In the premodern era, before the players association's extraordinary victories in collective bargaining and arbitration in the 1970s, the negotiating rules were simple. Under the traditional reserve system established in the late 1870s, a reserved player was bound to one club for his career or until that club assigned his contract to another club. Even under the reserve system, club owners lamented their fate. For example, in 1881 Albert Spalding would say, "Salaries must come down or bankruptcy stares every team in the face." Throughout the early years of the twentieth century and perhaps later as well, club owners enforced a uniform, leaguewide maximum salary for their best players.

Every time Organized Baseball faced a challenge from a rival league, the competition drove up player salaries, which would plummet again when the rival was conquered or co-opted. In lean years, for example, the 1890s, owners devised ways to hold player salaries in check while increasing revenue. Then, as clubs prospered in the 1920s, player salaries rose. But during the Great Depression of the 1930s, baseball attendance dropped precipitously—one year the St. Louis Browns averaged only 1,500 fans a game—and baseball player salaries slipped again. Never keen on promotion, club owners belatedly tried to create more fan interest in their commercial amusement. The Cincinnati Reds, for example, hosted the first night game at Crosley Field in 1935, a step long resisted by the magnates, although the technology had been available for decades. Arch Ward, the sports editor of the *Chicago Tribune*, offered the owners the opportunity to showcase their talent at the first

All-Star Game sponsored by the newspaper in Chicago in 1933. (It was fitting that Babe Ruth homered into the upper deck of Comiskey Park in what would be his last full season of competition.) Despite such efforts, the baseball enterprise suffered along with the country. There was simply not enough discretionary income around for fans to afford the fifty-cent admission for regular season games or even a five-cent hot dog.

Before the advent of the union, some owners controlled player salaries under the guise of benevolence. In his autobiography, *Veeck as in Wreck*, the inimitable Bill Veeck, at various times the owner of the Indians, Browns, and White Sox, explained how he negotiated salaries with his players: "I would just as soon give a player what he thinks he deserves, if I can afford it." He found his ballplayers' demands to be quite reasonable, perhaps because they appreciated their subservient economic position. In St. Louis, Veeck said that a half-dozen players signed blank contracts, letting their owner fill in the number, and in response Veeck felt a duty "to be more than fair."

Veeck told the story of how, when he owned the Cleveland Indians, he negotiated salaries with Hall of Fame pitcher Bob Feller:

> Bob and I would each write a figure for his basic salary on a piece of paper and split the difference. The first year, he wrote down $60,000 and I wrote $65,000, so he cost himself $2,500. The next year he wrote down my original $65,000 but my figure was $62,500, which meant he recouped half of his loss. He did a lot better than that, actually. I had Feller on an attendance-bonus clause those first two years, and in that record-breaking second year he earned himself an extra $27,500.

It is hard to know whether Veeck's tales are apocryphal. They do, however, attest to the players' dependency on his "fairness" and their lack of recourse if they were dissatisfied.

Even under the strict reserve system, occasionally club owners showed enormous generosity. Longtime Red Sox owner Tom Yawkey was so thrilled when Carl Yastrzemski led his club to the 1967 pennant that he doubled Yaz's salary. Yaz had carried the Fenway Park team with his Triple Crown performance—a .326 batting average, 44 home runs, and 121 runs batted in—the last time any player led his league in these three categories.

Not all owners have responded to excellence on the field with such beneficence. After an extraordinary sophomore campaign in 1937, in which he batted .346 with 167 RBIs and 46 home runs, Joe DiMaggio demanded a raise from $15,000 to $40,000. Colonel Jacob Ruppert, owner of the Yankee club, offered him $25,000, but not a penny more. DiMaggio stayed home, while the Yankees attacked him relentlessly in the New York press as "an ungrateful young man" who was "very unfair to his teammates." "If he doesn't sign," Ruppert said, "we'll win the pennant without him." In the end DiMaggio did sign and, for perhaps the only time in his glorious career, heard jeers from the Yankee Stadium crowd. A decade later, the Yankees made DiMaggio baseball's first $100,000-a-year player.

Before the advent of the modern protocols that offer options to players eligible for salary arbitration and free agency, ballplayers were left with a Hobson's choice—either accept the club's offer or holdout, hoping for more. Holdouts sometimes worked, but they usually took time—both Amos Rusie in the 1890s and Frank "Home Run" Baker in the 1920s sacrificed a year of valuable playing time at the peak of their careers to leverage an extra few thousand dollars out of their owners. The most celebrated holdout in recent times resulted from the 1966 arrangement between baseball's finest pitchers—Don Drysdale and Sandy Koufax of the Los Angeles Dodgers—to stand together in their contract demands. They sought $1,000,000 over three years, to be split evenly between them. Koufax explained to the press that they had joined forces seeking both "dignity" and "bargaining power." Dodgers owner Walter O'Malley, the man who had abandoned Brooklyn for riches on the West Coast, would not yield to the demands of mere ballplayers. Eventually, the parties compromised and reached a settlement favorable to the pitchers. Koufax signed a one-year contract for $125,000, Drysdale for $110,000, becoming, in the process, the highest paid players in the game at that time.

The joint Koufax-Drysdale holdout has historic importance in the baseball industry for two additional reasons. First, it led directly to the creation of salary arbitration and the contract prohibition on collusion. Second, the players' scheme had frightened the club owners, since a joint holdout of key players would produce enormous bargaining power. By the early 1970s, the owners' concern multiplied with the advent of an effective labor organization that could mobilize and orchestrate cooperation among players. In 1973, the club owners proposed to the players association a new procedure for establishing salaries when a club and a player reached an impasse in negotiations. By preventing all holdouts by players eligible for this process, the use of salary arbitration would insure that there would be no repeat of the Koufax-Drysdale power play. The union quickly agreed to implement the new procedure starting in 1974, sensing correctly that it had received a major gift from management. The owners voted 22–2 to approve the arbitration process, with Charlie Finley of the Oakland A's and Augie Busch of the St. Louis Cardinals voting in the negative. Over the next quarter-century, the salary arbitration system proposed by management would catalyze an enormous increase in player salaries.

To avoid a repeat of the Koufax-Drysdale affair, club owners also sought a flat prohibition of joint player holdouts. During collective bargaining negotiations with the players association in 1976 over the new free agency system, the owners demanded a pledge against player collusion. The union agreed, but only if management would also agree not to collude. The owners agreed to ban collusion because they could not imagine a situation where they would want to work together in such a way, since before 1976 there was no free agent market in which they competed for available talent. By the mid-1980s, however, the dramatic increase in superstar free agent salaries drove owners to conspire to hold down salaries, only to be penalized by labor arbitrators in the three collusion grievance cases based on the Koufax-Drysdale no-collusion clause.

To obtain the full economic benefits of a competitive salary market, the players association pursued litigation—first, based on the antitrust laws, in the federal courts in Curt Flood's valiant but doomed suit, and then privately within baseball's grievance arbitration system. In 1975, arbitrator Peter Seitz upheld a grievance filed by Dodgers pitcher Andy Messersmith and Expos pitcher Dave McNally in which they claimed that the standard baseball player contract contained only a one-year renewal option, rather than the perpetual reserve system management had devised a century earlier. After the owners' futile effort in federal court to overturn the Seitz award, they sat down with the players association to negotiate procedures for administering this new system of free agency. Union chief Marvin Miller, an economist by training, knew that wall-to-wall free agency for all players would depress salaries because of the ready availability of substitutes on the supply side of the market. He wanted to limit free agency, as did the owners, but for very different reasons. Miller wanted a limited number of players available each year so that the owners would compete against one another, rather than pitting player against player, which would depress free agent salaries. The owners wanted to retain their exclusive contract rights to the players for as long as possible. They agreed on a six-year major league service minimum for free agency eligibility. The result was as Miller had predicted: The competition between clubs for the limited number of free agents available each year drove up those players' salaries.

While baseball's superstars were cashing in on the bonanza of free agency, younger players were benefiting from an increase in the minimum salary their union had negotiated in the collective bargaining agreement. Even before the establishment of the modern players association, management had raised the minimum salary from $5,000 in 1946 to $7,000 in 1966. Marvin Miller's first contract with the owners in 1968 further increased the minimum salary by more than 40 percent, to $10,000. The guaranteed floor has escalated gradually in each subsequent collective bargaining agreement. Under the terms of the current collective bargaining agreement, the minimum salary for the 1999 and 2000 seasons is $200,000.

The Rules

Today, clubs and players negotiate salaries under three different sets of negotiating rules. The applicable rule depends upon the length of a player's major league service. Under Article XXI, the definition section of the collective bargaining agreement, 172 days on a major league club's roster constitutes a year of major league service. The negotiating rules are as follows:

1.   A junior player not yet eligible for salary arbitration negotiates his salary much as his predecessors did under the pristine reserve system. There is one purchaser for the player's services—the club that reserves the right to negotiate with him. Clubs obtain that right either by obtaining the player through the amateur draft, by signing an undrafted player, or by acquiring rights to the player by trade or purchase. Although the best junior players today are likely to have agents representing them, most amateur draft choices sign minor league contracts with little negotiating over compensation. When those players progress to the major leagues, they must be paid at least at the minimum salary specified by the collective bargaining agreement.

2.   The rules change substantially when a player becomes eligible for salary arbitration under the terms of the collective bargaining agreement and their club tenders them a contract seeking their continued employment at the major league level. The current collective bargaining agreement provides that all players with at least three years, but fewer than six years, of major league service are "arbitration-eligible." A player with at least two years, but less than three years, of major league service is eligible for salary arbitration if "he has accumulated at least 86 days of service during the immediately prior season" and if "he ranks in the top seventeen percent" of the players in the two-year service group in terms of length of major league service. The eligibility of these "super-two's," as the parties call them, is obviously the result of a compromise reached during collective bargaining negotiations between the owners and the players association.

The effect of eligibility for salary arbitration on player salaries is dramatic. In 1998, the average salary for a player with two years of major league service who was not yet eligible for salary arbitration was $337,425. For two-year players who fell into the top 17 percent of this group and thus were eligible for salary arbitration, the average salary was $734,297. What a difference a day of major league service might make!

Arbitration-eligible players not only have demonstrated their potential as professional athletes but have also made actual contributions to their clubs' success. Although the player must play for his club or not play at all, at the salary arbitration stage his salary is set in comparison with other players around the league with similar performance statistics and major league service. His prior performance on the diamond thus determines his slot in baseball's prevailing wage system, as we shall see in Chapter 7.

3. The rules change again after a player accumulates six years of major league service, when he is eligible for free agency and can negotiate with any major league club interested in purchasing his services. Normally, clubs compete with one another to sign prized free agents, a negotiation system we describe as the "free agent auction." We will explore its workings in Chapter 8.

Baseball's aggregate wage structure, therefore, results from the confluence of many factors. Individual player salaries reflect the negotiating rules that apply at different stages of their careers. Player salaries operate in a dynamic market—one that changes over time and that reflects individual player performance, club resources, and industry conditions. The salary paid players also is, in part, the product of the negotiating skills of both parties. We will focus on bargaining strategies in Chapters 5 and 6.

The Wage System

Superstar salaries make the headlines: Albert Belle, Barry Bonds, Randy Johnson, Bernie Williams, Mo Vaughn, Mike Piazza, and Kevin Brown are paid handsomely to entertain spectators and television viewers. Fans who follow free agent signings might think that all ballplayers earn $10,000,000 or more, but nothing could be further from the truth. One defining characteristic of baseball's wage system is the disparity between the highest and lowest paid players. The highest major league player salary is more than *eighty* times the lowest player salary.

Fans express dismay at the salary of the last man on the roster. How can a "banjo-hitting" reserve middle infielder earn hundreds of thousands of dollars a year? The answer, of course, is that a club owner thinks his services are worth that amount of money. (It may also be that the club is paying the player the minimum salary required under the collective bargaining agreement.) If the club had a better minor league player available at the same price, it would move him to the major league roster.

Before we explore the baseball salary negotiation process and the workings of salary arbitration and free agency, we should review the basic data of the labor market's salary system. How much are major league ballplayers actually paid? Fans sometimes have difficulty distinguishing fact from fancy, and we should ground our analysis on an accurate description of baseball's wage system.

The Superstars

Some ballplayers earn a fortune for the services they provide their clubs. Clubs value their stars' services highly because they are productive performers. As a result of their play, their clubs win games and attract more fans to the contests. Studies have shown that an elite player might add ten to fifteen wins to a ball club's season total. The revenue increase that results from higher attendance may more than cover that player's salary.

As any casual fan of baseball knows, the trend in player salaries has been upward for decades. The first million-dollar-a-year player was Nolan Ryan of the Houston Astros in 1979. The apex of the annual salary pyramid has since continued to rise:

Year	Player and Club	Annual Salary
1982	George Foster, New York Mets	$2,000,000
1989	Kirby Puckett, Minnesota Twins	$3,000,000
1990	Jose Canseco, Oakland A's	$4,000,000
1991	Roger Clemens, Boston Red Sox	$5,000,000
1992	Ryne Sandberg, Chicago Cubs	$7,000,000
1996	Ken Griffey, Jr., Seattle Mariners	$8,000,000
1996	Albert Belle, Chicago White Sox	$10,000,000
1997	Pedro Martinez, Boston Red Sox	$12,000,000
1998	Mike Piazza, New York Mets	$13,000,000
1998	Mo Vaughn, Anaheim Angels	$13,300,000
1998	Kevin Brown, Los Angeles Dodgers	$15,000,000

The highest paid players on each of the thirty major league clubs earned as follows for the 1998 season (including performance bonuses and prorated signing bonuses):

AMERICAN LEAGUE

Club	*Player and Position*	*1998 Income*
Anaheim Angels	Gregg Jeffries, of	$6,000,000
Baltimore Orioles	Mike Mussina, p	$6,755,492
Boston Red Sox	Pedro Martinez, p	$7,575,000
Chicago White Sox	Albert Belle, of	$10,000,000
Cleveland Indians	Kenny Lofton, of	$7,550,000
Detroit Tigers	Bobby Higginson, of	$2,425,000
Kansas City Royals	Dean Palmer, 3b	$5,825,000
Minnesota Twins	Paul Molitor, 1b	$4,250,000
New York Yankees	Bernie Williams, of	$8,300,000
Oakland Athletics	Kenny Rogers, p	$5,000,000
Seattle Mariners	Ken Griffey, Jr., of	$8,153,767
Tampa Bay Devil Rays	Fred McGriff, of	$5,500,000
Texas Rangers	Juan Gonzalez, of	$7,800,000
Toronto Blue Jays	Roger Clemens, p	$8,550,000

NATIONAL LEAGUE

Club	*Player and Position*	*1998 Income*
Arizona Diamondbacks	Andy Benes, p	$6,450,000
Atlanta Braves	Greg Maddux, p	$9,600,000
Chicago Cubs	Sammy Sosa, of	$8,400,000
Cincinnati Reds	Barry Larkin, ss	$5,300,000
Colorado Rockies	Larry Walker, of	$6,050,000
Florida Marlins	Alex Fernandez, p	$7,000,000
Houston Astros	Jeff Bagwell, 1b	$7,945,000
Los Angeles Dodgers	Gary Sheffield, of	$14,936,667
Milwaukee Brewers	Marquis Grissom, of	$5,000,000
Montreal Expos	Rondell White, of	$2,000,000
New York Mets	Mike Piazza, c	$8,000,000
Philadelphia Phillies	Lenny Dykstra of	$6,000,000

Club	Player and Position	1998 Income
Pittsburgh Pirates	Al Martin, of	$2,600,000
St. Louis Cardinals	Mark McGwire, 1b	$8,928,354
San Diego Padres	Greg Vaughn, of	$5,275,000
San Francisco Giants	Barry Bonds, of	$8,916,667

In addition to these top earners, the clubs paid $5,000,000 or more to each of the following players in 1998:

AMERICAN LEAGUE

Club	Player and Position	1998 Income
Anaheim Angels	Chuck Finley, p	$5,000,000
	Ken Hill, p	$5,000,000
	Tim Salmon, of	$5,000,000
Baltimore Orioles	Rafael Palmeiro, 1b	$6,515,828
	Cal Ripken, Jr., 3b	$6,400,000
	Roberto Alomar, 2b	$6,343,771
	Brady Anderson, of	$5,441,843
	Jimmy Key, p	$5,390,825
Boston Red Sox	Mo Vaughn, 1b	$6,625,000
	John Valentin, 3b	$5,250,000
Chicago White Sox	Frank Thomas, 1b	$7,000,000
	Robin Ventura, 3b	$6,100,000
	Jaime Navarro, p	$5,000,000
Cleveland Indians	David Justice, of	$6,500,000
	Travis Fryman, 3b	$5,400,000
New York Yankees	David Cone, p	$6,666,667
	Chuck Knoblauch, 2b	$6,000,000
	Paul O'Neill, of	$5,500,000
Seattle Mariners	Jay Buhner, of	$5,367,702
	Jeff Fassero, p	$5,016,667
Texas Rangers	Ivan Rodriquez, c	$6,700,000
	Will Clark, 1b	$5,812,595
	John Wetteland, p	$5,800,000

NATIONAL LEAGUE

Club	*Player and Position*	*1998 Income*
Arizona Diamondbacks	Bernard Gilkey, of	$5,050,000
	Jay Bell, ss	$5,000,000
Atlanta Braves	Andres Galarraga, 1b	$8,400,000
	John Smoltz, p	$7,750,000
	Tom Glavine, p	$7,000,000
Chicago Cubs	Mark Clark, p	$5,050,000
Colorado Rockies	Darryl Kile, p	$5,492,981
	Dante Bichette, of	$5,291,667
	Vinny Castilla, 3b	$5,050,000
Houston Astros	Craig Biggio, 2b	$6,145,000
	Randy Johnson, p	$6,000,000
	Moises Alou, of	$5,020,000
Los Angeles Dodgers	Bobby Bonilla, 3b	$5,900,000
	Raul Mondesi, of	$5,500,000

In 1998, a total of sixty-three ballplayers earned $5,000,000 or more. With team rosters capped at twenty-five, there are 750 player jobs at the major league level at any one time. Only 8.4 percent of these players earned incomes at these lofty heights.

Other Entertainment Superstars

The compensation of elite baseball players pales in comparison to the annual earnings of other entertainers. Discounting unique events, such as the sale of the *Seinfeld* television show into syndication, which made that sitcom's star *Forbes Magazine*'s 1998 top earner at $225,000,000, the top forty movie, television, and singing entertainers all earned from two to ten times as much as the highest paid baseball players. For example, at $28,000,000 a year Julia Roberts was at the bottom of the list of earnings of the top forty entertainers, Garth Brooks was midway at $54,000,000, and Oprah Winfrey was at the top, earning $125,000,000. Kevin Costner, who had played catch with a fire-balling hurler in *Bull Durham* and with the spirit of his long-departed dad in *Field of Dreams*, earned $41,000,000 in 1998. (Most recently, Costner triumphed on the Yankee Stadium mound as veteran Tigers right-hander Billy Chapel in *For Love of the Game*. His real earnings for 1998 were almost three times the salary of baseball's highest paid pitcher.) Yet no fans of these fine performers raise a hue and cry about such astronomical earnings, nor should they. These men and women entertain us, as do professional baseball players.

The Other End of the Bench

Now let's look down to the other end of the bench, at the salaries of the lowest paid major leaguers. In 1998, 125 players, or 16.79 percent of all major leaguers, were paid exactly at the contract minimum of $170,000. Every club had players on its 1998 roster who were paid at this level. Florida and Detroit carried the most players at the minimum, with thirteen and eight, respectively; Texas, Colorado, New York (Yankees), San Diego, and San Francisco had the fewest, with one each.

During every season, there are more than twenty-five players on a club's payroll as players move up from and down to the minors. Minor league players brought up to the majors earn the required minimum salary on a prorated basis for the days spent on the major league roster. During the 1998 season, the Florida Marlins employed thirty-three different players on the major league roster, twenty-nine of whom were paid $280,000 or less.

Why are these major league players (twice the number of those who were paid $5,000,000 or above) paid 2 or 3 percent of what the salary superstars earn? The economics is fairly simple. Most are young players not yet eligible for salary arbitration and are still bound to their clubs, which reserve their rights. They have no alternative employers competing for their services. The clubs can dictate the salaries they will pay, at least when it is at or above the collective bargaining agreement minimum.

Are junior players exploited by the reserve system? In a competitive labor market, workers are usually paid at their marginal productivity. Admittedly, these junior players may contribute more to their clubs by their performance than they are paid. This *excess productivity* accrues to the club owner. He may pass it on to the fans in the form of lower ticket prices, but that is not likely. Labor economists suggest that, in keeping with the human capital theory, clubs pay players who are bound by the reserve system less than their marginal value to the clubs in order to recoup their training and development costs. Only one out of fourteen minor leaguers ever makes it to the major leagues for even the proverbial "cup of coffee." Fewer still are able to stay at the major league level for an entire career. It costs a club almost $2,000,000 to train every successful product of its minor league system, considering all those who fail to make it to the major leagues.

The Change in Average Player Salary

The extremes of any wage system can be deceptive. One way to describe the baseball wage system is to examine average salaries, although this too can be misleading, because a few superstar salaries distort the average. Averages are useful, however, in comparing changes in aggregate salaries over time.

In 1947, the average player salary was $11,000, slightly more than four times the average American worker's pay. From the advent of free agency after the 1976 collective bargaining agreement until 1998, the average player salary increased 2,633 percent, to a level fifty times that of the average American worker. Again, however, this overstates the increase, because very high free agent salaries distort the average.

A more accurate gauge of salary distribution than average salary is median salary, for as many ballplayers earn more than this amount as earn less. From 1983 to 1998, the median salary doubled, while the average salary increased almost fivefold because of free agent contracts. The average and median player annual salaries for 1976–98 were as follows:

Year	Average Annual Salary	Median Annual Salary
1976	$52,300	*
1977	$74,000	*
1978	$97,800	*
1979	$121,900	*

Year	Average Annual Salary	Median Annual Salary
1980	$146,500	*
1981	$196,500	*
1982	$245,500	*
1983	$289,000	$207,500
1984	$325,900	$229,750
1985	$368,998	$265,833
1986	$410,517	$275,000
1987	$402,579	$235,000
1988	$430,688	$235,000
1989	$489,539	$280,000
1990	$589,483	$350,000
1991	$845,383	$412,000
1992	$1,012,424	$392,500
1993	$1,062,780	$371,500
1994	$1,154,486	$450,000
1995	$1,094,400	$275,000
1996	$1,101,455	$300,000
1997	$1,314,420	$400,000
1998	$1,377,196	$427,500

*Data not available

The statistics show that median salary increases flattened out in the mid-1980s. Management said this was the result of their realization that long-term guaranteed player contracts simply did not pay off on the field or at the box office. The players association had a different explanation—that the constraint on salaries was the direct result of a secret collusive arrangement by the owners that violated the Koufax-Drysdale provision of the collective bargaining agreement. After two arbitrators in three separate grievance cases in the late 1980s agreed with the union, salaries again began to climb.

Analysis of salary data from the 1990s shows the impact of the dramatically escalating free agent salaries. Average salaries are distorted by these "high rollers," who earn $10,000,000 or more a season. By contrast, the relatively flat median salary is not similarly affected and instead reflects player earnings in the middle of the major league salary pyramid, whose height has risen substantially as a result of free agency.

Although players on every club earn at least the contract minimum, and some earn at the multimillion-dollar level, baseball's thirty clubs have vastly different total payrolls. In 1998, the Orioles' payroll ($75,185,921) was more than nine times the Expos' payroll ($8,317,500), and the Yankees' payroll ($65,764,367) was nearly eight times as high. In 1998, there were five players—Gary Sheffield, Albert Belle, Greg Maddux, Mark McGwire, and Barry Bonds—who earned individually more than all Expos players combined.

Although this variance in club payrolls may raise concerns about competitiveness within the major leagues, it has been a characteristic of the baseball business since its inception. The free agent revolution of the last quarter-century, however, has made the financial disparities more apparent. Small-market or lower-revenue clubs always were long shots to win a pennant. For the most part, however, attendance has remained steady or increased for the have-not clubs as well as the haves. Today, low-payroll clubs have become the land of opportunity for younger players who might not receive a second look from more prosperous and successful teams.

Pay by Position

A ballplayer's compensation depends in part upon his contribution to the success and performance of his club. As we have seen, not all players can demand high salaries. In fact, the data indicate that there are markedly different average salaries for ballplayers based on the position they play.

The highest paid baseball players play first base. In 1998, the 25 major league first basemen who played a hundred games or more earned, on average, over $3,700,000. The 10 American League designated hitters who played in eighty games or more averaged over $3,300,000. Outfielders earned an average of $2,900,000. On the other end of the scale were the shortstops, at about $1,500,000; the third basemen, at about $2,000,000; and the catchers at $2,200,000. The 128 starting pitchers with nineteen or more starts averaged about $2,200,000.

Relief pitchers (the 188 pitchers with ten or fewer starts and twenty-five or more relief appearances) were the lowest paid players on the major league roster, averaging $850,000 for the 1998 season.

Bonus Babies: The J. D. Drew Precedent

Although they boast about their successes, big league scouts historically have a losing record in predicting the future performance of teenage athletes. Only 5 to 7 percent of all prospects who sign professional contracts make it to the major leagues. Branch Rickey, who was lauded for being able to place "a dollar mark on muscle," thought he could predict success based on a prospect's character and raw physical attributes. Rickey knew that a coach could teach a pitcher to control his pitches, but he could not increase the speed of those pitches. Traditionally, young ballplayers have received very modest signing bonuses. Even so, Rickey thought the signing bonus was the bane of baseball: "If things come easy," he said, "there is no premium on effort. That's the great deep fault of the signing bonus in my business. There should be joy in the chase, zest in the pursuit."

Today clubs pay significant signing bonuses to their surest picks, but have no guarantees of their success. Bonuses for top draft picks have edged upward as major league salaries have soared. In 1982, the highest bonus was $100,000. By the late 1990s, top draft choices commanded multimillion-dollar bonuses. But although the bonus amounts increased, drafted players still remained tied to a single purchaser for their services. On the other hand, if many clubs could bid for the services of a promising rookie, the price for his services would increase.

In 1998, agent Scott Boras tried to turn his client, J. D. Drew, into a free agent rookie. The Philadelphia Phillies had drafted the twenty-one-year-old Drew as the number two pick overall in the 1997 amateur draft. At that point he had completed a sparkling college career as an outfielder at Florida State University, ninety miles south of his hometown of Hahira, Georgia. On Drew's behalf, Boras declined Phillies general manager Ed Wade's offer of $2,000,000, instead demanding a four-year guaranteed contract for $10–11,000,000. Several Phillies regulars, including Lenny Dykstra and Curt Schilling, publicly ridiculed Drew's demands and intransigence. The Phillies' management denounced Drew and his "Machiavellian" manipulator, the "evil" Boras, in the local press, and it appeared that the future star might have overplayed his hand.

Drew refused to sign with Philadelphia and instead spent the 1997 season playing for the St. Paul Saints in the independent Northern League. Boras's strategy was to have the major leagues declare Drew a free agent, but no one on the management side was prepared to do Scott Boras any favors. When Drew reentered the amateur draft for 1998, the St. Louis Cardinals selected him as the fifth pick. In the end, Boras's strategy worked, at least in terms of his client's salary, for in July 1998, Drew signed a four-year contract guaranteeing him $7,000,000, which, with incentives, could be worth a total of $8,500,000. Agent Scott Boras had shown once again that he was a force with which to be reckoned in the baseball business.

With appropriate hoopla, J. D. Drew joined the Cardinals' AA Little Rock farm team, the Arkansas Travelers, on the Fourth of July, 1998. He moved up to the Cardinals' AAA club in Memphis after forty-six games. By September 8, Drew had made it to the major leagues, where in twelve games with the Cardinals he hit .417 with five home runs, three doubles, and one triple in thirty-six at-bats.

A Single Team: The 1998 World Champion New York Yankees

Baseball players amass performance statistics—hits, runs, and runs batted in—as individuals. But none of these figures really matter if the player's club does not win. No team has won as many regular and postseason games in one championship season as the 1998 New York Yankees. This remarkable club won an American League record 114 games in the regular season, swept the Texas Rangers 3–0 in the Division Series, bested a tough Cleveland club 4–2 in the League Championship Series, and then swept the San Diego Padres in 4 games to win the World Series. The Yankees' team salary structure, although obviously on the high end of the major league spectrum, offers a good example of the compensation spread on every baseball club.

The 1998 Yankee offense was led by Bernie Williams (paid $8,300,000), the league's batting champion at .338 with 97 RBIs, although he missed thirty-one games midseason with a sprained right knee. The Yankees' leading run producer was first baseman Tino Martinez ($4,300,000), who powered 28 homers and 123 RBIs for the club, only the fourth Yankee to have back-to-back 120-plus RBI seasons. (The others were Ruth, Gehrig, and DiMaggio.) The steady play of right fielder Paul O'Neill ($5,500,000) made him the most reliable Yankee. The Yankees' middle infielders were Chuck Knoblauch ($6,000,000) at second base and Derek Jeter ($750,000) at shortstop. Scott Brosius ($2,650,000), the World Series' Most Valuable Player, anchored the infield at third base.

The Yankees rotated players in left field: Veterans Tim Raines ($1,300,000) and Chad Curtis ($1,250,000), and rookies Ricky Ledee ($170,000) and Shane Spencer ($170,000) shared playing time. Veteran Chili Davis ($4,333,333), injured most of the year, filled the designated hitter role at the season's close.

Joe Girardi ($2,850,000) and Jorge Posada ($250,000) platooned behind the plate. Girardi caught David Cone ($6,666,667) and Andy Pettitte ($3,800,000), while Posada caught David Wells ($4,666,666) and Orlando Hernandez ($750,000). Yankee closer Mariano Rivera ($750,000) led the most effective bullpen in the major leagues, which included Jeff Nelson ($1,766,666), Ramiro Mendoza ($275,000), Graeme Lloyd ($875,000), Mike Stanton ($1,916,000), and sometime starter Hideki Irabu ($2,925,000). The Yankees filled out their roster with other players used only occasionally.

The Yankees' wage system shows the enormous salary disparity among players on the same team. It also raises doubts as to the correlation between pay and performance. Obviously, for the 1998 season Derek Jeter was underpaid and Chuck Knoblauch was overpaid. Was Bernie Williams's contribution to the club's success nearly thirty-five times that of Jorge Posada? Orlando Hernandez was a powerful addition to the Yankees staff at a bargain price compared with the inconsistent Hideki Irabu.

Player salaries reflect more than projected performance, even when that prediction is prescient. Salaries are in fact a function of a player's

status under the collective bargaining agreement, his on-field performance, and the bargaining effectiveness of his representatives. All
salaries (except those imposed through salary arbitration, but none of
the Yankees' junior players actually completed the arbitration process
in 1998) are the product of voluntary negotiations between parties with
different bargaining power. The salaries may not be fair, but they are
the result of an efficient exchange between the owner and his players.

THREE

It is more profitable for me to have a team that is in contention for most of the season but finishes fourth. A team like that will draw well enough during the first part of the season to show a profit for the year, and you don't have to give the players raises when they don't win.

CONNIE MACK

The Baseball Marketplace: Economics and Game Theory

The man-child from Baltimore, Babe Ruth revitalized the national pastime after the Black Sox scandal. His colossal paycheck reflected his extraordinary contribution to the game, but when his skills waned, his salary level followed suit. (National Baseball Hall of Fame Library, Cooperstown, N.Y.)

Economists use econometric models made up of supply and demand factors to describe the business behavior of participants in baseball's world of high finance, deferred payments, and guaranteed contracts. Their assumptions and conclusions about economic behavior are not always accurate, of course, but they are useful nonetheless as one way to talk about these complicated events. Economic models will help us understand the process of salary determination.

Within the baseball salary marketplace, club owners and players engage in strategic behavior, exchanging information about their needs, financial limitations, and alternatives to agreement. Following basic principles of economics and using negotiation strategy, the clubs and players address the central term of the employment contract—what the player will be paid for his services as a professional athlete. Clubs and players often interact in predictable ways, conduct we can describe using the tools of game theory and strategic analysis.

Economists value gains that can be achieved by a voluntary exchange between two parties. The baseball player sells his services for a salary the club is willing to pay for those services. Each benefits from the exchange. The player could not do anything else that would bring him more satisfaction and enjoyment, or he would do so. Money is only one way to measure gratification, however. Participation in baseball brings what economists call *nonpecuniary advantages*. Think of the psychic benefits of turning a smooth double play at Yankee Stadium on a lovely night in late September or striking a home run into Waveland Avenue over the ivy-covered walls of Wrigley Field. A club owner, no doubt, could spend his money doing something else and probably reap a higher profit. But baseball brings joy beyond money to owners and players alike.

Connie Mack was correct when he admitted in an unguarded moment that he could realize a larger profit by fielding a cheaper, less competitive team. Even the stoic Mack, however, might concede that owning a perennial loser club that earns more money is less fun than owning a contender that breaks even at the box office. Former Cleveland Indians owner Richard Jacobs, who brought the Tribe back from the abyss, said, "We won't make any money, but we'll have a damn good team." In fact, he had a damn good team *and* he made money.

And what does the economist or game theorist gain by studying the salary-for-services exchange between owners and players? With hard work and clear vision, he or she will reap the satisfaction of understanding how the baseball business operates.

The Basic Economics of Setting Salaries

Before the advent of salary arbitration and free agency, ballplayers and owners enjoyed much simpler lives. Players faced an employment market restricted by rules unilaterally imposed by the clubs under an anticompetitive agreement among the employers. There was one purchaser for each player's services, the club, which reserved the right to contract with him. Economists term a situation such as this, where there is only one purchaser for a commodity, a *monopsony*.

The club owners set forth the rules of this reserve system in the charter of their enterprise, the Major League Agreement. They charged their commissioner (and, before him, the three-member National Commission) with the responsibility of enforcing that arrangement. Under the reserve system, the club offered the player a stark choice—play under the terms the club proposed or decline to play major league baseball. The clubs' monopsonistic market power prevailed throughout baseball's first century.

In the eighteenth century, Adam Smith had postulated that an "invisible hand" sets the market prices for commodities as individual sellers and buyers, acting in their own self-interest, determine what goods and services are worth. In this way, the operation of the market achieves efficiency, the economist's paradigm. Because people act according to their personal incentives and values in addition to pecuniary motives, in the aggregate, the theory states, society benefits.

Today the "hands" that control the salary market of baseball—thirty general managers and a relatively small number of influential player agents—are not "invisible." How then do these participants in baseball's business determine the market value of a player?

Baseball's salary-setting process follows the model used to determine the price of any commodity in the marketplace. Players have a carefully measured record of their performance. We know the batting and fielding performance of field players and innumerable statistics for starting and relieving pitchers. Economists have proven what baseball people recognize intuitively: There is a clear relationship between player productivity and the success of a ball club on the field, at the gate, and in collateral markets, such as local television contracts, team endorsements, and royalties. Better players produce more profits, and thus owners have an incentive to pay more for their services.

Before we examine the salary-setting process further, it will be useful to review some elementary principles of economics. *Price*—here the salary the owner pays a ballplayer—is a function of *supply*—the number and quality of similar players available—and *demand*—how much the owner desires a particular player's services and the number of owners who seek to sign that player. The greater the demand, the higher the price. The greater the supply, the lower the price. When the offering price is accepted by the player, markets *equilibrate*.

Demand, in turn, is a function of the *utility* of the commodity for the purchaser based on individual preferences and the availability of acceptable substitutes. Even with unlimited financial resources, a club owner cannot sign every free agent. The collective bargaining agreement caps the active club roster at twenty-five players from the start of the season until midnight August 31, and at forty players from September 1 until the end of the season.

To be more precise, a player's price is a function of his *marginal utility* to the club. For example, a team with five great starting pitchers would not receive much added value from signing a sixth starter, but would likely find use for an additional slugger who could produce more runs for those pitchers. On the other hand, a team with only two starters of true major league quality would find significant marginal value in signing a third and fourth starter.

Supply is often defined by, among other things, the uniqueness or distinctiveness of the commodity sold. There is but one Mark McGwire (although there is also the 1998 Most Valuable Player, Sammy Sosa, and the future home run king, Ken Griffey, Jr.). There are many players capable of hitting home runs each season, but none is at the level of McGwire, Sosa, or Junior. And there are untold number of men and women who would play major league baseball at virtually any salary.

(I would play for free.) Each potential seller of baseball services brings different qualities to the table, and each purchaser places a different marginal value on each potential seller.

The economic analysis of the baseball business begins with three basic assumptions: (1) Clubs and players act rationally; (2) they seek to increase their private satisfaction (happiness, consumption, and profits); and (3) they have different tolerances for risk. At times, considering the behavior of some owners and some players, rationality appears to be a major area of question. But we must remember that we do not know their subjective preferences, their sources of information, or how they process it. If we did, it is likely their conduct would appear more rational.

A central problem in negotiations and indeed in any economic interchange is incomplete information, or what economists refer to as *information failure*. Participants may think they appreciate what their opposite number wants or needs, but, without an effective communication system, those aspirations and goals are only hunches. People draw inferences from behavior, but their conclusions are inexact. In fact, participants in negotiations may not really know what they themselves want or need. Even if they do, how do they signal that information across the table?

In general, people want more *things*—whether they are items that can be bought with a higher salary or greater profits or intangibles such as more peace of mind that might not flow from money at all. We are all human. But how much more is enough? How much is it all worth to you?

Risk aversion is a fundamental factor in the salary negotiation process. All contracts involve some measure of risk. Will the player perform? Will he excel to a point where he is underpaid by his club? Some owners and players are comfortable taking risk and reap major benefits when the chances they take pay off. Others are risk averse and seek to control the factors that contribute to uncertainty. Because negotiating is a process fraught with uncertainties, parties better able to accept risk are more likely to prevail.

Soap in the Clubhouse Shower

As Yogi Berra once said, "Ninety percent of the game is pitching and the other half is hitting." Although his mathematics were not as accomplished as his on-field performance, Berra knew the value of good pitching. But today's pitchers complete only a few games each season, and starters are almost always replaced by relievers before the game is over. It is said that they are being "sent to the showers," and unlike athletes in most other sports, a player removed from a baseball game might as well take a shower, since the rules prohibit his return to the game.

There is a wonderful story told about Christy Mathewson and a shower during the 1908 season, when he pitched brilliantly for John J. McGraw's New York Giants as a starter and an occasional reliever. It was a hot Chicago midsummer's day. After warming up in the late innings in case he was needed to relieve rookie pitcher Otis Crandall, Mathewson went into the locker room to take a shower. The Giants were coasting toward a 4–1 victory, with Crandall very much in control. The rookie walked the bases full in the ninth inning, however, and McGraw called for Mathewson, who was just emerging from the shower. Dripping wet, Mathewson dressed back into most of his uniform. (His wet feet could not get back into his baseball spikes, so he wore his street shoes. He also could not find his cap.) Out on the mound, he quickly disposed of the final two Chicago batters.

We can assume Mathewson, a fine gentleman of the game, had used soap for this notable shower. What should a club pay for a bar of shower soap? Soap has a definite utility to the dirty consumer and a modest cost to produce for the manufacturer; there are no readily available substitutes, and there are many producers of the commodity in the marketplace. The market price for soap is set by supply and demand. If offered soap for sale at $100 a bar, would anyone (even Jerry Colangelo, Arizona's owner with apparently unlimited resources) buy it? The consumer has alternatives—wash without soap (assuming he or she can afford the water) or make his or her own soap (the common substitute before the twentieth century). Another option is to go without washing, which is not a viable alternative for most folks who want to participate in modern American life, but was the preferred choice a century ago when a bar of soap cost almost half a day's wage.

Turning from soap to sluggers and hurlers, we can follow a similar analysis. In the free agent market, price is determined by utility. A player's utility can be determined, at least in part, by examining his performance statistics. Baseball is a game of statistics, but, as they say, "There are lies, damned lies, and statistics." For a club interested in purchasing the services of a player, the bottom line is the impact of the acquisition of that player on attendance and on the overall performance of the team. Unlike in football, the gate is a critical variable in the baseball revenue picture. In fact, some bonus provisions in negotiated free agent contracts are tied directly to attendance figures. Mark McGwire's contract for his historic 1998 season, for example, included a dollar for every home attendee over 2,800,000 at Busch Stadium. (He earned $395,021 under that provision.) For most contracts, the connection between attendance and salary is indirect. Management must project what the acquisition of a player might do at the turnstile. Will more fans come to see him? The acquisition of a talented player enhances the prospects of a team. More people pay to see a winning ball club. How is this fact converted into the market value of a player?

Although fans would like to believe that every club owner would want to be able to buy the services of available superstars, the economic reality is far different. There are budgetary constraints, and, as noted, the league limits the size of the major league roster. It may not be to an owner's financial advantage to sign every available free agent.

Determining the marginal utility of a player is not an exact science. Baseball intuition plays a critical role, as does the money pitch of the player's agent. Often, the chemistry of a team can be affected, both positively and negatively, by the acquisition of a free agent. The impact of a player on the atmosphere in the clubhouse can turn a good deal bad and vice versa.

It is easier to calculate the marginal utility of starting pitchers. Fans do come to the ballpark to see a particular pitcher perform, which is why clubs announce who their starters will be days before the game. At the 1999 Hall of Fame induction ceremony for Nolan Ryan, Texas Governor George W. Bush, former co-owner of the Texas Rangers, commented: "Fans came to see Nolan Ryan. If you said, 'Nolan's pitching,' the people came. They expected something special—and they got it." Similarly, attendance figures soared for the Houston Astros in 1998 after they acquired six-foot-ten Randy Johnson from Seattle on July 31. In the "Big Unit's" first start, the Astros drew a regular-season record crowd of 52,071 fans to the Astrodome. Johnson's performance on the mound—he went 10–1—assured the Astros an appearance in the play-offs and added about 20,000 additional fans in each of his home starts, more than enough to cover the $1,920,000 the Astros paid for his services in August and September.

Basic principles of economics thus apply in baseball as they do everywhere else in a free market economy. Club decisions are driven by incentives, which in the case of baseball is to field a competitive team and to make a profit. Owners of sports teams also factor noneconomic gains—psychic benefits—into the mix. For example, a club owner may want to acquire the contract of a free agent simply because of the acclaim he thinks it will bring him, not because, by any reasoned analysis, the free agent will improve the club's bottom line. The owner might try to work a favorable deal for the player's services, but money alone will not always control his decision-making.

The Babe's Salary Curve

Because player salaries continue to escalate, seemingly without limit, fans lose sight of the fact that the same economic principles that drive salaries up eventually will drive them down. Players who do not produce will earn less money within the limits set by the collective bargaining agreement's provisions on minimum salaries and maximum annual salary cuts. If their marginal value is lower than these constraints allow, the player will be *released*, or as it is called in nonsports labor relations, terminated. The downturn of the salary curve attracts less media attention than the upswing, but it happens to every player at some time in his career. No one plays baseball forever.

Babe Ruth's salary rise and eventual fall is a useful example of the operation of basic economic principles in America's game. Some sportswriters were quick to proclaim the 1998 Yankees club the greatest baseball team of all time. Baseball aficionados, however, bestow the mantle of "best ever" on the 1927 Yankees, led to immortality by the greatest Yankee of them all—probably the greatest player of them all—George Herman "Babe" Ruth.

Larger than life and true to his image, Ruth revitalized the national pastime during the 1920s after the Black Sox scandal had besmirched the game's reputation. He changed the nature of baseball with mighty blows from his bat, and the game has never looked back. Babe was well compensated for his magnificence both on and off the field. Babe's financial statistics demonstrate both the disparities in salaries within a single club even under a single negotiating rule—the reserve system—and the rise and fall of baseball's salary curve.

Compare the Babe's salary with those of his teammates on the mighty Yankees of 1927. Babe earned $70,000 that year, but other Yankees regulars earned much less: Herb Pennock ($17,500); Bob Meusel ($13,000); Joe Dugan and Waite Hoyt ($12,000); Earle Combs ($10,000); Lou Gehrig ($8,000); Tony Lazzeri ($8,000); Mark Koenig ($7,000); and Wiley Moore, who won nineteen games ($3,000).

The comparison to Lou Gehrig, who followed Ruth in the Yankees' "Murderers Row" batting order, is particularly telling. Gehrig was a remarkable athlete, but he did not share the Babe's crowd appeal or spontaneity. Gehrig was stoic and solemn. Throughout his career, he never was paid even a third of what Ruth had earned. (Much the same occurred three decades later during the Yankee years of Roger Maris, the erstwhile holder of the single-season home run record. The Fargo, North Dakota, native earned only $42,500 in 1961, his sixty-one-homer season in which he won the league's Most Valuable Player Award for the second year in a row. The much more beloved Mickey Mantle, however, earned more than twice that amount.)

Babe Ruth's rise as baseball's redeemer is well known. A hulking scamp from the Baltimore waterfront, recognized early by Brother Matthias at St. Mary's Industrial School for his unique physical attributes, Ruth began playing professionally as a pitcher with Jack Dunn's local minor league club, the Baltimore Orioles. Babe's first contract with the Orioles in 1914 was for $600 for the season, about the annual earnings of the average workingman. He used his first paycheck to buy a bicycle, which he gleefully rode around his hometown. By midseason, Babe was performing so well that Dunn raised his annual salary to $1,200 in May and $1,600 in June, the amount he paid his veterans. Local sportswriters referred to him as "Dunn's Baby," or more simply "the Babe." By July, however, Dunn had hit the financial skids. Competition for attendance from the Baltimore Terrapins of the new Federal League cost the Orioles dearly. Dunn was compelled to sell Ruth's contract, along with those of two other players, to the Boston Red Sox for $25–30,000.

Before joining the Red Sox, Babe served a brief stint in the minors with the Providence Greys (called "the Clamdiggers" by locals) to cure his bad habit of tipping off his curve ball by curling his tongue in the corner of his mouth. When called up to the parent club in 1915, Ruth, at age twenty-one, became one of the major league's finest pitchers, winning eighteen games and losing only eight for the Red Sox, whom he helped to win the World Series that year. In the next three seasons, he compiled a 60–32 record while the Red Sox won two additional World Series, including their 1918 victory over the Chicago Cubs, the last time the Boston American League club triumphed in the fall classic.

For the 1919 season, Ruth told new Sox owner Harry Frazee he wanted $15,000 (only Detroit's Ty Cobb was paid more), more than double his 1918 salary of $7,000. Alternatively, Ruth offered to take a three-year contract at $10,000 a year. Frazee said no; Ruth held out, threatening to quit baseball and work on his Massachusetts farm. Appreciating Ruth's value as a box office draw, Frazee increased his offer to $8,500. Before the club left for spring training and a profitable barnstorming tour with the New York Giants, Frazee gave in to Ruth's alternate demand, a three-year contract at $30,000. Perhaps Frazee knew even then that he would never have to pay Ruth the full contract price, for on January 3, 1920, he sold Ruth's contract and his reserve rights to the New York Yankees for $125,000 in cash and a loan of $300,000, which the Boston owner used to finance his Broadway shows. Ruth, the greatest Broadway show of all time, became a Yankee.

Ruth knew that 2,500,000 people had each paid between 55 cents and $2.20 to get into the Polo Grounds in 1920 and 1921 primarily to see him play for the Yankee club. The Yankees, netting about $1,000,000 profit each year, offered Babe $50,000 a year for five years. Babe said that, if the club would make it $52,000 a year, he would take the offer because he had "always wanted to make a grand a week."

Babe Ruth's performance on the field as an everyday player—his bat was more valuable to his club than his pitching arm—was as prodigious as his economic performance. The next highest paid player on the 1922 Yankees was Frank "Home Run" Baker, who had to hold out for almost two seasons in order to win an annual salary of $16,000. Wally Schang, one of the best catchers in the league, earned $10,000; Bob Shawkey, a three-time twenty-game winner, earned $8,500; and first baseman Wally Pipp, in his ninth season, who had led the league twice in home runs, earned $6,500.

Babe's Decline and Fall

Before the 1930 season, Babe spoke with Lou Gehrig, whose contract was also expiring, about a joint holdout. Gehrig refused; he was too well disciplined for such collective action. Ruth was on his own. In negotiating his 1930 contract with the Yankees, Ruth told the club's magnate, brewery owner Jacob Ruppert, that he wanted $100,000. Ruppert refused, offering only a $5,000 raise from $70,000 to $75,000. Ruth rejected this, held out, and sent a letter to the newspapers saying he was "good for $25,000 a year for life even if I quit baseball today." Babe eventually reduced his demand to $85,000 a year for a three-year contract, Ruppert upped the offer to $80,000 on a two-year deal, and Babe agreed. It was his last big contract.

By this point, Ruth's bat had begun to lose some of its magic. As his playing skills began to erode, he would fall from salary prominence. In 1932, Ruth still hit a notable .341, but relinquished the league's lead in home runs, which he had held in twelve of the prior fourteen seasons. The country was experiencing the worst of the economic depression, baseball attendance was down, and most other ballplayers were taking pay cuts. In 1932, when Ruth's two-year, $80,000-a-year deal expired, Ruppert sent him a $70,000 contract for the season. After two months had passed without an agreement, both compromised at $75,000. The die was cast, however. Ruth's value to the Yankees was on the downswing, as was his salary curve.

By 1933, the bargaining power had shifted as Ruth's powers continued to decline. Ruppert sent Ruth a contract in January with a one-third salary cut to $50,000. Ruth returned the contract unsigned, and they "negotiated" in the press. Babe said he would accept a 10 or 15 percent cut, "but $25,000 is no cut, that's an amputation." He and Ruppert met in spring training in Florida, and Ruth offered to accept $60,000, but Ruppert refused to budge. Babe came down to $55,000. Ruppert stood pat and told the press: "If Ruth does not sign by March 29, he will not be taken north with the team. Furthermore, if he does not come to terms by then, the present offer of $50,000 will be lowered. Ruth has come down in his demands, but I told him I cannot possibly sign him for more than $50,000." Four days later, on March 22, Ruth caved in. Ruppert let him save face, however, by telling the press: "We have reached an agreement. I asked Ruth what he wanted, and he said, 'I'll take $52,000.' I told him that was all right, and that ended the matter."

The following year, 1934, after Ruth's batting average had slipped again to barely above .300, the Yankees offered him $25,000 as their "top offer." At this salary, Babe would still earn more than twenty times the average worker's salary during the depths of the Depression. Babe again visited Ruppert at his brewery, and they reached an agreement. Ruppert told the press: "I asked Babe if he would sign for $25,000 and he said he thought he should get $35,000. After further discussion, I agreed." In two years, Babe's annual salary had been cut $45,000. The next year, after a dismal performance in 1934, Ruppert released Ruth, who was signed by the Boston Braves as assistant field manager, an honorary title with no duties. He appeared as a player in twenty-eight games. The end of Babe's career was as pitiful and precipitate as his rise to fame and fortune had been mythic and meteoric.

Game Theory

An analysis of Ruth's success and failure in salary negotiations shows the operation of game theory, the systematic study of conflict and the strategies used to resolve disputes. Every conflict is a "game" of sorts, with the participants as the "players" and the negotiation strategy and tactics as the resolution methodology. These are games not of chance or even skill but of strategy.

Each participant seeks to maximize the expected payoff of the nego-tiations. Agreement is not inevitable, of course. Baseball salary negoti-ations might end in an impasse without a signed contract. In fact, the potential for no agreement and the costs the parties might then incur are forces that press the parties toward agreement.

Games are conducted under conditions of uncertainty. All games require communication, the conventions the parties use to exchange information (and disinformation) and to launch negotiation tactics such as threats, promises, and commitments. Game theorists refer to some communications as "cheap talk," pronouncements that are costless, nonverifiable, and nonbinding, even though they may convey informa-tion. Without a communication system, negotiations will fail. In base-ball salary negotiations, much time is spent in this information exchange, some of it very public, much of it merely puffing, and some of it absolutely vital.

Negotiating a baseball player's salary normally is a form of what game theorists term *distributive bargaining*. As Howard Raiffa, one of the orig-inal thinkers in game theory, wrote in *The Art and Science of Negotiation*, in distributive bargaining "the parties have almost strictly opposing interests on that issue: the more you get, the less the other party gets, and—with some exceptions and provisos—you want as much as you can get." This negotiation protocol describes win-lose bargaining, the bane of modern commentators who preach principled win-win negotiations. We will employ both approaches in analyzing negotiation strategy in Chapter 5.

In game theory parlance, the player is the "maximizer," seeking to sell his services at a higher price. The club is the "minimizer," seeking to buy the player's services at a lower price. Both act within limits, how-ever. Too much success in negotiating creates attendant risks of loss to both parties.

The "exceptions and provisos" to the theory of distributive bargain-ing that Raiffa mentions have real meaning in the baseball context for four reasons: First, as we have seen, the collective bargaining agree-ment sets the absolute floor price in all salary negotiations; second, although a club may not want its player to get rich at its expense, it does want the player to be sufficiently satisfied with his compensation to perform at his highest level; third, a club does not want its player to sign with a rival club; fourth, a player may want more, but not so much more as to keep the club from assembling a squad of other talented players who can compete for the pennant.

Baseball salary negotiations differ from pure distributive bargaining in a number of other important ways. Salary negotiations are not a one-time-only, isolated process. Each negotiation has vertical impacts on future negotiations with that player and horizontal impacts on concurrent negotiations with other players. Psychological wounds inflicted during one set of negotiations may not heal in time for subsequent negotiations between the club and the player. Furthermore, because a club negotiates contracts with many players at the same time, the results of one salary negotiation affects the others.

In *The Strategy of Conflict*, Thomas C. Schelling's monumental 1960 work, the author explored the theory of strategic behavior as applied to international relations. His insights are valuable in understanding baseball salary negotiations as well. Schelling emphasized that games of strategy must assume rationality on the part of both parties to a negotiation, since total irrationality on either side would raise grave doubts as to the enforceability of any bargain reached and would undermine future negotiations between the parties. Similarly, mutually damaging behavior jeopardizes the efficacy of the negotiations.

Negotiating contracts under a regime in which the enforcement of contract promises is uncertain or very expensive also undermines the bargaining enterprise. Parties must discount such promises on the possibility that they may prove unenforceable. This is not the case with contracts between a player and a club, however, since they are legally enforceable after they have been approved by the commissioner's office. There is also an efficient, low-cost method of enforcement included in baseball's collective bargaining agreement—grievance arbitration before a permanent arbitrator.

During the course of negotiations, each party employs strategic behavior to influence the conduct and expectations of the other. The most powerful strategic tactic, but one fraught with risks, is the irrevocable *commitment*, whereby a player or an owner announces that he will not accept anything less, or pay anything more, than a stated amount.

In order to make such a tactic powerful, it must attach to the party's prestige or reputation or entail a significant loss if found to be a bluff. In baseball salary negotiations, this can be done by making the commitment in a public forum, such as the press.

Schelling uses the following story to illustrate what it means to make a strategic commitment. Assume two trucks are hurtling toward one another on a one-lane road, with neither ready to give way by driving off the road. To emphasize his commitment, one driver pulls off his steering wheel and tosses it out the window. By relinquishing his power to alter his course, that driver forces his approaching counterpart to choose either a crash or a concession.

Tendering a commitment effectively ends bargaining and converts negotiations into a "take-it-or-leave-it" game. This may produce either an agreement or a stalemate. A commitment must be communicated persuasively in order to be effective. (In Schelling's hypothetical, the opposing driver must see the steering wheel fly out the window.) It must also be the first use of the tactic. If an owner publicly commits that he will pay only $1,000,000 and not a penny more, and if the player at the same time commits that he will accept only $2,000,000 and not a penny less, the parties are at loggerheads. On the other hand, if only one party uses the tactic, it may be effective in producing a solution to the game, albeit under duress. If negotiations deadlock despite one party's commitment, negotiators will have to find an excuse to allow that party to move off his commitment if there is to be an agreement. One common way of doing this is to produce additional data that, when analyzed, could justify a readjustment in the committer's position.

In baseball bargaining, an owner can present to the player an argument based on the constraining impact of the horizontal, intersecting player negotiations: "If I do this for you, I must do it for all my players." It is then incumbent on the player (through his agent) to explain why this principle of equity allows for different treatment for this player. Like cases should be treated alike, but all players are not alike.

The solutions to games often, but not always, involve compromises. Of course, one party can stick with its opening position, or even refuse to enter into negotiations at all. Most antagonists cooperate to some degree, however. The extent of cooperation depends upon their bargaining power within the negotiation framework. Alternatively, creative bargaining—for example, brainstorming options or pairing issues to create a means of compensation for concessions—can alter the matrix and produce agreement.

How do you know who wins in salary negotiations? It is likely that both sides will claim victory, and they may be right. Winning is not an objective measure but rather depends on each party's subjective value system. An owner who keeps a player's salary below $2,000,000 may, under his own value system, have succeeded beyond his expectations. For the player, a salary above $1,000,000 may be a dream come true. It is possible, then, for both parties to win although neither achieves all his goals.

Salary Arbitration Criteria

Game theorists do not prescribe the criteria parties should use in reaching a settlement. In fact, the fairness of contract outcomes, assuming any agreement is reached, is left for others to judge. Rather, game theorists describe behavior and analyze the efficiency of processes in terms of whether they move the parties toward or away from settlement. They worry about the stability of outcomes and their effect on external events. These commentators remain value neutral, able to serve as objective spectators who critically evaluate bargaining protocols and working rules.

The club owners and the players association have specified the relevant terms of their economic marketplace for those players eligible for salary arbitration. The contract factors are a good starting point for describing the determinants of the baseball player marketplace. (We will explore the operation of baseball's unique process for resolving disputes over the salary of eligible players in Chapter 7.) Article VI, Section F(12), of the collective bargaining agreement lists the criteria their arbitrators must use to determine disputes in salary arbitration as well as the factors they may not consider. Although these market criteria are not mandated beyond the salary arbitration process, clubs and players may use similar factors to set salaries for players who are not eligible for salary arbitration because they have insufficient years of major league service or are eligible for free agency.

Article VI, Section F(12), provides as follows:

(A) The criteria will be the quality of the Player's contribution to his Club during the past season (including but not limited to his overall performance, special qualities of leadership and public appeal), the length and consistency of his career contribution, the record of the Player's past compensation, comparative baseball salaries . . ., the existence of any physical or mental defects on the part of the Player, and the recent performance record of the Club including but not limited to its League standing and attendance as an indication of public acceptance . . . .

(B) Evidence of the following shall not be admissible:

   (i)   The financial position of the Player and the Club;

   (ii)   Press comments, testimonials or similar material bearing on the performance of either the Player or the Club, except that recognized annual Player awards for playing excellence shall not be excluded;

   (iii) Offers made by either Player or Club prior to arbitration;

   (iv) The cost to the parties of their representatives, attorneys, etc.;

   (v)   Salaries in other sports or occupations.

Player Performance and Comparables

In the baseball business, the performance and salary of each player serve as the benchmarks for what other players are paid. Although it would be interesting to attempt to define the precise skills and abilities needed to perform at each player position on a team and set a bench-mark rate for each one, much as is done under an industrial workplace job evaluation system, the negotiating parties in baseball do not demand such specificity. They have adopted the principle of pay com-parability, however, and it is the controlling factor in baseball salary determination. This concept in fact has been the principle catalyst for the rise in player salaries over the past twenty-five years.

With junior players not yet eligible for salary arbitration or free agency, the club holds the upper hand in negotiations. An agent might argue comparability, but a club is free to ignore his protestations. As long as the club offers at least the minimum level of pay required by the collective bargaining agreement, the player has no option but to play for the salary offered or not play at all.

The Subsidiary Factors

The parties' collective bargaining agreement lists other factors to be used in the salary arbitration process, including "the existence of any physical or mental defects." Under this criterion, players who have substance abuse problems will suffer in the salary negotiation process. In 1982, for example, Dodgers pitcher Steve Howe filed for salary arbitration after three solid seasons as a relief pitcher—the first in 1980 as the National League Rookie of the Year. Howe had become addicted to cocaine, however, mixing the illegal drug into his alcoholic binges. After the 1982 season, at the urging of his wife, his agent, and his club, Howe went to the Meadows in Arizona, a well-known rehabilitation center. At the same time, Howe's club tendered him a contract for the coming season, and he chose to have his salary determined through the arbitration process. He did not prevail, however, undoubtedly because of his well-documented "physical or mental defect."

Similarly, players who regularly spend extended periods of time on the disabled list will likely fail to achieve all their salary aspirations either in arbitration or in free agency. At some point, of course, a player is not worth anything to his club, and, like other employees in a similar situation, may lose his job.

It is difficult to gauge what effect, if any, the other subsidiary criteria might actually have on salary arbitrators or in negotiations. For example, it is difficult to identify any arbitration case where the "recent performance record of the Club including but not limited to its League standing and attendance as an indication of public acceptance" has affected the outcome. Because salary arbitrators make decisions without written opinions, we may never know if these ancillary criteria are considered at all.

There are factors other than those listed in the collective bargaining agreement's salary arbitration clause that also play a significant role in salary negotiations involving free agents. The club's resources, the fact that there are other players the club must also sign, the personal qualities of the player, his agent, and management's representative all come to bear in the complex process of setting salaries in baseball's marketplace.

The Geographic Market

Depending on its nature, a product can have a geographic market ranging from a neighborhood to the entire global economy. Unique items—a rare diamond or a painting by Van Gogh—are likely to have the same market in Anaheim, London, or Bahrain, because they can be transported worldwide and maintain their value. Perishable commodities, on the other hand, have a market as narrow as their transportability for sale. Milk and other fresh foodstuffs are perfect examples.

The market for personal services normally is regional, again except for unique individuals whose services might have national or worldwide appeal. But for fungible employees without such unique skills, a localized market, bounded by forces of supply and demand, prevails.

Baseball players sell their personal services within the highly imperfect market created by the sports enterprise of major league baseball, under rules controlling that nationwide economic unit. While there are other potential purchasers of these services—Japanese professional baseball clubs, for example—the transaction costs attendant to trans-Pacific sales and league limits on the number of non-Japanese players per club make this an alternative in only a few situations.

Normally, persons are paid differently for the same personal service provided in different markets. The higher cost of living in cities on the East and West Coasts, for example, produces higher salaries for those employees willing to live there. By comparison, the cost of labor is significantly lower in Midwestern labor markets. This fact of economic life does not operate within the baseball business, however.

Baseball players are compensated based on a nationwide market. Under the baseball salary system, once a player reaches salary arbitration eligibility, he is paid the same in St. Louis as he is in Boston. Based on the cost of living differential, his paycheck will stretch much further in Cleveland than in San Francisco.

Baseball management waged the 1994–96 labor conflict with the players association in an effort to place significant limitations on the existing salary market structure, although it was not just interested in helping the "have-not" teams. Owners first sought to place a cap on total player salaries per club, a cap that would have benefited the Yankees as much as the Pirates. (In fact, it would likely have helped the Yankees more because the Pirates' payroll was far below the cap.) Pressed by the union to agree to an alternative formulation—one more likely to provide added financial resources for the lower-revenue clubs—management settled for a luxury tax on total club salaries that, when fully implemented, will collect millions of dollars from the five clubs with the highest total player salaries. This pool, combined with resources accumulated from other forms of revenue sharing, is then to be distributed to lower-revenue clubs according to a complex formula set forth in the collective bargaining agreement. The clubs that receive this corporate welfare are under no obligation to spend it to improve the teams they put on the field, although that was clearly the parties' expectation. However, initial experience with the luxury tax and revenue sharing raises serious doubts whether the revised market will have any dampening impact on player salary levels.

The Prohibited Factors

The parties' collective bargaining agreement prohibits salary arbitrators from considering a series of factors that many would consider relevant in the determination of salary. The arbitrators, for example, may not consider the "financial position" of either the player or the club. Thus an employer's ability to pay, which is a customary consideration in setting workers' salaries in most businesses, lies outside the foul lines of baseball salary arbitration. This prohibition reinforces the basic understanding that there is one thirty-team market of fungible employers.

On the other hand, an owner's ability to pay plays a significant role in salary negotiations with players not yet eligible for salary arbitration and with free agents. Clubs will bemoan their financial fate, parade unverified figures of annual losses before agents and players, and seek cooperative compromises from their talented employees. There is no way a player not yet eligible for salary arbitration and bound to his club by the reserve system can respond effectively, except by threatening to withhold his services, rarely a good option. A free agent can shop for another purchaser.

The collective bargaining agreement also prohibits salary arbitrators from considering media comments about players. If a player has performed well, it is thus reasoned, his statistics will tell his story, not the local sportswriters. Perhaps the parties who inserted this prohibition knew that once the floodgates were opened to press accounts, there would be no stopping point. Press comments tend to come in matching pairs: A player who is a bum to some is a Babe to others. In salary arbitration, there is one exception to this ban: recognized annual player acknowledgments for playing excellence, such as the Gold Glove Award for fielding, the new Hank Aaron Award for hitting, the Cy Young Award for pitching, and other statistically based honors.

As is common in all forms of arbitration, various offers made by either the club or the player prior to arbitration cannot be raised at the hearing. As we shall explore in depth in Chapter 7, the owners and the players association have created a process of adjudication designed to encourage settlement. If attempts to settle could later be offered as evidence in arbitration, it would chill that private resolution effort. Similarly, during salary arbitration the parties are banned from mentioning the costs of their representatives and attorneys, an issue that is really irrelevant to the arbitrator's job.

Finally, the parties have wisely excluded evidence of salaries in other sports or occupations from salary arbitration. Again, within the closed marketplace of baseball, where salaries are supposed to be based on baseball player performance, the earnings of a basketball player or a movie star are not relevant. There is no way for baseball salary arbitrators to evaluate what the performances of these other entertainers contribute to their enterprises, since the arbitrators face enough of a challenge trying to measure a baseball player's contribution, especially because the critical permissible factors tend to point in different directions.

A Marketplace of Plenty

Baseball's salary marketplace is overflowing with salary dollars for those players able to establish their value to their clubs. The process of allocating those resources consumes time and money, and, as might be expected, it does not operate perfectly. Clubs make mistakes, much as players make errors on the field of play. Unlike a ballplayer's faux pas, however, management misjudgments do not appear in blinking lights on the centerfield scoreboard. Rather, they appear on profit-and-loss statements in the club's boardroom.

Although many young men want to perform at the major league level, relatively few are called up from the minors. Those who do make to "The Show" are the best at the game. Assuming an uneven allocation of talent among the thirty clubs and their farm teams, we might estimate that, at any given time, no more than two thousand athletes are capable of performing at this highest level. Their salaries reflect this limited supply of actual and potential major leaguers. Baseball may have a marketplace of plenty, but there are not plenty of players of major leaguer quality.

The economics of the national game has been substantially revised by events of the last quarter-century. The sport has grown in profitability at the same time its players have reaped the benefits of increased bargaining power and a strong labor organization. We turn now to a closer examination of the participants in this marketplace and examine in more detail their successes and their failures.

FOUR

There ain't much to being a ballplayer, if you're a ballplayer.

HONUS WAGNER

The Ballplayers, the Owners, the Agents, and the Union

Escaping from the coalfields of western Pennsylvania, Honus Wagner filled "the place of honor" in the Pirates lineup for decades and refused lucrative offers of cash to jump to rival leagues. (National Baseball Hall of Fame Library, Cooperstown, N.Y.)

Honus Wagner, "the Flying Dutchman," escaped from a life of working in the coalfields of western Pennsylvania at the end of the nineteenth century by playing professional baseball. A truly decent gentleman and among the finest ballplayers of his era—some say the best ever—Wagner enjoyed a twenty-one-year major league career from 1897–1917 and led the league in batting eight times. (Before the advent of the Most Valuable Player Award, the supreme annual honor went to the league batting champion.) He retired with a .327 average. He played every position on the field except catcher until settling in at shortstop in his seventh year in the majors. Throughout much of his glorious career, Wagner batted fourth in the lineup, the position now called "cleanup" but then termed "the place of honor."

Major league baseball players have come from all walks of life—many, like Wagner, from humble beginnings, others from prosperous suburbia. Players hailed from the inner-city streets, the farms, and the small towns of America. Some—like Christy Mathewson (Bucknell), Frankie Frisch (Fordham), and Lou Gehrig (Columbia)—pursued a baseball career after completing college; other players signed a professional contract right out of high school and served their apprenticeships in the minor leagues. Carl Hubbell spent nine seasons pitching in the minors before he began his Hall of Fame major league career with the Giants. Al Kaline went directly from high school to the majors as an eighteen-year-old, never stopping in the minor leagues. Increasingly, major league players come from other countries, most importantly, the Dominican Republic. They share a love of, and ability for, playing the game, but they recognize that it is more than a pastime. Baseball is their profession. It is how they earn a living.

Wagner was fortunate to have played for Barney Dreyfuss, the owner of the Pittsburgh Pirates. Unlike many of his contemporaries, Dreyfuss treated his players like family, offering to invest their pay and guaranteeing they would not lose their nest egg. During the good years, Dreyfuss would share team revenues with his players. On the road, the owner would rent rooms in a fancy $5-a-night hotel and pay for theater tickets if the scheduled games were rained out. Dreyfuss's beneficence paid off. In 1901, when raids by the new American League ravaged other

National League clubs, the Pirates stayed intact. As a result, the club won pennants in 1901, 1902, and 1903.

Not all owners are saints, of course. A recent example of a despicable magnate is Cincinnati's tightwad, Marge Schott. In his new book, *Leveling the Playing Field,* Harvard law professor Paul Weiler relates startling information about the former general managing partner of the Reds. She would regularly refer to her partners as "money-grubbing, beady-eyed, Jew bastards" and to her black players as "dumb, trouble-making, million-dollar niggers." When the commissioner's office learned of Schott's "offensive and intolerable" language and behavior, she was suspended from the game. A business enterprise that had systematically excluded players of color for more than seventy years would not countenance such overt racism in the modern era.

THE PLAYERS IN THE BUSINESS OF BASEBALL

A fan needs a scorecard to identify the players on the field, especially in a year when league expansion brings many new ballplayers to the majors. A scorecard would also help identify the "players" in the business of baseball. There are four groups involved in the establishment of player salaries—the professional athletes, the owners, the agents, and the union. Each group brings different interests and qualities to the negotiating table.

Today, ballplayers are unlikely even to appear at the table in person. (In fact, the current collective bargaining agreement between the club owners and the players association states that an owner can demand that a player appear in person at only one salary negotiating session annually.) Instead, an agent serves as the player's negotiating representative. The corporations and partnerships that own the thirty major league clubs are represented in negotiations by their agents as well, who are typically their general managers.

The terms of the collective bargaining agreement between the club owners and the players association, an extraordinarily complex document, set the framework for salary negotiations. That agreement establishes, among other things, the minimum salary that clubs must pay major league ballplayers and the basic benefits to which all players are entitled. The union's negotiations with management not only deter-mine the floor for salary negotiations but also establish the rules under which the salary-setting process is conducted. Although the players association's role is vital, the collective bargaining agreement does not set the salary of any player above the minimum, nor does it insure that any ballplayer has a spot on the roster.

THE BALLPLAYERS

Baseball players are a varied group brought together to provide sports entertainment for the North American public from April to October. Many players are highly compensated for their efforts, although more than 90 percent of all the young men who sign a professional contract never make it to the major leagues. Most in fact never make it above a minor league A club. Some toil for years in the minor leagues. A very few, like Shane Spencer of the 1998 Yankees, explode on the major league scene for a September worth remembering. But for every Shane Spencer, there are others who only see the inside of a major league park by paying the price of admission.

There are a limited number of jobs in the major leagues—750 at any one time during most of the season. Athletes compete with one another to advance through the minors to the major league level. And most of those few who do make it stay only a short time, for there is always another player ready to compete for his valued spot on the roster. Rook-ies compete with minor leaguers, starters compete with players on the bench, and everyone competes with players who might arrive in a trade or through a free agency signing. As Satchel Paige said, "Don't look back. Someone may be gaining on you."

Modern players are stronger, taller, and more agile than their coun-terparts of fifty or one hundred years ago. They enjoyed a better diet growing up and use better conditioning equipment on a year-round basis. They bring to the game their athletic abilities—their strength, speed, agility, and coordination—and their commitment, or what base-ball folks call "hustle." Veteran players are better than novices, having learned how to play the game through experience. Statistical analysis of player performance shows that batting averages peak in a player's sixth and seventh year in the major leagues. A player's physical condition tends to diminish over time, however, as do his reflexes. Only a few special players are able to maintain a high level of performance over a two-decade career.

Because of the competition for a limited number of roster spots, major league players must continuously refine and improve their skills simply to stay where they are. Pitchers must learn to throw another pitch to fool the batters, and hitters must practice to keep their batting eye and their swing. A long slump for any player at any time may foretell the end of his career.

The International Pastime

Professional baseball has always attracted the finest Latin American athletes, although before Jackie Robinson only very light-skinned Latinos need apply. The past two decades, however, have witnessed the Latinization of the major leagues. Many of the sport's greatest stars now hail from the Caribbean basin. At least a dozen major leaguers list a small mountain village in the Dominican Republic, San Pedro de Macoris, as their hometown, including the Cubs' Sammy Sosa, the Red Sox' Jose Offerman, and the Blue Jays' Tony Fernandez. Today, more than 20 percent of all major leaguers are Latino, reflecting the significant increase in the Latino influence across American society and culture.

Baseball prospects from outside the United States, Canada, and Puerto Rico are not subject to the annual amateur draft. Thus, with good international prospecting the clubs can find gold at discount prices. Clubs legally sign children as young as sixteen to contracts for a few thousand dollars (and illegally sign even younger prospects with fraudulent birth certificates). By comparison, players subject to the amateur draft cannot be signed until they have finished their senior year in high school. Enterprising clubs, like the Los Angeles Dodgers, maintain Dominican baseball academies to develop their own prospects.

The great, virtually untapped resource for talented young ballplayers remains Cuba, where the game has been played at an expert level for decades. Fidel Castro was a right-handed breaking-ball pitcher with the Havana Almendares in his prerevolutionary days in the mid-1950s.

About thirty Cuban ballplayers—most importantly the Hernandez half-brothers—have defected to play professional baseball in North America. Others have allegedly been enticed by baseball scout Pablo Peguero to escape to the Dominican Republic, where they matriculated at the Dodgers training academy in Campo Las Palmas outside Santo Domingo.

Baseball's efforts at recruiting Latin talent have proven spectacularly successful. Sammy Sosa, whose 1998 performance made him the treasure of the Latin American community, signed with the Texas Rangers organization in 1985 for $3,500. The Dodgers signed pitcher Pedro Martinez in 1988 for $5,000. Today, they are two of the game's most prominent stars in performance and earnings.

The 1998 Yankees were a good example of the diverse origins of modern ballplayers. Eight players hailed from the Caribbean or Latin America—Bernie Williams, Ricky Ledee, and Jorge Posada from Puerto Rico; Chili Davis from Jamaica; Orlando Hernandez from Cuba; Ramiro Mendoza and Mariano Rivera from Panama; and Luis Sojo from Venezuela. Two players came from the Pacific Rim—Hideki Irabu from Japan and Graeme Lloyd from Australia. The remaining fifteen players came from across the United States—from California, Indiana, Illinois, Florida, Louisiana, Maryland, Missouri, New Jersey, New York, and Texas.

Entering the Profession

Until recently, all baseball players began their professional careers by signing contracts for modest salaries. For example, a scout signed Bob Feller off his family's Iowa farm for $1 and an autographed baseball. Ted Williams at seventeen played for the San Diego Padres of the Pacific Coast League at $150 a month. Before the advent of farm systems in the 1920s and 1930s, independently owned minor league clubs would scour the countryside for prospects, developing their potential, and, for the few who panned out, selling their rights to major league owners. In 1940, the Dodgers' Lee MacPhail bought the minor league contracts of two players, paying $75,000 for Harold "Pee Wee" Reese's contract, a very good deal in the long run, and $100 for Pete Reiser's, an even better deal in the short run. Reiser, who led the National League in batting with a .343 average in his first full year in the majors, would, however, play only four full seasons for the Dodgers. On the other hand, Reese would perform at Hall of Fame caliber for sixteen years in Dodger blue, including steady play in seven World Series.

After Carl Yastrzemski hit .650 in high school on Long Island, seven major league clubs bid to sign him. In those days before the amateur draft, clubs could compete for teenage talent, and many clubs recognized the promise of this strapping youngster. The Yankees, for whom Yaz had always dreamed of playing, offered him $40,000. Each competitor club raised the ante, until the Boston Red Sox gave him a $108,000 signing bonus plus a two-year $10,000 AAA contract and also paid his college tuition. Yaz's twenty-three-year Hall of Fame career proved this was a wise investment for the Sox.

Today's major league player development system is a costly and risky venture. Only one out of every fourteen minor leaguers even makes it to "The Show," and most who do only stay for a "cup of coffee." Considering this modest success rate, it costs a club more than $2,000,000 overall to develop a single successful major league ballplayer.

Sources of Player Revenue

A ballplayer's primary source of income is his regular season payroll check. In an earlier age, players would also barnstorm after the close of the season and play exhibitions for pay on off-days during the season. Members of successful teams would share in World Series receipts, welcomed income during an era of very modest player salaries. In 1911, the Philadelphia Athletics' winners' share was $3,655 each, the New York Giants' losers' share $2,436, both more than the average player's full-season salary of the time.

From the earliest days of the professional game, players leveraged their on-field celebrity to increase their off-field earning potential. Players, for example, toured on the vaudeville circuit in the nineteenth and early twentieth centuries. While managing the New York Giants, John J. McGraw earned $3,000 a week for fifteen weeks in the off-season delivering his monologue on the secrets of "Inside Baseball." Pitchers Rube

Waddell and Bugs Raymond starred in a play entitled *The Stain of Guilt.* Even Ty Cobb took $10,000 to tour in *The College Widow* in 1911, but quit after six weeks, claiming the stage lights were affecting his batting eye.

Babe Ruth perfected modern player endorsement marketing. He lent his name and his fame to a broad variety of products—cereals, candy, cookies, soap, men's underwear, and cigarettes. He was not the first ballplayer to sell the commercial use of his name and picture, however. Honus Wagner endorsed an array of comestibles, plus baseball gear, gunpowder, and "nonexplosive" analgesic balm. Coca-Cola, he said, "assisted my mental and physical activity." He drew the line at tobacco products, however, even though he himself chewed and smoked. When he discovered that American Tobacco intended to insert cards featuring his well-known visage in cigarette packages, Wagner protested. A small number of such cards were printed nonetheless, and today each of the few dozen that still exist is worth close to $500,000.

Some players invested their baseball earnings wisely. Ty Cobb bought Coca-Cola stock from his Georgia pals at $1.18 a share. Honus Wagner bought oil wells in West Virginia, and a chicken farm, real estate, and an automobile dealership in his hometown of Carnegie, Pennsylvania. He also tried to start a traveling circus—admission thirty cents—but it folded. John J. McGraw bought saloons, restaurants, and pool halls where he entertained his gambling buddies. He also lost $100,000 in a disastrous Florida land deal.

In 1924, Christy Walsh, who had ghostwritten World Series reports under Babe Ruth's name, persuaded Ruth to invest some of his huge earnings. Babe bought an annuity for $35,000 cash. When the insurance company from whom he purchased it held a ceremony to congratulate him and to tell him he was a lucky man for having invested so wisely, Ruth responded, "Yes, I guess so. There's no doubt I'm lucky. There is also no doubt that you have my $35,000."

A Quick End to a Promising Career

Compared with collision sports like football and hockey and contact sports like basketball, the gentle ways of baseball appear tailor-made for long playing careers for those players with major league abilities.

Longevity in the major leagues is a valuable prize, especially in an era when ballplayers are well paid. Sometimes, however, the end of a major league career comes swiftly and unexpectedly.

On August 16, 1920, New York Yankees submarine pitcher Carl Mays hit Cleveland shortstop Ray Chapman in the head. He died shortly thereafter, the only batter killed by a pitched ball in the history of the game. Herb Score, the Indians' brilliant lefty, was hit in the eye by a blistering line drive off the bat of Yankee Gil McDougald in 1957, effectively ending what was destined to be a Hall of Fame career. In 1967, during the Red Sox marvelous run for the pennant, Tony Conigliaro was hit in the head by California Angels pitcher Jack Hamilton. The pitch shattered Tony C's cheekbone and would have killed him had it been an inch higher. Conigliaro tried to resume his career two seasons later without success. He died in 1990 at age forty-five.

Baseball players have not been immune from the contagions that laid waste to large sectors of the American public. Typhoid fever, influenza, tuberculosis, appendicitis, brain tumors, heart disease, pneumonia, and cancer have all claimed major league ballplayers in their twenties and thirties. Harry Agganis, "the Golden Greek" at first base for the Red Sox, hit .281 with 24 home runs and 108 RBIs in his rookie year in 1954. Shortly after the start of the 1955 season, with his average above .300, Agganis took ill and died of a massive pulmonary embolism.

Fans will certainly remember those modern baseball heroes whose brilliant careers were cut short by tragic accidents. Roy Campanella, three-time MVP and sturdy backstop of the Brooklyn and Los Angeles Dodgers, was paralyzed for life as a result of a driving accident in January 1958. Roberto Clemente, MVP in 1966, died in a plane crash while on a mercy mission in December 1972, carrying food, clothing, and medical supplies to earthquake-ravaged Nicaragua. Thurman Munson, the Yankees captain and catcher throughout the 1970s, including his MVP year of 1976, perished when he crashed his new plane while practicing landings and takeoffs at the Akron-Canton airport in August 1979.

We see our baseball heroes as immortals, but they are not. They are paid well to display their athletic abilities, but like all of us, they are not immune from an injury or accident that can put a quick end to their careers. The brevity and insecurity of a ballplayer's career are what make contract negotiations so critical and put a player's high salary in perspective, since the contract under negotiation may be his last as a major leaguer.

THE OWNERS

Unlike entrepreneurs who build businesses from the ground up, baseball owners purchase ongoing businesses, except, of course, those few who are granted expansion franchises. Historically, baseball owners were individuals who brought to the national pastime the business savvy and financial resources they had accumulated in many different fields. William Hulbert was in the coal business in Chicago when he purchased the White Stockings in 1875 and formed the National League the following year. John T. Brush, the owner in turn of the Indianapolis, Cincinnati, and New York Giants baseball franchises, was a clothing manufacturer and department store owner from Indianapolis. Brush sold the Giants to Charles Stoneham, who made his money during the Roaring Twenties by speculating on stock market investments. J. Earl Wagner was a Philadelphia butcher before he bought the Philadelphia and later the Washington baseball clubs. Many owners were brewers—Harry Von der Horst and Chris Von der Ahe of the St. Louis Browns in the early days, Jacob Ruppert of the Yankees during the first half of the twentieth century, and Augie Busch of the St. Louis Cardinals in the modern days. Charlie Finley sold malpractice insurance to physicians in his native Indiana before buying the Kansas City Athletics and moving them to Oakland. Atlanta Braves owner Ted Turner was a yachtsman. George Steinbrenner of the Yankees owned American Shipbuilding, headquartered in Cleveland and then in Tampa until it went bankrupt in 1993. With few exceptions, the owners have been experienced, astute businessmen, but at times something has happened to them when they purchase a franchise. As Cincinnati Reds general manager Jim Bowden said in 1998, "History should tell us that smart folks become stupid in a hurry when they buy a baseball team."

Starting in the 1960s, baseball ownership began to shift from indi-

vidual owners toward corporate control, in particular by media enterprises. From its inception, professional baseball had enjoyed a symbi-
otic relationship with the press, which needed daily copy to fill its pages
and sell advertisements. Modern broadcast media appreciates baseball's dependable, if sometimes unspectacular, ratings. In August 1964,
CBS purchased the New York Yankees for the then astounding price of
$11,200,000. Today, the Chicago Tribune Company, which owns news-
papers and television stations, owns the White Sox franchise; Time-
Warner owns Turner Enterprises, which, in turn, owns the Atlanta
Braves; Walt Disney owns the Anaheim Angels baseball club, the ABC
network, and cable's premier sports channel, ESPN; Rupert Murdoch's
News Corp. media empire purchased the Los Angeles Dodgers in
March 1998 for $311,000,000. Murdoch also established a network of
local American television stations that controls the local television
rights to almost all baseball games. His buying spree, during which he
also purchased European soccer clubs and an entire Australian rugby
league, has made him the world's most influential person in the media-
sports conglomerate.

In 1999, the New York Yankees merged its business operations with
basketball's New Jersey Nets in a move designed to afford the two
clubs additional leverage in negotiating a local television package. The
"YankeeNets" holding company is a partnership valued at
$1,400,000,000. Nets owners Raymond Chambers and Lewis Katz paid
the Yankees owners $225,000,000 in exchange for a 50 percent interest
in the merged entity. (For purposes of the merger, the Yankees franchise was valued at $600,000,000, the Nets at $150,000,000.) George
Steinbrenner continued to run the Yankees and the Nets' owners operated the basketball franchise. The new combined entity, however,
would negotiate contracts with the local media, marketing agreements,
sponsorships, and advertising, and handle ticket sales for both clubs.
This unprecedented intersport merger may be the harbinger of future
sports marketing combinations.

There has been at least one exception to the corporate ownership
trend in baseball. In June 1998, Cleveland Indians owner Richard
Jacobs, a wealthy shopping mall developer, sold 4,000,000 class A
shares of his club to the public for $15 each. The stock, traded on the

NASDAQ exchange under the letters CLEV, is now selling at $10 a share. Jacobs maintained voting control of the baseball operation, as required by major league rules, by retaining all of the club's 2.28 million class B stock, with each class B share having 10,000 times the voting rights of class A shares. The Indians thereby joined the Boston Celtics, Florida Panthers, and Green Bay Packers as professional sports franchises publicly traded. There was talk in 1999 that other major league franchises would consider similar public stock offerings to raise additional capital.

The Indians' financial records are open because its stock is traded publicly. In 1998, the club earned net revenue of $12,700,000 on $144,500,000 in gross revenues, including $55,8000,000 from game attendance (the Indians have sold out every game in Jacobs Field history), $16,200,000 from concessions, $9,400,000 from luxury boxes and club seat rentals, and $9,800,000 from advertising. The Indians' post-season revenues from the 1998 playoffs—when the club lost to the Yankees in the American League Championship series—totaled $8,7000,000. Club records indicate that Richard Jacobs earned $467,424 in salary from the club and that his ownership stake earned him 49 percent of the club's pretax operating income of $19,000,000 in 1998.

In May 1999, the seventy-three-year-old Jacobs announced that his Cleveland franchise was for sale. He and his late brother David had purchased the club in 1986 for $36,000,000, and they had almost doubled their investment with the $60,000,000 public stock offering in 1998. With the market pegged in 1998 by the sale of the Dodgers at $311,000,000 and the sale of the Texas Rangers at $250,000,000, Jacobs explained that he thought it was a good time to sell. Indeed it was. On November 4, 1999, Cleveland lawyer Larry Dolan purchased the Indians for a record $320,000,000.

The inflation in the purchase price of major league baseball franchises has extended down into the minor leagues. Today, a class A club sells for more than $2,000,000, a class AA club for $4–6,000,000, and a class AAA club for $10–15,000,000. Of the 158 clubs in the minors affiliated with major league franchises, only a handful are profitable, perhaps a third break even, and the remainder lose money annually. Owning a minor league club, it seems, is a matter of ego, not economics.

Owner Expenses and Revenues

The purchaser of a baseball club receives a roster of players, an exclusive franchise for a territory, and a set of contracts with concessionaires and broadcasters. Although the player payroll constitutes the largest share of a club's budget, a franchise has many other expenses. First, the club needs secure a place to play its contests either by leasing or owning its ballpark. Increasingly, franchises have received public funds for stadium construction as part of lucrative deals to keep clubs in town or to lure others away from their current location. Times have long past when Mr. Ebbets was able to build his glorious park in Brooklyn for $750,000 in 1913.

A major league club has significant operating costs, for example, in transportation, hotels and meals, and administrative overhead. And, like any business, a baseball franchise must advertise and market its product. Each club also maintains a minor league system to develop future major leaguers.

Club revenues in baseball come from four main sources: ticket sales; sales of television and radio broadcasting rights (both local and national); concession sales at the ballpark, including food, souvenirs, and parking; and royalty rights from sale of the use of the team's logo and other intellectual property interests.

In their National Agreement, club owners have agreed to a set of rules to protect their revenue stream. Most importantly, the owners control the entry of rival entrepreneurs at the major league level. The nation's three largest metropolitan areas—New York, Los Angeles, and Chicago—have a sufficient population base to support two clubs each, and the San Francisco–Oakland area also hosts two franchises, but they have both faced financial adversity. The other clubs in the thirty-team major leagues enjoy territorial exclusivity. Their markets vary in size and wealth, and baseball club owners always face competition for the sports entertainment dollar from other professional sports.

Ticket sales for attendance at the games, "the gate," remain the most significant source of club revenue. Professor Gerald W. Scully of the

University of Texas at Dallas, an accomplished baseball economist, has established through data analysis that game attendance is a function of three independent variables: (1) area population; (2) team success on the field; (3) and the age of a club's home stadium. Big-city franchises draw larger crowds and earn more money than small-city franchises with the same winning percentage. Winning teams outdraw losing teams with the same population base. Teams with new stadiums significantly outdraw those with older facilities. All of baseball's high-revenue clubs have new stadiums except the Yankees, Cubs, Mets, Angels, and Dodgers, which all are in very large population centers. All low-revenue clubs play in old stadiums, but that will change as the Brewers, Tigers, Giants, Astros, Reds, and Pirates obtain new stadiums (incidentally, all designed by HOK Sport of Kansas City, the preeminent architect of retro-styled ballparks). These clubs will seek to replicate Cleveland's remarkable turnaround from a baseball also-ran to a perennial power-house as the result of the construction of Jacobs Field, the infusion of needed capital, and the clever managerial decision to invest in long-term contracts for junior players.

Starting in 1961, with the addition of two teams to the American League, the sale of new franchise rights and the expansion of the major leagues have been significant sources of revenue for existing clubs. Owners have always been careful, however, not to expand to all available cities, because the mere threat to relocate their franchises to these suitable alternatives provides them leverage in bargaining with their home cities for new facilities and other concessions. On the other hand, the major leagues have expanded sufficiently to leave only a few markets open for the creation of a rival league. Expansion is not cost-free for existing teams, of course, since they must share the revenue from national television and radio contracts with their new partners. Expansion also reduces the quality of competitive play, which may affect attendance.

For over a century, club owners defended the strict player reserve system as essential to maintaining on-field parity among clubs with different financial bases. The allocation of player resources is of vital concern, but the reserve system had nothing to do with fostering competition. Instead its main objective was to keep player salaries under control, and it accomplished that goal quite well.

A great player is worth more in a big market than in a small one because his potential to increase attendance is greater in the larger market. Without a reserve system, the best players would be attracted to richer teams who could pay them more. Economic principles suggest that this movement to richer teams should also occur under the reserve system, and it did, as owners moved the best players where their abilities had the highest income potential.

Throughout the history of the major leagues, smaller-market clubs have sold players to larger-market teams, a practice that continues today. The old Kansas City Athletics, the St. Louis Browns, the Washington Senators, the Philadelphia Phillies, and the Pittsburgh Pirates used to market their talent every year. Purchaser clubs (in particular the New York Yankees and Brooklyn Dodgers) were willing to pay these seller clubs more for their best players than the sellers could earn by using them on their small-market teams, but less than the purchaser clubs could earn by using them on large-market teams. The only, albeit important, difference between player movement under a strict reserve system and under free agency is the party who pockets the financial gain—either the seller club (under the reserve system) or the free agent (under the current system for those players with at least six years of major league service).

Baseball club owners appreciate the economic realities of their business. As co-ventures in two circuits consisting of clubs with very different financial capabilities, the quality of the product sold by all the owners leaguewide is always a significant issue. This is not a new problem in organized baseball, for Branch Rickey lamented the economic state of the sport more than seventy-five years ago:

> Poverty means that you have a ball club low in the standings of the race, and it naturally follows that but very few fans turn out at the gates to see the boys play ball. If the fans fail to attend games, then your bank account is positively nil. And without money a baseball owner not only will find himself in a whale of lot of trouble, but positively unable to raise even a finger to help rebuild his team. We have heard a great deal about economics lately, and this is the part it plays in major league baseball.

To attract fans, each club must have the capability of both winning and losing. If some clubs cannot field a competitive team, the entire commercial amusement suffers. The outcome of each contest must be uncertain in order to maintain the interest of fans. While spectators "root, root, root for the home team" and "if they don't win, it's a shame," the fact that their team has the possibility of either winning or losing is vital to the fan appeal of the game. More than any other professional team sport, baseball fulfills this *uncertainty principle* because the best club rarely wins more than two games out of three, and the worst rarely loses more than two out of three. In other words, any club can beat any other club on any given day.

The media have made much of the apparent correlation between a club's payroll and its performance on the field. In the 1998 season, for example, no club with a payroll less than $40,000,000 won more games than it lost. Although high spending did not insure success—the Orioles' $70,000,000 payroll in 1998 did not produce a postseason appearance for the club—low spending seemed to assure failure. The 1999 season, however, showed that the correlation was less than perfect. Clubs such as the Cincinnati Reds and Oakland A's performed admirably with modest payrolls. Others, such as the Los Angeles Dodgers, faltered despite their generous salary levels.

Auxiliary Revenues

In addition to the gate and concessions, major league clubs earn revenue from a number of auxiliary sources—television and radio rights (both national and local), promotional rights (sponsors' rights to use the club's name and logo), sponsorships, and naming rights to new sports facilities.

All major league clubs share equally in national broadcasting and licensing revenue, which, in 1998, amounted to $16,500,000 for each franchise. The first radio broadcast of a baseball game was the 1922 World Series between the Yankees and the Giants. Stations WJZ in Newark and WGY in Schenectady transmitted the program. The great sportswriter Grantland Rice served as the first play-by-play announcer. Early radio games were rarely broadcast live from the ballpark. Instead, announcers re-created the contest by reading a ticker-tape transmission of the game with canned fan noises in the background. There is the famous story of Ronald "Dutch" Reagan's innovative performance as a baseball announcer in Illinois when his ticker tape malfunctioned. Reagan improvised a monumental parade of foul strikes, perhaps the longest in the baseball history. Eventually, the tape resumed and with it a more accurate re-creation of the game.

Television discovered baseball in August 1939, when the Dodgers-Reds game from Ebbets Field was broadcast to those few New Yorkers who owned a television set. From the inception of televised contests, club owners expressed concern about their impact on attendance. Why would fans come out to the park and pay admission (as well as buy refreshments and souvenirs) if they could watch the game at home for free? As a result, televised home games were the exception, rather than the rule, and in some cases they still are. On the other hand, some owners thought that television spurred fan interest in the team and brought patrons out to the ballpark to see their heroes in action.

Local rights to televise games produce significant revenue for some owners and very little for others. Steinbrenner's Yankees, for example, are completing a twelve-year, $486,000,000 contract with the MSG Network. MSG, in turn, sells a portion of those rights to a noncable New York television station, currently a station owned by Fox. Traditionally, these local television revenues have not been shared among the owners.

Steinbrenner also has a ten-year, $95,000,000 contract with Adidas to license the Yankees name on the manufacturer's sports products. When the relationship was announced, the baseball commissioner's office objected. Steinbrenner in turn sued, and the matter was settled in favor of the very independent owner from New York City.

In recent years, clubs have cashed in on a new source of revenue—the naming rights to their ballparks. Purchasing these rights is an effective corporate marketing strategy, and baseball clubs have willingly accepted the largesse. For example, the Detroit Tigers' new downtown stadium will be called Comerica Park for the next thirty years in exchange for $66,000,000, the same price and terms the Colorado Rockies will reap from Coors Brewing Company and the Arizona Diamondbacks will collect from Bank One. Pittsburgh's new field was a comparative steal for PNC at $20,000,000 over twenty years, about half of what the Seattle Mariners will receive from Safeco Insurance and the

Milwaukee Brewers from Miller beer. The new Fenway Park is likely to fetch a record fee of some $40–50,000,000 for a limited fifteen-year term from the corporation licensed to attach its moniker to the re-created Green Monster adjacent to the existing stadium, the oldest in baseball. By 1999, half the thirty major league franchises had sold their stadium naming rights.

The Bottom Line

Is baseball profitable? Total gross revenue in the sport in 1998 amounted to $2.7 billion, but the clubs did not share equally in these receipts. The high-revenue clubs—Yankees, Braves, Indians, and Orioles, for example—averaged at least $140,000,000 in gross revenue, compared with $46–47,000,000 for the lowly Expos and Twins. Owners claim annual loses, but their bottom-line conclusions leave many questions unanswered. Professor Allen Sanderson, a sports economist from the University of Chicago, has said that any decent accountant can make a team look like it is losing money.

Owners have always used their baseball operations to support their other businesses. Their baseball enterprises helped Augie Busch sell beer in St. Louis and Ted Turner convert a small local UHF television station into the first nationwide superstation, with programming provided by his Atlanta Braves. Harry Frazee leveraged his Red Sox club as a source of financing for his Broadway productions. To do this he sold off his players, mostly to the Yankees, including the notorious 1920 sale of Babe Ruth for $125,000 and a $300,000 loan. (That year, Babe hit fifty-four homers, twenty-five more than in 1919 and more than all but one entire team in the major leagues.)

Forbes Magazine reported that in 1998 thirteen clubs lost money: the Los Angeles Dodgers ($11,700,000), the Kansas City Royals ($10,900,000), the Toronto Blue Jays ($9,500,000), the Seattle Mariners ($8,600,000), the Milwaukee Brewers ($8,800,000), the San Diego Padres ($8,000,000), the Chicago Cubs ($7,900,000), the Boston Red Sox ($7,600,000), the Minnesota Twins ($7,100,000), the San Francisco Giants ($6,400,000), the New York Mets ($5,200,000), the Detroit Tigers ($4,500,000), and the Houston Astros ($3,700,000). The losses of the Mets, Dodgers, and Red Sox resulted from their transfer payments to other clubs under the luxury tax provision in the current collective bargaining agreement.

On the other hand, *Forbes* reported that eight clubs earned significant profits in 1998: the New York Yankees ($23,000,000), the Arizona Diamondbacks ($22,500,000), the Tampa Bay Devil Rays ($20,600,000), the Colorado Rockies ($19,500,000), the Cleveland Indians ($19,000,000), the Atlanta Braves ($16,400,000), the Florida Marlins ($8,600,000), and the Montreal Expos ($5,600,000). Montreal ended in the black after receiving $13,000,000 through revenue sharing. The remaining nine clubs broke even or enjoyed modest operating profits.

Public financing of baseball stadiums is a relatively new phenomenon. In 1909, Barney Dreyfuss used his own resources to build a new stadium for his Pirates, Forbes Field, to replace the outmoded Exposition Park, at a cost of $1,000,000. Similarly, Ebbets Field, Fenway Park, and Wrigley Field were built with private money. No public money was sought or used. The "House That Ruth Built" was actually built by beer magnate Jacob Ruppert for $2,000,000 in 1923. Walter O'Malley built Dodgers Stadium in Chavez Ravine in Los Angeles almost a half-century later for $20,000,000.

For the most part, baseball clubs now play in stadiums constructed at public expense. They pay modest rents and generally retain the revenues from parking, concessions, advertising, luxury suite rentals, and the naming of the facility by other commercial enterprises. Even today, however, there are a few exceptions to reliance on public financing. The Detroit Tigers club privately constructed a new downtown stadium for its lowly franchise. The San Francisco Giants ownership spent $300,000,000 to build a new less-windy stadium for its team.

Franchise Values

The value of baseball franchises, as determined by the reported sale prices, has skyrocketed at the same time as player salaries have increased. The increasing price of a franchise should be a function of the future expected profits, including gains realized when it is sold. Many people obviously think baseball is a good investment.

The net worth of a baseball club has changed dramatically over the years. Harry Wright's Boston Red Stockings were valued in 1874 at $833.13, jumped to $3,261.07 the next year, then fell to $177.74 in 1880. By comparison, the cost and value of modern baseball franchises have only gone up. The investors awarded the National League expansion franchise in New York in 1962 paid $3,750,000 for the right to field a team. (There can be a legitimate argument that the 1962 Mets were not actually a "major league" team. They won but 40 of the 160 games they played.) The investors sold their interest in 1980 for $26,000,000. Six years later, new owners purchased the Mets for $100,000,000.

The value of major league franchises is bolstered by the fact that there are only a limited number of such business opportunities. There are thirty major league franchises, and in 1997 (before Rupert Murdoch purchased the Dodgers) a club's average value was estimated at $134,000,000. In 1999, the controversial Marge Schott sold her controlling shares in the Cincinnati Reds, the club in the geographic area with the smallest population base in the major leagues. Schott's 36.7 percent of the Reds cost Carl Lindner and her other limited partners $67,000,000. Extrapolated, this would mean the Reds franchise value was $181,800,000.

As is apparent, annual income and loss figures have little relation to the value of the franchises. *Forbes Magazine* estimates the current value of the marginally profitable Montreal franchise at $84,000,000, while the Los Angeles franchise, operated at an annual loss, sold in 1998 for $311,000,000. The disparity in franchise values is enormous. The Yankees, Indians, Braves, and Orioles are currently valued at more than four times the amount the Expos, Twins, and Royals are said to be worth.

Even businesses that annually lose money may be a valuable asset at tax time, because baseball losses can reduce an owner's tax liability for income earned in other corporate entities within a complex business structure. And some businesses—including baseball franchises—that show losses may be using creative bookkeeping methods to pay their profits to their owners in the form of salary or loan repayment.

Bill Veeck's greatest contribution to the business of baseball may not have been his exploding scoreboard in Chicago but rather his creation of a tax shelter for professional sports teams by devising the concept of depreciating a player's contract as an intangible asset over the useful playing life of the player. Although Congress and the Internal Revenue Service later imposed some limits on this scheme, it remains a viable source of financial relief to club owners, courtesy of the American taxpayers.

The profitability of baseball has been a matter of public discussion and private study for decades. From the early days of organized professional baseball, owners have bemoaned their financial fate. The real story of the economic health of the enterprise is far more complicated, and it varies from club to club. During the 1920s, without radio or television revenues, fifteen of the sixteen clubs showed a profit. The Ruthian Yankees made over $3,500,000. Stanford economist Roger Noll agrees with Texas economist Gerald Scully that today's baseball business is profitable for most club owners. Some small-market clubs, however, seem destined to experience annual red ink, at least until they become the beneficiary of publicly financed or publicly assisted stadiums like Jacobs Field in Cleveland.

THE AGENTS

The third base on the negotiating diamond is covered by sports agents. As denizens of this "hot corner," whose occupant is in the direct line of fire of a right-handed hitter, agents need a quick and creative mind, steady reflexes, and patience. Regretfully, there have only been a few truly distinguished agents in the history of the game. In fact, until fairly recently, owners flatly refused to deal with agents. Although under the terms of the collective bargaining agreement owners are compelled to meet with a player's agent, they remain unnerved by having to swim with people they see as sharks. Even agents do not like other agents, who are potential competitors for their clients' business. Agents make the money pitch, and it is not always a pleasant hanging curve. It is often a high, hard, and inside fastball.

Although sports agents' most visible role is in negotiating contracts, they serve their clients in a variety of other ways as well: They handle the financial side of a player's life—paying bills and taxes and offering investment advice; they counsel a player on personal issues; and they market their client's image for endorsements. Agents also face a great deal of job insecurity, for even when they produce revenue for their clients, they may lose out to rival agents with a better sales pitch. An agent who overpromises, however, will lose credibility with his current and future clients and with the ball clubs. Ballplayers understand production. The player who hits home runs in batting practice but strikes out in the actual game will not long remain in the major leagues. Likewise the agent who promises enormous salaries but produces far less will not long remain in the profession.

Sports agents come from varied backgrounds, although increasingly they are trained as attorneys. Not all have had a legal background, however. For example, hockey superstar Wayne Gretzky was represented by Mike Barnett, who owned a bar in Edmonton. Almost all agents are male, although that may be changing as women's professional sports become more stable and lucrative. There are 736 agents registered with the National Football League Players Association; only 17 are women.

Mark McCormack's Cleveland-based International Management Group, a billion-dollar-a-year business with 2,500 employees worldwide in seventy offices, was the forerunner of modern sport agencies. McCormack began in the 1960s by representing his friend, golfer Arnold Palmer. Agents tend to specialize in particular sports: David Falk in basketball, where he represents Michael Jordan and Patrick Ewing; Leigh Steinberg in football, where he represents a bevy of quarterbacks, including Steve Young, Troy Aikman, and Drew Bledsoe.

Scott Boras is a former baseball player who went to law school after a short career in the Cardinals' minor league system. Representing athletes is both a lucrative business and a personal calling for Boras, who has been vilified by club owners and fans. His seven-year deal with the Dodgers for $105,000,000 for free agent pitcher Kevin Brown in December 1998, baseball's first $100,000,000-plus contract, was only the latest in a string of successes that have made him a champion to his talented young clients and a pariah to baseball management. In 1984, Boras negotiated his first big contract, a $7,500,000 deal with the Toronto Blue Jays for his former minor league teammate Bill Caudill, who went on to achieve obscurity, winning six games and losing ten with seventeen saves in his final three years in the majors. More recently, Boras won a $65,000,000 contract for Atlanta's future Hall of Fame pitcher Greg Maddux. His work for rookie J. D. Drew may have drawn the scorn of Philadelphia fans, but it recalibrated the salary market for untested rookies.

Boras does not bargain in the traditional sense of give-and-take. He instead prepares statistics to make the case for what he sees as the market value of his clients, and then entertains offers from clubs interested in the players he represents. If an offer is unacceptable, he simply turns it down. There is no haggling. Boras's share is 5 percent, at the high end for agents, but apparently the players he represents believe he is well worth it. Is he "the most hated man in baseball," as the 1998 *New York Times* article about him said? He is certainly not a favorite of baseball management, but his clients have few complaints about his tireless and fearless representation.

Agents must register with the unions in those major team sports in which they want to represent players, including major league baseball. They must also pay a licensing fee in all major team sports except major league baseball. In addition, about thirty states now have laws regulating agents, focusing on their interaction with college athletes. Often, successful agents have athletic backgrounds themselves and start their careers by representing their former teammates and friends.

Many agents find clients at their source, by developing ties with college coaches. However, in those major league team sports that use colleges and universities as cost-free minor leagues—basketball and football—an agent can easily run afoul of the NCAA regulations. Their potential clients, for example, may expect and demand a bag full of illegal gifts. Occasionally, the worst agents are exposed—Norby Walters and Lloyd Bloom come to mind—but the payoffs are too great to deter all misconduct. Still, of the more than one thousand registered agents in baseball, basketball, and football, only four were suspended for misconduct in 1998.

THE UNION

Although sports agents are vilified by fans in the public morality play about soaring players' salaries, the Major League Baseball Players Association comes in for its share of scorn as well, especially during the periodic labor disputes that have disrupted the continuity of the game. As a result of the collective bargaining process, the players association and the club owners have created a bargaining framework within which players have been able to reap cosmic salaries. But in fact, the union never negotiated even one of those player contracts.

Unlike most collective bargaining relationships, unions in the entertainment industry (of which professional sports is a part) do not negotiate with management over the precise salaries performers receive. The National Labor Relations Act provides that a union, as the workers' exclusive bargaining representative, has the right to demand negotiations over "wages, hours, and other terms and conditions of employment." However, the players association (and all other unions in the entertainment field) chose not to exercise this power with regard to negotiating individual salaries. Article II of the collective bargaining agreement between the players association and the club owners provides that *an individual player*—and not the union—"shall be entitled to negotiate . . . an individual salary over and above the minimum." Why did the players association relinquish its legal right to negotiate salaries?

To maintain its status and legitimacy, a union must design a collective bargaining strategy that meets the needs of its membership. Otherwise, the union will not last long in its representative capacity. In professional sports, it is essential for the union to command the allegiance and support of the superstars in the bargaining unit. When the football players union failed to do so during the 1987 strike, some superstars crossed the picket lines, thereby dooming the union's collective job action. (Joe Montana and Tony Dorsett did cross, Dan Marino and John Elway did not.) A bifurcated system of salary setting—with player agents negotiating for individual salaries and the union negotiating for minimum salaries—allows the superstars to win the highest salaries possible from their clubs while still remaining loyal to their union, which then protects the rank and file with minimum guarantees.

In baseball, the potential market value and resulting salaries of players within the bargaining unit vary widely. As we discussed in Chapter 2, many players are paid at or near the contract minimum, modest compensation at least when compared with the multimillion-dollar salaries of the game's superstars. The highest paid players receive more than eighty times the salary of the lowest paid players.

A single union could not bargain effectively for the salaries of performers who cover such a broad spectrum of value to their employers. Unions attempt to maximize the interests of the unit as a whole, but if they negotiated a comprehensive wage system, they would risk losing support from those players who would likely benefit more from a free-market, price-setting mechanism. Performers bring unique talents to their work; they all believe they will benefit from a market that can respond to those talents. Unions rightfully worry about great disparities in pay between members of the bargaining unit, but too much attention to that concern in the sports industry would be dangerous to the unions' continued effectiveness.

Appropriate Bargaining Unit

By law, a union must represent the interests of *all* its members, not just those who support its continued status. For this reason, among others, the National Labor Relations Board, in conducting representation elections, looks to devise an "appropriate bargaining unit" of employees who share a "community of interest." Workers who face the same day-to-day working conditions, receive generally the same level of compensation, and bring to the workplace a similar set of skills and experiences would be placed together in the same bargaining unit. This is a unit a union could represent effectively in bargaining, since its members have similar interests, expectations, and aspirations. In most collective bargaining settings, a union tries to maximize the interests of all its members.

Of course, all bargaining units are heterogeneous to some degree and contain persons with different abilities and interests. There are always some employees with more valuable production skills who are better compensated than others. Other employees have more seniority and thus benefit from a collective bargaining agreement that allocates economic rewards based on years of service. On the other hand, an entertainment industry bargaining unit is so diverse in terms of individual earning potential as to present an impossible challenge to any labor organization.

Even employees with vastly divergent earning potential share some interests in certain terms of employment, such as medical insurance or vacation provisions. All also benefit from a grievance and arbitration procedure that can be used to resolve disputes that arise during the term of the agreement. Baseball's collective bargaining agreement is no exception and contains many terms that profit all members. For example, Article XIV states that players (except for pitchers, catchers, and injured players) need not report for spring training more than thirty-three days before the season's start. This is as important to a lower-paid junior player as it is to a seasoned veteran. All players also have a common equal interest in Article II, which allows them all to negotiate individual salary terms.

In the business of baseball, more modestly paid players retain the opportunity to progress to the higher levels of compensation. (These are not simply daydreams. Both Hollywood mythology and baseball reality are filled with stories of those who are "discovered" after years of hard work and then suddenly thrust into superstardom.) Remember, each player has beaten long odds just to make it to the major leagues. Thus, a wage system that allows all employees the opportunities to prosper financially based on their individual productivity can meet the needs and the aspirations of every member of the unit. Proof of this is that no player is ever heard complaining publicly about the high salaries paid his teammates.

Individual bargaining over salaries does impose "transaction costs" on management. Paying players under a universal wage scale would save time and money. It would also reduce the risk that a single employer might skew the market with a particular unwise free agent signing. In fact, during the 1990 and 1994 negotiations the owners proposed a wage-scale alternative to individual bargaining. The players association understandably declined to jettison a pay system that had proved so successful to its members.

The Floor

There is one important restriction in baseball's wage system of individualized bargaining—the "floor," or the guaranteed minimum salary level for all players as established by the collective bargaining agreement. It is the players association that bargains for the floor. Employees at or near that level need to know that even if they do not reach superstardom, they will still be well compensated for their services. The minimum salary has increased over the years in step with the prevailing average of negotiated salaries; the current collective bargaining agreement set the minimum at $170,000 for 1998 and at $200,000 for 1999 and 2000. It will remain at $200,000 for 2001 if the players association exercises its option to extend the agreement. If it does not, the minimum will be increased by a cost-of-living adjustment.

Job Security

Collective bargaining agreements do not guarantee employees a job; they simply set forth the procedures that must be followed if an employer seeks to separate an employee from his or her job. Typically, this requires an employer to establish "just cause" to terminate a worker. Almost all collective bargaining agreements include a procedure for contesting a dismissal through a grievance and arbitration mechanism. The "just cause" standard means that an employee who fails to live up to his or her side of the employment bargain—for example, by repeated insubordination, work disruptions, absenteeism, or poor performance—will be held to have forfeited his or her job.

In the entertainment industry, however, talent serves at management's will. One employee becomes a star because of management's intuition, and another loses a position through the same process of discretionary decision-making. Traditionally, management retains broad latitude to decide who will stay and who will go. (Think of the opening number in the Broadway musical *Chorus Line:* "I hope I make it . . . .")

The counterpoint to high entertainer salaries and the chance at instant stardom is the risk of instant failure and the loss of a job. Were there only one potential employer in the entertainment industry, this might be an intolerable situation, exactly the kind a union is formed to confront. Management discretion can, and has been, abused at times. Because there are many employers of entertainers, however, someone whose television show is canceled on one network might appear the following season on another network. As long as producers do not collude to blacklist performers, a system of artistic judgment and managerial discretion may operate fairly. Traditionally, management need not prove "just cause" to terminate an entertainer from a role.

These same protocols have always operated within professional team sports. A player with the talent to perform at the major league level can be assured by the union that he will be compensated fairly at least at the minimum level set forth in the collective bargaining agreement. He knows that if his skills improve further, he has the opportunity to earn considerably more in salary, especially when he qualifies for free agency. The union negotiates the system of rules that will be used to determine his salary and sets a minimum floor. If club management does not believe the employee has the skills and ability to play at the major league level, however, he has no right to keep his job.

Section 7(b) of the Uniform Player Contract negotiated by the players association and the club owners allows a club to terminate a contract if the player "shall at any time . . . fail, in the opinion of . . . management, to exhibit sufficient skill or competitive ability to qualify or continue as a member of the . . . team." At termination, the club's continuing obligation to pay the player is regulated by the collective bargaining agreement and, of course, by any provision of his individual contract that guarantees salary payment.

Although the club management's decision is final, league rules and the player contract do provide some insurance for a player who faces termination yet retains the skill and ability to play at the major league level. If a club intends to terminate a player's contract, it must first request the other twenty-nine teams to "waive" their right to claim him at the price of $1.

This procedure of requesting "waivers" affords other clubs the opportunity to claim a player who might meet their needs. If such claims are filed, priority goes to the club with the poorest team record.

Spring Training per Diem

The 174-page collective bargaining agreement between the players association and the club owners contains many valuable benefits for all major league ballplayers. One such benefit with a long history in the baseball business is the spring training per diem. Under their individual employment contracts, players are not paid until the commencement of the regular season. However, under the collective bargaining agreement, players invited to spring training camp in 1997, for example, were paid a weekly allowance of $211. A player living away from spring training headquarters also received a supplemental weekly allowance of $34, daily meal money and tip allowance of $60, and a daily room allowance of $25. These amounts were adjusted for 1998–2001 according to increases in the cost of living. For a player earning $13,000,000 a year, such as Mike Piazza of the Mets, these allowances are trivial. But for a rookie trying out for a spot on the major league roster, however, these per diem payments may be vital.

Club owners first provided spring training allowances in the late 1940s, after they crushed a player unionization effort spearheaded by Robert Murphy, a Harvard-trained lawyer from Pittsburgh. Murphy's American Baseball Guild of 1946 sought increases in the minimum player salary and improvements in the pension plan, which the owners granted, but only after Murphy, who had been roundly ignored, was gone from the scene. The players still refer to spring training allowances as "Murphy money."

Pension Plan

One of the players association's primary goals since its earliest days as a real union has been to improve the ballplayers' pension plan. It was, in fact, the major issue in the 1968 and 1970 negotiations. Although the pension was not a significant concern during the labor disputes of the 1990s, the parties included modifications to the Major League Baseball Players Benefit Plan and its Funding Agreement in Exhibit 5 attached to the current collective bargaining agreement. They continued the current plan for an additional six years, and the clubs agreed to pay $68,000,000 annually into the plan through 2002. Retired players receive pension payments in accordance with the terms of the plan, the amount depending upon their years of accumulated major league service.

Safety and Health

Article XII of the collective bargaining agreement addresses safety and health issues. It establishes a joint advisory committee to address emergency safety and health problems; sets forth the procedure for placing a player on the disabled list; provides players the opportunity to obtain—at the team's expense—a second medical opinion concerning any condition being treated by the club's physician, and requires each club to employ two full-time certified trainers. As an example of the detail included in the agreement, Section E lists the equipment each visiting locker room shall have: whirlpool, hydroculator, ultrasound machine, and examining table.

Parking

For any fan who has been frustrated trying to find a place to park around the stadium, Article XV (B) of the collective bargaining agreement is perfectly understandable:

> Each Club shall provide or arrange for appropriate automobile parking spaces for Players and, to the extent practicable, van and small truck parking spaces for Players, at its home ballpark on game or practice days, without cost to the Players.

Spanish Translation and ESL Courses

Recognizing the increased importance of Latino ballplayers, the collective bargaining agreement and all other important notices are now translated into Spanish, with the players association and the clubs sharing the cost. Each club must make available an English-as-a-second-language (ESL) course, if at least one player on the roster requests the sessions.

POSTGAME WRAP-UP

Following each contest, baseball announcers and commentators offer a summary of the game's action. The next morning, the sportswriters have their turn at bat, analyzing the play from the night before. What then should we say about the economics of the baseball business in our postgame wrap-up?

All participants in the business of baseball have the opportunity to prosper as long as they have the skill and ability to compete at the major league level. Club owners need managerial skills; ballplayers need athletic skills; agents need interpersonal skills; and the players association needs organizational skills. That said, some succeed, some do not. In part, that is the result of luck.

Branch Rickey's famous line, that "luck is the residue of design," has great significance in the baseball business. Success in the enterprise comes to those with ability who work at it with diligence. The profits of the game, what economists call "the economic rents," are there for the taking. Within the highly imperfect and highly restrictive internal markets of the baseball business, masterful business strategies combined with tenacity can reap enormous dividends.

FIVE

I do not love [money]. I have not been near enough to it to build up any affection to speak of.

ROY HOBBS

Roy Hobbs and the New York Knights: A Salary Negotiation

In Bernard Malamud's novel The Natural, *an aging Roy Hobbs confronts his life's demons on the baseball diamond. Hobbs was portrayed in the movie by Robert Redford. ("THE NATURAL," 1984 © TriStar Pictures Inc. All Rights Reserved. Courtesy of TriStar Pictures)*

Some claim that a good negotiator is born and not trained, and that may be the case. Certainly, some bargainers innately understand the dynamics of the negotiation process. They possess the interpersonal skills needed to appear reasonable while standing fast and persuading adversaries to concede. They know how to get what they want from others through negotiations. In the business of baseball, negotiating player salaries is a fine art. In this chapter we shall describe some of the masters' strokes: how negotiators interact at the table and how their tactics move the parties toward agreement.

The participants in a baseball salary negotiation are not enemies out to destroy one another. In fact, the opposite is true. Management wants to satisfy its player (within limits, of course), and the player wants the club to prosper both on and off the field. Both sides will benefit from a financially secure club, which will be able to pay higher salaries, sign better players, and increase its opportunity for postseason play. The participants in salary negotiations thus might be termed *cooperative antagonists*. Although they have different interests and value systems, they both can achieve their goals through cooperation.

In this chapter, we will construct and apply negotiation models and evaluate good bargaining tactics and bad ones. This brief primer on negotiating baseball player salaries is based on empirical evidence of how the process actually operates. It cannot capture the complete essence of the bargaining interchange, however. Like a Jackson Pollock drip painting, any portrait of baseball salary negotiations leaves much to the imagination.

Roy Hobbs

To help describe the negotiation process, we will use a hypothetical, a common recourse in every law school classroom. Most baseball fans will remember the legendary Roy Hobbs, the star of Bernard Malamud's brilliant first novel, *The Natural,* and the complex, even obsessed, character played by Robert Redford in the 1984 movie of the same name. At the majestic conclusion of the film (as opposed to the novel, where Hobbs strikes out), a severely injured Hobbs, bleeding from wounds in his stomach, hits a towering home run, exploding the lights of Knights Field, to win the pennant for the mythical New York club and its manager and co-owner Pop Fisher. But what if Hobbs had not then retired to the midwestern wheatfields to play catch with his son? What if he had wanted to pursue his baseball career? How would Hobbs and Pop Fisher have negotiated the terms of his contract?

According to Malamud's story, set in the early 1950s, Hobbs's major league contract was for $5,000, actually below the leaguewide minimum of $6,000. Now shifting the Hobbs hypothetical to the present, we know that in today's market, of course, he would have commanded a significant increase in salary simply by making it to the major league club; he would have received at least a prorated share of the $200,000 minimum now required by the collective bargaining agreement for the portion of the season he was on the Knights roster. Based on his stellar performance for the club, his agent would likely demand a superstar's salary for the coming season. The Knights might respond that Hobbs was a one-shot phenomenon worth far less than the league average salary, especially considering his advanced age.

Hobbs, you may recall, never made it into the game as a sparkling nineteen-year-old hurler—he was sidetracked on his way to a Cubs tryout by a mysterious woman in a black veil carrying a .22 pistol. Now, as a thirty-four-year-old rookie, he has become a baseball sensation. It was Knights coach Red Blow who gave him the nickname of "the Natural." When Hobbs first came to bat in the majors, Pop Fisher told him to "knock the cover right off the ball." He took Pop's directive literally and did just that. He carried the Knights on his shoulders from eighth place (then the league's cellar) to the pennant.

Hobbs, as a second-year player, would not be eligible for salary arbitration or free agency under the current collective bargaining agreement, for he is covered by the vestige of the traditional reserve system. There is only one purchaser for his services, the New York Knights, and only one option if Hobbs is unwilling to accept the club's offer: He may retire from the game.

Prenegotiation—Information-Gathering and Self-Assessment

Long before Hobbs, his agent, and Pop Fisher sit down to negotiate a contract for the forthcoming season, they will have done a considerable amount of homework. Both parties will have researched the salary market for power hitters like Hobbs, collecting data about comparable players. Although they will work from the same information, it would not be surprising if they reach different conclusions about the economic value of Hobbs's services.

The initial estimates of the parties differ because their underlying interests and perceptions differ. Of course, players seek higher compensation and owners seek lower compensation, but that is only the threshold of analysis. Players are not paid for their past performances, but for their expected future performances. But each party makes different predictions as to the future productivity of a player, and estimating value is not an exact science. Salary figures also will not be the only issues on the table; there will be discussion about the length of the contract, bonuses, no-trade provisions, and a variety of other concerns.

Negotiations present a complicated matrix of issues involving individual aspirations, perceptions of reality, and noneconomic psychic elements, such as pride, altruism, gratitude, and self-esteem. Reflecting on prior negotiations (none in Hobbs's case) and considering portents for future negotiations (perhaps unlikely in Hobbs's case), salary negotiations begin with a snapshot of a player's career: What has he done, and what does that past performance suggest for the future?

For the club, any single salary negotiation is one of many defining events in the annual process of conducting a profit-making enterprise. While the Knights are negotiating with Hobbs, they must be aware of the horizontal implications of this set of transactions on their entire business. They know they must also sign southpaw hurler Al Fowler, their flashy center fielder Juan Flores, and their dependable catcher Dave Olson. They likewise must predict how the fans will react to the performance of the Knights' cadre of twenty-five players.

If everything else were equal, of course, the Knights would want to make each of their players as happy as possible. Satisfied players play better baseball. But everything else is not equal; financial resources are limited, and much of the club's business plan for the coming season remains indeterminate. The first variable is Roy Hobbs and his salary. Without their star outfielder, the Knights are cellar dwellers. With him, they might repeat as pennant winners. The Knights ownership must seek an agreement that will secure the services of their valuable star player, but at a price that allows the club to field a solid team and earn a profit.

One crucial variable in the negotiations will be the interests and perceptions of both parties in continuity and flexibility. The club will be concerned about Hobbs's age (which the team knows) and his health (which the team may not know, although they have reason to worry). When age catches up to Hobbs—as it does to all ballplayers—he will lose his ability to contribute to the club's success and, with it, his slot on its major league roster. Under the standard uniform player contract signed by all ballplayers, team management retains broad discretion to determine whether their employee continues to possess the skill and ability to perform at the major league level. An older player like Hobbs will be interested in security and will likely prefer to have his salary guaranteed for a number of years.

Management probably recognizes that Hobbs does not have many years left in the professional game. He did have a remarkable season, however, leading the league in both home runs and triples, a combination matched in all of baseball's "real" history only by Willie Mays in 1955. Now thirty-five, Hobbs is unlikely to get any better. (By comparison, Mays in 1955 was only in the fourth year of his Hall of Fame twenty-two-year career.) Because Hobbs will fade as a player, the Knights' interest is in avoiding a long-term financial burden while retaining their star's services in the short run.

These bargaining positions would be reversed for an up-and-coming player like the young Willie Mays, who had not yet realized his full potential. A long-term contract would lock him in at an established pay level for an extended period. In a change in the bargaining rules that will have an impact on the salary level of solid performers, junior players today become eligible for salary arbitration after three years and free agency after six. With a long-term contract, management would "buy out" the player's right to pursue salary arbitration or free agency. (This was the strategy the powerful Cleveland Indians used so successfully in the early 1990s to hold together the nucleus of the club that had elevated the franchise out of three decades of decay.) Obviously, extended-term contracts come with a premium, but they may be worth management's investment.

Assessing Alternatives to Agreement

Before entering into negotiations, each party assesses the cost of a failure to reach an agreement. What are the alternatives to agreement? I am reminded of a 1999 *New Yorker* cartoon where the snarling Easter Bunny is seen negotiating with an obstinate chicken. Thrusting the contract across his desk, the Bunny barks, "May I remind you that we can always go with duck eggs!"

There are always alternatives to reaching an agreement, although, like duck eggs, they may not be particularly appealing. A player may chose to end his professional baseball career and do something else. But for almost all players, work outside the game is not as rewarding either financially or emotionally. The club, on the other had, can always sign another player, although not necessarily someone with the same skills and in the same price range.

The lowest salary the player would accept, which is his *reservation* or *walkaway price*, is a vital bit of information, since by definition, his club need not offer a dollar more for the player to sign, because to him playing at that salary is preferable to not playing at all. The highest salary the club would pay, its reservation price, is equally critical information, since the player need not accept a dollar less than this amount. The challenge in bargaining is in hiding or strategically revealing these subjective reservation prices. The negotiation process involves an encounter to divide the increment between the most the club would be willing to pay and the least the player would be willing to accept.

For Roy Hobbs, the alternatives to an agreement are not particularly attractive. For fifteen years, he floated from one job to another—a circus clown in a painted face, a semi-pro ballplayer, and a knockabout with no money. Hobbs has no marketable skills other than swinging his homemade bat, the mighty Wonderboy. (Even the bat is now gone, splintered in his last at-bat of the regular season. In Malamud's book, Hobbs touchingly buries the pieces of Wonderboy in left field.)

The Knights have few alternatives of Hobbs's caliber. At the start of the prior season, hard-hitting Bump Baily had led the team, but he died tragically after running into (and through) the outfield wall. Frankly, there is no one in the baseball marketplace who can match Roy Hobbs's productivity, and the Knights' reservation price equals what he would bring through their turnstiles. If Hobbs only knew this amount, he would demand it and reap the benefits.

Hobbs is one of a small, elite group of virtually irreplaceable baseball players. Catchers Mike Piazza and Ivan Rodriquez; home-run kings Mark McGwire, Sammy Sosa, and Ken Griffey, Jr.; Yankees stalwarts Bernie Williams and Derek Jeter; and starting pitchers Pedro Martinez, Greg Maddux, and Randy Johnson all fit this category. Any club can find another batter or pitcher at a lower price, but these players have unique market value because there are no readily available substitutes.

The object of negotiations is to produce for both of the cooperative antagonists an outcome with greater value than their no-agreement alternatives. If a player can pursue another rewarding career, then the failure to reach an agreement leaves him able to take advantage of that opportunity. Life is filled with opportunities but offers only a limited amount of time. When a person pursues one opportunity, such as playing baseball, over another, he incurs *opportunity costs*, that is, the marginal price of using the time that might be spent elsewhere. Similarly, because players have limited playing careers, they may decide to explore other opportunities later in their lives.

For ballplayers and club owners, the game means more than just money, however, for they receive nonmonetary, psychic rewards over and above the income. Baseball is fun to play even with so much money at stake. Many players will accept salary decreases to stay in the game for one more season before retiring, even if the immediate no-agreement alternatives might bring them more economic gains. Likewise, baseball clubs are fun to own and operate. Club owners may be recognized as civic assets. Although they can neither hit nor throw a ball, they are honored fiduciaries of the national game, at least as long as their team plays competitive ball. Each season, hope is renewed, and owners bask in the public's attention.

Apparent Conflict

Benjamin Franklin, an early American "game theorist," cautioned negotiators to avoid unnecessary disagreements:

> Trades would not take place unless it were advantageous to the parties concerned. Of course, it is better to strike as good a bargain as one's bargaining position permits. The worst outcome is when, by overreaching greed, no bargain is struck, and a trade that could have been advantageous to both parties does not come off at all.

Baseball club owners are willing to "trade" salary for services, as are their players. Good bargaining requires an earnest effort to strike a bargain and thus avoid Franklin's "worst outcome," an unnecessary stalemate.

Parties start salary negotiations in apparent conflict. The Knights' owners may think that Hobbs wants the world, but he really only wants a piece of it. Their conflict may not be real, or at least not as extreme as they might think at first. The parties may actually agree on the range of possible values for a player's services. Through effective negotiations, they communicate their assessments and seek cooperation.

No two sets of negotiations are exactly the same because the people, their interests, and their negotiating tactics are different. The process of interaction can be stressful or placid, rancorous or professional, prolonged or expeditious. Parties will attempt to manipulate information, disclosing some of their subjective evaluations of the risks, aspirations, and reservation points, while molding the understandings of their opposite number. Some effective negotiators are bombastic, others seem respectful and polite, still others appear confused. Whatever the personae, the bargaining process follows a predictable format, which Howard Raiffa has termed "the negotiation dance."

Salary negotiations combine reality and fiction, real facts and purported events, candid assessments and deceptive maneuvers. There is trading to do, but the amount and the timing vary with each set of negotiations. Of course, there is no mathematical certainty to the parties' valuations. Their beliefs, estimates, and predictions are likely reshaped during the dynamic negotiation process in which issues, interests, and reference points keep changing.

Personal satisfaction, the ultimate yardstick for measuring the success of negotiations, is harder to define than the infield fly rule. The negotiation process itself is not cost-free to the participants; it can have a lingering effect on both the player's performance and the club's plans for that player. A single negotiation should not be viewed in isolation; one set of negotiations is informed by previous interactions and affects future negotiations as well. There are what economists call "transaction costs" in the interchange. It is possible, as Professors David A. Lax and James K. Sebenius argue, to "create value" through negotiation, while the parties also "claim value" in every deal.

Principled Negotiations

Hobbs, his agent, and Pop Fisher would do well to read the classic text by Harvard professors Roger Fisher and William Ury, *Getting to Yes*, the 1981 negotiating guidebook that proposes using *principled negotiations* in lieu of traditional positional bargaining. The protocol provides a more efficient and less stressful method of achieving what the authors call "wise" agreements. Under the Fisher-Ury approach, parties focus on their shared and opposing interests, create a variety of possibilities to satisfy those interests, and base their negotiation interchanges on objective standards rather than emotions, pressure, and ego, which often leave participants "angry, depressed, fearful, hostile, frustrated and offended."

Few baseball salary negotiators use the Fisher-Ury approach, choosing instead to bluster and threaten, cajole and pressure, and maybe even lie and cheat. Our description of the Hobbs-Knight negotiations will relate how salary negotiations actually take place, but suggest, where applicable, how the Fisher-Ury concept of principled negotiations might facilitate agreement.

Public Posturing

Baseball salary negotiations contain an important public aspect, since the players are public figures in the entertainment industry, stars who attract the public's attention. A whole section of the daily newspaper is devoted to sports, much of it these days about the business of sports. While fans generally do not know when negotiations between a movie star and a film studio fall through, they do know when a star baseball player remains unsigned for the coming season. They want their heroes on the field. For that reason, salary negotiations usually commence with a very public conversation about the positions of the parties.

Roy Hobbs quickly became a public figure in New York. He boasted that he would be the best ever to play the game, and, for at least one season, he was. His performance was not unlike Shane Spencer's month of September 1998 for the New York Yankees, when he became an "overnight" sensation after spending nine years in the minors. Batting .373, Spencer hit ten home runs with twenty-seven RBIs in twenty-seven games and two more homers and four RBIs in five postseason games. Spencer, however, could not maintain the charm. He slumped in the World Series and then spent much of the 1999 season commuting back and forth to the Yankees' AAA club in Columbus.

Until Hobbs arrived in New York City, gamblers, bums, drunks, and crackpots inhabited Knights Field. His performance put solid citizens in the seats, and the club played to full houses at home and away. Fans came to Knights Field just to watch Hobbs's exploits. As Malamud writes, "The fans no longer confused talent with genius. When they cheered, they cheered for Roy Hobbs alone."

Much of what goes on during the public stage of salary negotiations is "posturing and prancing." The parties know this, but that does not mean that this warm-up to bargaining is irrelevant. To the contrary: It sets the stage for the real game. The player's agent or the player himself may announce to the press that he will demand an "appropriate" salary for his continued services with the ball club. Once Hobbs's agent holds a press conference and announces a figure of "what this hero is worth," he has thrown down the gauntlet. The club may respond with similarly extreme posturing about the player's ungratefulness for the club's willingness to offer him this opportunity and his lack of understanding of the club's current financial limitations. The club may also denigrate the player's potential contribution to the club's success and suggest that it may no longer be very interested in his services. Management may leak stories about the player's uncertain physical condition. These opening salvos, duly reported by sports reporters who are hungry for controversy, set the stage for negotiations.

Hobbs's nemesis (in the book and the movie) is newspaper reporter Max Mercy. Mercy would certainly amplify the wattage on these public positions. Mercy unearthed Hobbs's dark history, learning how, at a railroad stop on his way to his tryout with the Cubs as a teenager, Hobbs had challenged an aging, Babe Ruth–like figure, Wammer Wambold, to a three-pitch contest. He fanned the national idol, but that only attracted the attention of the star-struck witness, the mysterious, shrouded Harriet Bird, who had been stalking the Wammer. Later, in a Chicago hotel room, Bird shot Hobbs, ending temporarily the pilgrim's progress toward baseball stardom.

What impact does this preliminary stage of posturing have on subsequent negotiations? How will Max Mercy's stories play at the negotiation table? That depends, in part, on the public's reaction to the posturing and on whether the negotiation process will respond to public input. In general, experienced negotiators appreciate that this stage is similar to the feather display of a peacock, designed to soften an opponent's resolve. On the other hand, negotiators are real people whose feelings can be hurt by negative public statements. The pain can linger and inhibit real bargaining, once that stage begins. A kind word, or what Lax and Sebenius call "the simple pleasure one derives from being treated with respect," can go far in facilitating negotiations. A public outcry in favor of Hobbs would make the no-agreement alternatives less attractive for the Knights. Public derision of Hobbs, on the other hand, diminishes his value to the club.

Fisher and Ury would counsel against any public posturing in stating a party's position. Hobbs's agent's ego may become identified with the salary he cannot achieve for his client through negotiations. The club's response in the form of personal attacks on Hobbs will sour the bargaining relationship before it has even begun. Both would do well to focus on their interests on the problem they must solve together by setting a fair salary for Roy Hobbs.

Worthy of Respect

Moving briefly from the fictional to the real world of baseball bargaining, the public posturing by the Boston Red Sox and their All-Star first baseman, Mo Vaughn, during the 1998 season presents a perfect example of the harmful potential of this phase of negotiation. Vaughn was completing his eighth year with the Bosox. With his contract expiring, he was entitled under the collective bargaining agreement to declare free agency and explore the market of competing ball clubs. Vaughn was a "good public citizen," respected by the people of Boston. The fans loved their husky, powerful first baseman. His Mo Vaughn Youth Development Center in Dorchester, Massachusetts, provided after-school activities for inner-city youth. Vaughn was as fine a performer as there was in the game, and a model of a gentleman and an athlete. The Elias Sports Bureau statistics would later confirm the fact that during the 1998 season he was the premier first baseman in the game.

For months before any real contract negotiations had begun, the Boston newspapers were filled with quotes from Vaughn and the Red Sox management. Vaughn professed that he was not focused on money. He only sought "respect" from the club, and sportswriters who had followed Vaughn for years knew he was sincere. The club thought that their reported offer to Vaughn of $10,000,000 a year represented barrels of "respect." But in fact, at the All-Star break, the club had offered Vaughn (through his able agent, Tom Reich) less than that, a four-year, $37,000,000 contract. Finally, disturbed by his club's public derision, Vaughn announced in midseason that he would not re-sign with the Red Sox.

The posturing stage of the Vaughn salary negotiations drew to an abrupt close, but it had caused significant damage to the bargaining relationship. The Red Sox had publicly abused their star first baseman in the middle of a pennant race by failing to give him the intangible acknowledgment he sought. That simple act of unkindness might have soured the deal for good. At the same time, Vaughn lost some public affection from Boston fans who now thought he was just another mercenary preparing to desert them. (Red Sox fans, of course, still burn with the memory of another slugger shipped south eight decades earlier when owner Harry Frazee sold Babe Ruth to the Yankees.) Although Mo only was seeking a courteous regard for his contributions to the club over his career, his antics might have been seen as just another play for more money. The Red Sox must have known that they could re-sign Vaughn if they were willing to offer him the respect he so richly deserved. As owner John Harrington told the Boston Globe: "When the year is over, we will lock in on getting Mo. But it is my responsibility to do what is in the best interests of the organization." Harrington genuinely believed that Mo Vaughn would come crawling back to Fenway.

After the close of the season, Vaughn declared his free agency, as expected, and he was not alone. Following the 1998 season, there were 169 free agents, including many of the game's finest players—for example, American League batting champ Bernie Williams of the Yankees, and two of the National League's premier starting pitchers, Kevin Brown of the Padres and Randy Johnson of the Astros. In addition, the talented but troubled Albert Belle of the White Sox was available. Belle had hit more home runs after the 1998 All-Star break than Mark McGwire and led his league in batting average, runs batted in, and home runs in that half-season. His contract with the White Sox had a clause that allowed him to entertain offers from other clubs during a month-long window period.

The 1998 postseason featured the best free agent class since 1992–93, when Barry Bonds, Greg Maddux, and David Cone were on the market. Thus, perhaps the Red Sox thought they were right to lay back in the Vaughn negotiations until he realized there were other sluggers in the marketplace. In fact, however, the club's delay in pursuing Vaughn proved disastrous. The player dealings of 1998 would provide an extraordinary example of baseball's free agent auction in operation, which we will analyze in Chapter 8.

Vaughn used the remainder of the 1998 season to display his on-field skills, although his club did not need any additional evidence of his value to the team. Vaughn would lead the Red Sox into the divisional playoffs as a wild card team. The hiatus in negotiations gave the parties an opportunity to cool the rhetoric. After the close of the season, on October 30, 1998, in an interview given to Will McDonough of the Boston Globe, Harrington set forth the Red Sox' position in straightforward terms:

> Our people have been in touch with Mo's agents. They will be in Orlando over the weekend talking, but I don't think anything will happen until next Thursday or so. Up to that point, teams are not allowed to give a specific offer to a free agent from another team. So I think Mo's people will wait until that time to see what offers they have from other teams and every detail of those offers. At that time, we think we will find out for the first time exactly what it will take for us to re-sign Mo. We don't know now how much money he'll be looking for. We don't know how many years he wants to sign for. We'd like to sign him for three. But we offered him four years last summer at the All-Star break, and if he wants four, we'll go four. If we can't meet what they want, then we will move on and get someone else signed with the money we have slotted for Mo. If there is no one player, then we will use it to get two very good players. Our top priority [after Vaughn] is still a frontline pitcher. We asked [Red Sox manager] Jimy [Williams] and his wish is for more pitching.

Baseball's salary structure had changed, however, since July 1998, when Vaughn and the Sox were last in contact. The week the World Series ended, the New York Mets signed their future Hall of Fame catcher, Mike Piazza, to a seven-year, $91,000,000 contract, the largest in baseball history up to that time, although it would not remain so for long. When asked about the impact of the Piazza deal on the Vaughn negotiations, Harrington responded:

> I think Piazza is the standard for this year. I don't think anyone [else] is going to get that kind of money. I look around baseball and I don't see it coming from any other team. The Mets are in a unique situation. They are fighting for the back pages in New York [referring to the sports headlines of the *New York Post* and *Daily News*] with the Yankees, and they've been losing. They have to try to keep themselves in the news to generate positive publicity. That's why they went out right away and got Piazza this deal and signed [their star pitcher Al] Leiter. And I'm sure they will spend more money before they are finished. But they are the only team that I can see that is in that kind of situation.

Harrington would prove a poor prognosticator, and his attitude had doomed negotiations with his star player.

Vaughn's main interest in negotiations was the security of a long-term deal. On Friday, November 6, 1998, now backed by the financial resources of the Disney organization, the Anaheim Angels proclaimed the start of competitive bidding with a blast by offering Vaughn a six-year contract for around $72,000,000. In response, Vaughn said he was awaiting offers from the Dodgers, Orioles, Yankees, Rockies, and White Sox. In a weekend television interview, he expressed the hope of wrapping up the matter in a few days, saying, "I don't plan to string this out." Vaughn continued to express his desire to complete his career in Boston, but, he explained, there would no longer be a "home town discount."

It is likely Boston could have signed Vaughn at any time in the 1998 season for a four-year, $44,000,000 deal. The club tendered its first post-season offer to Vaughn's agent on Monday, November 9, three days after the Angels made their six-year, $72,000,000 bid. Although not announced publicly, Boston's offer was said to be for five years at a total of $63,000,000. In part because of the damage done in the posturing stage of negotiations, the Red Sox' offer would not be sufficient for the club to keep its most popular player.

Initial Positions

Negotiations commence when the parties meet to communicate their initial positions. A face-to-face encounter is a prerequisite to real negotiations. Studies show that negotiations in writing or even by telephone simply do not have the same prospects of success. There is something about sitting across the table from your "cooperative antagonist" that promotes an effective exchange.

Opening positions influence how the parties perceive the negotiation challenge. They display each parties' aspirations, but are rarely tendered with any genuine expectation of immediate agreement. Opening moves present an opportunity to capture information about the bargaining opponent, set the ground rules for later negotiations, and reduce bargaining uncertainty.

The initial offer and demand have a *boundary effect* on negotiations, which means that once a party makes a demand or tenders an offer, it implicitly promises never to demand more or offer less as long as the factual circumstances do not change. Without this understood protocol, parties do not know when bargaining has begun. You cannot negotiate with a moving target, although you can negotiate from a position that is initially unacceptable.

Let us assume that Hobbs's agent tenders an initial salary demand of $6,000,000. The agent might explain the basis for the demand: His client wants to be paid an amount equal to his contribution to the major league club. Hobbs always said he would be the best, and he proved it; now he wants to be paid accordingly. He is not asking to be paid as much as the other superstars, however. Although arguably the best power hitter in the game, at $6,000,000 there would be forty or so major leaguers paid as much or more in annual salary.

The agent's initial demand is based on an objective criterion, the player's contribution to the club. He does not explain, however, how he reached the $6,000,000 estimate for Hobbs's "contribution." Interestingly, this initial demand also rejects an alternative measure that many players use, namely comparability of pay to other ballplayers with similar levels of performance. Perhaps Hobbs's agent appreciates that his client is not similarly situated to other players because of his age and physical condition. In any case, a process of negotiations has commenced.

The Knights respond to Hobbs's demand by offering the major league average salary of $1,500,000. This too is an objective standard, although Pop does not explain why he thinks Hobbs is only worth what an average ballplayer earns. Hobbs's agent now knows that the star player is worth at least this amount to the Knights, something he did not know before the club's initial offer. His client can always say "yes" to $1,500,000, more than seven times the contract minimum of $200,000, although that is not likely to happen soon. Likewise, the club knows that its salary exposure for this player is capped at $6,000,000, far below the going rate for the game's superstars. It can draft a contract in that amount and be assured of the services of the Natural.

Neither side is likely to accept the other's initial position, but this opening gambit begins the process of communication. It also sets a presumptive settlement point of $3,750,000, which is midway between the opposing opening positions. This is why the counteroffer is often critical. Subjectively, the parties may focus on this midpoint. They have begun to negotiate. Although the parties know that initial bargaining positions are just openers, they have found them quite useful.

Of course, absurd initial positions can disrupt subsequent negotiations. Bargaining positions must fall within the range of possibility, even if they are not immediately acceptable. If a player demanded $100,000,000 just for the coming season and the club offered $50,000 (below the minimum set by the collective bargaining agreement), the parties would have shown such bad faith as to make fruitful negotiations impossible. Such initial positions signal an unwillingness to reach an agreement on any terms. Although the multimillion-dollar spread in the opening positions of Hobbs and the Knights leaves plenty of room for bargaining and presents a real challenge for the negotiators, today's ballplayers are paid salaries at both the $1,500,000 and $6,000,000 levels. There is work to do at the bargaining table, but the well has not been poisoned by the spread between the parties' initial positions.

Each party enters negotiations with a set of subjective personal preferences, which economists sometimes refer to as a *preference curve*. For example, let us assume that Hobbs would receive an enormous amount of personal satisfaction from a $6,000,000 a year contract. (Wouldn't you?) Fixing a value for our purposes, let us say this is worth a hundred units of satisfaction to the player. A $5,000,000 contract is also a very good thing to Hobbs and might be worth eighty units. A $4,000,000 contract is more modestly valued at twenty units, but at the initial stages of negotiations anything less is not acceptable and would bring Hobbs no satisfaction at all.

The club's preferences might be the mirror image of the player's. Let us assume the New York Knights will receive the greatest degree of satisfaction from a settlement at its initial offer price of $1,500,000, some satisfaction from a $2,000,000 settlement, a minimum amount of satisfaction from a $3,000,000 settlement, but no satisfaction at all from paying Hobbs anything more than $3,000,000 a year. (Remember the Knights also must negotiate with a full roster of players. Paying Hobbs more than $3,000,000 might require paying these other players more money as well. Salary negotiations thus have a spillover effect on a ball club.)

Under the current collective bargaining agreement between the owners and the players association, when a team's total salary is one of the five highest in the league, the team is "taxed," and this amount is pooled with other revenues and distributed to other clubs. Thus, a multimillion-dollar contract for Hobbs may actually cost the Knights more than its specific amount if it is taxable under the collective bargaining agreement.

Hobbs receives no satisfaction with a salary below $4,000,000, and the Knights receive no satisfaction with a salary above $3,000,000. At this initial stage, the satisfaction curves do not intersect. There is no settlement point at which both the player and the club reap utility of any amount. If the parties' curves had overlapped, there would be a "contract zone" within which they could agree and both be better off than with their no-agreement alternatives. Without a contract zone, no agreement is possible, but remember that the negotiation process has only just begun. There is work to be done if Hobbs and the Knights are to reach an agreement.

Information Exchange

Parties need information before they can recalibrate their interests and preferences. By supplying information to and eliciting information from the opposing party, a negotiator alters his and his opponent's perceptions, interests, and behaviors. Effective communication consumes time, however, and salary negotiations must often simmer for a while. The club and the player will reassess their levels of satisfaction and their reservation prices as they learn more during the course of negotiations. But what information is trustworthy? If the general manager and the player's agent have dealt productively with one another before, there may be mutual trust in the information exchange; alternatively, a prior bad experience between the two might have destroyed all confidence in information supplied.

Information communication is vital for negotiations, but it also can be used as an effective strategy. One party always knows more than the other about some things, a situation economists call *asymmetric information distribution*. Hobbs's agent may have the most reliable information about his client's medical condition, for example, whereas the Knights ownership knows about potential substitutes for him—minor league prospects, trade possibilities, and other free agents—and their potential prices.

Parties use information (and misinformation) as a bargaining tactic in an effort to affect the perceived value of no-agreement alternatives and the likelihood of reaching an agreement. The Knights might reveal to Hobbs's agent that they have an interest in other free agent outfielders. (Bobby Bonilla always seems to be available.) These substitutes may not be of Hobbs's caliber, but they also might not carry his price tag. Hobbs suggests in response that he might just retire and live on residuals from the movie that is certain to made of his life.

Information communication has an ethical dimension as well. Should the agent tell Pop that Hobbs's physician has given him a clean bill of health? That would appear to be vital information, but what if this is not completely true? Can the agent lie in the interest of his client? How does this affect the negotiations? The parties expect hyperbole, but they cannot countenance disingenuousness.

Patience and a Deadline

Negotiations require patience and, at times, obstinacy. As Branch Rickey said: "You can't solve everything in a minute. Make time your ally. Delay sharp action." The party with the greater patience and the lesser risk aversion is more likely to prevail. The negotiator who is not in a rush to consummate an agreement likewise has a distinct advantage. At the same time, deadlines tend to move negotiations forward. In collective bargaining, for example, there is the date a contract expires or the date after the expiration when the union threatens to strike or the employer threatens to lockout its employees. It is only when such a deadline is reached that a *cost of disagreement* is imposed on the other side. Without a deadline, there is no motive power to compromise. In other words, why give in if nothing will happen if you do not?

In salary negotiations under the reserve system for players not eligible for free agency or salary arbitration, the start of the season sets a functional deadline. Only then does the player start losing salary and the club start missing the player's contribution to the team. Under the collective bargaining agreement, the owners and the players association have set a precise deadline in mid-March by which players must be signed for the forthcoming season.

Other time limits apply with regard to players eligible for free agency. Under the collective bargaining agreement, an eligible player "may give notice of his election of free agency within the 15 day period beginning on October 15, or the day following the last game of the World Series, whichever is later." After that notice, other clubs may negotiate terms with the player. The player's former club has until December 7 to offer the salary arbitration option to its free agent. If it does not, the club forfeits all rights to negotiate with and sign the free agent until the following May 1. If it does offer salary arbitration but the free agent refuses, the club has until January 8 to re-sign the player. Again, if the club does not meet this deadline, it loses the right to contract with the free agent until May 1.

These fixed contract deadlines can have a dramatic effect on negotiations. Similar deadlines are in place regarding junior players eligible for salary arbitration, as we will discuss in Chapter 7. In all instances, the deadlines make negotiations work, because threats can then be realized and costs imposed. Deadlines also provide the parties with a safe period in which to reach an agreement. Until then, the status quo prevails.

In the old days, before player agents and free agency, negotiations were much simpler for both owners and players. Normally, they did not require much time or patience. The club owner or his general manager told the player what his salary would be. If the player balked, the owner might sweeten his offer to show he was a nice guy who cared for "his" players. Alternately, the owner might ask the player how much he wanted to get paid, and the naive country boy—too embarrassed to ask for what he was really worth in terms of his contribution to the club's revenue—would almost always ask for too little.

Strategic Negotiations: How to Throw a Preference Curve

Roy Hobbs and the New York Knights remain $4,500,000 apart after exchanging their initial bargaining positions. For the economic purist, the object of negotiations should be to reach agreement at a point of maximum satisfaction for both parties. (This goal, termed *Pareto optimality*, is the settlement point at which there is no alternative agreement that makes Hobbs better off without hurting the Knights, and vice versa.) Hobbs and Pops are not purists but rather realists, earnestly seeking to find their way to a contract. What do they do now?

Hobbs and the Knights are bargaining over what is called a *continuous variable*—money. A continuous variable is comparatively easy to adjust. There are multiple settlement points between the extremes, although at this stage of the Hobbs negotiations none of these is acceptable. Hobbs wants more money; the Knights want to pay less money. Anything Hobbs receives over his reservation price, the lowest salary he is willing to accept, is seller surplus. Anything the Knights pay under than their reservation price is buyer surplus. The negotiation process allocates these surpluses.

Parties use negotiation tactics to create a contract zone within which an agreement on salary is possible. These tactics can be positive or negative, and are likely to be both during the course of a successful negotiation. Each party wants want to disguise its own reservation prices and ascertain their opponent's reservation price. By presenting arguments, making threats, and taking commitments, each side attempts to alter the satisfaction curves of the other side. In short, they seek to inflate the cost of disagreement. The most obvious means of doing this, of course, is to threaten to break off negotiations.

The most difficult aspect of any threat or even an inflexible commitment is to make it believable to the opposing party. Hobbs cannot threaten to live off his savings, since he has no savings. (By comparison, as we shall see in the next chapter, Ty Cobb used his baseball earnings to make profitable investments, in particular by purchasing Coca-Cola stock; when he stated he would leave the game were he not paid as much as he wished, the Detroit Tigers could not ignore his threat.)

Negotiations are not only a series of negative threats. Participants may alternatively use the "carrot" in an attempt to increase the perceived payoff to the opposite party if an agreement is reached. Hobbs's agent, for example, can make promises. He legitimately can claim his client will again be the backbone of the club, since without him the Knights were in last place. With him, they won the pennant, and he is ready to lead the Knights to another championship. It seems rather simple, doesn't it? Compare attendance figures with Hobbs and without him. Hobbs made money for the Knights, and he will do so again this coming season.

The Knights know very well what Hobbs meant to the club. What they do not know, and what Hobbs's agent cannot tell them with any certainty, is how well he will perform this coming season and how much he is worth. His checkered past makes that prediction hazardous, and even without considering Hobbs's unique history, there are always uncertainties in predicting player performance. Pop does not want to embarrass or demean his star outfielder in negotiations, but he does not want to overpay him either.

Hobbs explains once again how many fans will pay to see him destroy the lights in Knights Stadium. The Knights respond that Hobbs will always be a hero, and they remind him of the many endorsement opportunities he would have by staying in New York to play baseball. (Of course, some fans might see him as just a money-hungry, and aging, ingrate.)

The Fisher-Ury alternative approach to bargaining offers Hobbs and Pop another way to work toward an agreement. First, the parties would explain what they seek from bargaining not in terms of dollar amounts but of principles and goals. Each should clearly communicate. If either side is uncertain about what the other is saying, it should ask questions. At this stage, the negotiators should listen actively, acknowledge what is said, and not argue with the other side.

Hobbs might explain that, after all those years in the wilderness, he really wants to be paid well. He sees what other, more fortunate ballplayers are earning, and that upsets him. Pop might explain that he has all these other negotiations to complete with players on his club, and he is worried about the uncertain finances of his franchise. Also, because Hobbs came to the Knights like lightning out of a blue sky, Pop is afraid his good fortune could leave just as abruptly. Neither party should blame the other for its own problems, and each should recognize the interests of its counterpart as legitimate.

How then can these two parties reconcile their interests? Fisher and Ury would suggest using a process of inventing options that provide mutual gain. With this system, there is no single right answer. The parties should instead explore solutions that would leave their opposite number satisfied; any option should be considered valid, as long as it is based on an objective principle.

Fans normally envision the salary negotiation process as an acerbic, negative, verbal fistfight. This image does reflect part of the reality. There are real costs involved in the typical process, because, unfortunately, the parties rarely follow the Fisher-Ury approach of principled bargaining. Hobbs is a ballplayer, not a negotiator, and Pop is a baseball man. They both are spending valuable off-season time haggling over a salary. The anxieties and uncertainties of negotiation impose a real psychic cost on the participants.

Hobbs and Pop appreciate each other's role, however. They may even wear their platitudes on their sleeves, praising each other for his contributions to the club and the game. Each protests that all he wants is a fair deal. Pop may blame others for his inability to accede to what are Hobbs's otherwise "reasonable demands." Hobbs may respond that he owes it to the Knights' fans to be their hero, which requires the club to pay him like the superstar they think he is. At times, logic may take a backseat in the exchange. At other times, malevolence may rule. Pop, for instance, may offer as "facts" information that cannot be verified, or press Hobbs to take his offer or leave. These may all be bargaining ploys, or they may be real. How do you know?

Promises, Trust, and Cooperation

In our Hobbs hypothetical, there is still no contract zone within which both parties would obtain more satisfaction from making a deal than from losing one. The parties must shift their preferences if there is to be an agreement. A reevaluation of their interests and needs may foster a reassessment of their reservation prices. The agent has presented "evidence" of his client's worth to the club using statistics similar to those employed in salary arbitration. Unlike salary arbitration, however, where the player's performance and salary are compared with those of all other comparable players, here the statistics are likely tailored to meet the needs of the particular ball club. The Knights, who are looking for a power hitter to drive in runs from the fourth position in the lineup, appreciate Hobbs's power figures and run-producing ability. The player's agent should know the Knights' weaknesses and explain how Hobbs's strengths meet those needs. Effective salary negotiations require fluency both in the game of baseball and in the characteristics of the party across the table. Clear thinking is a premium asset.

The Knights, of course, have the same statistics on their player and know their team needs. A skilled player agent, however, can massage performance statistics in a way the negotiating club might not have fully appreciated. The agent is offering promises to the club: "If you sign my man at the right salary, he is likely to do this or that for you." No one can promise with certainty what will occur, only what is likely to occur given the prior experience. These promises may enhance the club's appreciation of the player's value, however, and thus shift the club's preference curve toward creating a contract zone.

The agent must build trust at this stage of the negotiations by spinning his statistics into a comprehensive picture of the player—warts and all—or his tailored figures will be ignored as hyperbole. Every player has weaknesses, and admitting those weaknesses may play a critical role in creating an atmosphere within which settlement is possible. On the other hand, such admissions may shift the player's preference curve in the direction of the club's. In any case, a balanced presentation of the statistics will help move the negotiating process along.

In baseball salary bargaining, parties negotiate to advance their own interests, not to diminish the interests of their opposing party. The parties need each other if they are to produce the entertainment package fans purchase when they come out to a game. No one would attend a game if there were no players on the field. No one would watch an individual player standing alone on a sandlot hitting baseballs over the fence, except perhaps for Mark McGwire or Sammy Sosa. Cooperation between the club and its players is therefore essential, and neither players nor owners want to be so triumphant in negotiations as to drive the other out of the business. But even though the club and the player have shared interests, this does not mean that any particular club must sign any particular player. There are always substitutes, although perhaps not of the same value to a club. The prospect of no deal makes both parties more reasonable.

A negotiator who works to keep hostility under control and negotiations on track may be more successful in the end than one who erupts. A negotiator who shows empathy for the opposite party's concerns and circumstances (even if spurious) may strike gold. A successful negotiator learns the relationship between the issues on the table and seeks key concessions by linking issues together. Hobbs's agent might say: "If you want some give on salary, you need to give us something on the length of the contract." This form of *integrative bargaining* produces joint gains and more stable agreements.

Hardball

Baseball salary negotiations rarely follow the cooperative model of negotiations sketched out above. In some cases, the use of hardball tactics akin to a chin-high inside fastball is more prominent. Listening carefully, negotiators discover their opposite numbers' core values and interests. Effective negotiators then hold their opponents' key values hostage.

The tough bargainer learns how to make a commitment in negotiations and convince the opposing party he cannot be moved. In this situation, a party's position is no longer a matter of willingness. It becomes instead a matter of ability, and there is bargaining power in relinquishing the options of conceding or compromising. A credible commitment effectively communicated can be effective, but it is an enormous gamble. If Hobbs's agent says his client will not sign for anything less than $6,000,000 and tells the Knights that they should not contact him again unless they are ready to meet that figure, the die is cast. This is not a risk-free strategy, of course. Accepting a settlement at any lower level will involve a substantial loss of face. Commitments enhance the risks of a deadlock. The Knights may look elsewhere and not contact Hobbs again.

Less dramatic than a commitment is a threat, a conditional commitment: "If you do not move your offer (or demand), then I will break off negotiations." Once again, if communicated and believed, this tactic can move an opposing party's preference curve. However, threats must be carried out on occasion if they are to be taken seriously and not seen just as a case of "crying wolf." They also may sour negotiations sufficiently to produce a deadlock.

Although baseball's ethos as an American idyll includes the core values of truth-telling and genuineness, parties also prevail in negotiations, at least in the short run, by telling lies and exploiting the opposition's ignorance. Baseball players rarely had agents until the 1960s. Players were untutored, easy targets for management, especially within a negotiating system where the rules favored the clubs.

In the long term, fair dealing likely is rewarded. Clubs, players, and their agents develop reputations that they carry into later negotiations. Parties face an ethical challenge in negotiations, which converts into strategic power. If they "do the right thing," they may sacrifice present advantage. If they "don't do the right thing," they may never be trusted again.

Personal interaction between representatives of the parties often determine whether there is a deal or no deal. Some sports agents are legendary for their irascible personalities. Does that tactic work? It depends, of course, on the experience and fortitude of the club's representatives and on the value the club places on the agent's clients. There is no excuse for a negotiation that should have succeeded because it would have benefited both the club and the player yet failed because of bad negotiating on the part of one or both parties.

Creative Bargaining

Because of the inherent cooperative impulse of baseball salary negotiations, clubs and players may pursue creative strategies to move toward agreement. If Hobbs's agent and the Knights discuss their real interests—those they share and others they do not—and explore options for fulfilling those interests, they will move toward agreement. The parties may not yet be able to agree on a salary, but they might be able to agree that any salary reached must fairly compensate the player as compared with his peers in the game and reflect the profits made by the team because of the player's services. Throughout the negotiations the parties can then return to this norm as the measure of any particular proposal.

As Lax and Sebenius point out, differences between the interests and perceptions of the parties play a key role in negotiations. Parties have different tastes, capabilities, attitudes towards risk, and concepts of the passage of time. They also make different predictions as to the future. Good negotiators seek to discover and exploit these differences. If a player is risk averse—that is, if he seeks certainty—he may be willing to accept a smaller, although certain, salary. Other players, perhaps many, have inflated views of their own potential, and may be willing to accept less "sure" money in exchange for higher performance-based bonuses.

A club makes predictions about the future performance (and fan attractiveness) of dozens of players each year. It may be less risk averse than individual players because it can spread those risks across the group of players. Some players will have astonishing years, while others will suffer downturns in performance. Here the parties can use their differences to jointly gain through negotiations. From the outside, the outcome of negotiations may look like a win or a loss to one party or the other, yet from the inside, both parties may be happy because they are interested in different things, which the agreement addressed.

A perfect example of a creative way for parties to achieve their joint interests is a *contingent agreement,* such as bonus provisions in a player's contract. Here is where Hobbs and the Knights may find the key to their settlement. After Hobbs's agent has spent hours extolling the virtues of his client, management might respond that, in this case, the player should be willing to allow his bat and glove demonstrate his ability and determine his pay. In short, let him earn his salary as he goes by using contract bonus provisions. The same response works for the Knights' concern about their star's durability as a player. Let the length of his contract be contingent on his annual plate appearances or games played.

Players, as a rule, are paid a flat salary, but many player contracts contain bonus provisions that reward performance during the contract year. Bonuses come in two different forms—"makeable" bonuses and "fantasy" bonuses. The players association's study of bonus provisions from 1986 until 1998 found that potential performance bonuses (makeable bonuses) in player contracts totaled $470,523,956, but that only $217,959,272, or 46 percent, were actually earned.

Rewarding an everyday player for accumulating a certain number of plate appearances in a season is an achievable bonus. If he stays healthy and plays at his expected rate of play, he should earn that bonus. A bonus for winning the Cy Young Award as the best pitcher in each league, on the other hand, is for all but a very few select starters not a realistic bonus. The contracts of many starting pitchers contain a bonus provision for winning the Cy Young Award, but only one pitcher can do so in each league each year. On the other hand, the Cy Young bonus provision for Roger Clemens has been money in the bank. By winning his fifth such honor after the 1998 season, he received a $250,000 bonus. Even Kevin Brown's $15,000,000-a-year contract with the Los Angeles Dodgers contains an additional incentive provision for his rank in the Cy Young voting. Management will offer these fantasy bonuses without too much concern in response to an agent's claim that his client is in fact the best pitcher in the league. "If he's the best pitcher," the club argues, "then he will win the Cy Young!" Sometimes fantasy bonuses come true. For example, under the terms of his contract, Scott Brosius earned a $100,000 bonus for being named the 1998 World Series MVP.

Bonuses whose achievement is within the total discretion of management are troublesome. If a pitcher's bonus is triggered by the number of games started and that number is sufficiently high, a manager's decision not to start a pitcher may mean the player cannot achieve that goal. There are historical examples of such misdealing.

White Sox owner Charlie Comiskey, a stingy tyrant, demonstrated to his players how to cheat by manipulating contract bonus provisions. In 1919, Comiskey's contract with star pitcher Ed Cicotte provided for a $5,000 salary plus a bonus for winning thirty games. After Cicotte had won his twenty-ninth and the Sox had clinched the pennant, Comiskey told manager Kid Gleason not to start Cicotte. He finished the season 29–7 with a 1.82 earned run average. Cicotte learned his lesson well: He was a ringleader in fixing the 1919 World Series and received $10,000— doubling his salary—for doing so.

Although a player who can establish management's bad faith in terms of a performance bonus now may have recourse through the grievance procedure under the collective bargaining agreement, it is preferable for an agent to foresee such a possibility and write contract language to protect his client. For example, for purposes of a performance bonus a pitcher could be credited with a start that he did not receive but that would have been his in the normal rotation unless the club can establish that he was not physically fit to pitch.

Fisher and Ury emphasize that the negotiating parties should attempt to separate the *people* who are bargaining from the *problem* they seek to resolve. It is realistic to assume that both parties want to find a way to reach an agreement acceptable to both sides. Despite their competitive spirit, they do not win by besting the opposing party, but by solving the problem they both have—here, setting an appropriate salary. If the cooperative antagonists work together, they may be able to solve that problem. As a harmonic ideal, such side-by-side bargaining is certainly worth the effort.

As a result of the use of bargaining tactics, the preference curves of the parties may shift to create a contract zone. The player agent may become more realistic about the potential settlement point when the club explains other financial contingencies. If the player has no other legitimate offers from competing clubs, his demands may moderate. Hobbs, of course, has no options with other clubs because he is only a second-year player in the majors.

Signaling

Both parties in the Hobbs case recognized that their initial positions were starting points, and both want to reach an agreement. Both also want to avoid what game theorists term *decision regret*, resulting from either failing to reach an agreement or agreeing to an unsatisfactory settlement. Both parties would be much better off with Hobbs in uniform, and they know it. It is time for the waiting game to end. How can Hobbs and the Knights inform each other that they are about to reveal genuine and credible concessions? How do they signal the opposing party that it is time to reach a deal?

Baseball signals are an age-old art form. Watch the third base coach relay signals to the hitter and the runner before a hit-and-run play. He touches the bill of the cap, then his belt, and the next signal is the real one . . . or maybe not. A catcher's signals to the pitcher with a runner on second base are supposed to confuse opponents. However difficult baseball signals are, bargaining signals are even more so.

The transition from sparing to genuine give-and-take negotiating is complex, especially if earlier public or private interchanges between the parties have been caustic. Hobbs and Pop have always shown each other mutual respect, which should make communications easier, but neither wants to lose face.

Hobbs's agent will not have to spend the coming season in the dugout with Pop and Roy. As an experienced negotiator, he can reveal more of his client's true position in the interest of reaching a deal and suggest ways to bridge the gap between the parties. He can take more of the heat, shielding his client from the owner's belligerence. Signaling cues are subtle, but, like those to the base runner, they must be read correctly. A missed signal on the field will lead to a sure out. A missed signal in negotiation may lead to an unnecessary impasse.

The lessons of good negotiating are really quite simple: Communicate the message you want the other side to hear. Have patience, because salary negotiation is a complex behavioral game. If you want to win big, you must be willing to accept risk, but no more than is absolutely necessary. A good negotiator knows where that line should be drawn.

Fenway Farewell

For Boston's Mo Vaughn and his potential suitors, negotiating salary was not particularly difficult. The Red Sox' offer to Vaughn as publicly announced was substantially lower in numbers and shorter in duration than the offer already made by the Anaheim Angels. More importantly, as far as Vaughn was concerned, the Red Sox' offer showed a lack of respect and appreciation for his career-long contributions to the club and the city. One newspaper commentator opined that the club's proposal was just high enough to convince the Boston fans that the club had made an earnest effort to sign their much admired star, but low enough to make sure Vaughn would reject it, which is exactly what happened.

On the day before Thanksgiving, after the Red Sox had publicly flirted with the Yankees' free agent Bernie Williams, Vaughn agreed to a six-year, $80,000,000 contract with the Angels, a deal that, on an annual salary basis, propelled him above Mike Piazza's record-breaking deal. Vaughn became the highest paid player in baseball, a record he would hold for less than a month.

"Hobbs to Play Again for the Knights"

Once the parties have revealed their genuine positions and, through the use of effective communications and bargaining tactics, repositioned their preference curves and created a contract zone within which any settlement point is preferable to their no-agreement alternatives, it is time to reach an agreement.

The headlines on the *New York Daily Bugle*'s back page reassured the many new fans of the New York Knights that their dashing hero would again be patrolling the outfield in the coming season. The parties had agreed to a contract guaranteeing Hobbs many millions of dollars in salary, with millions more in performance bonuses. If he stays healthy the entire season, for example, by accumulating 500 at bats during the year, the contract extends for another year with a 10 percent salary increase. With grit and determination, Pop's boys will once again compete for the pennant with their best players.

SIX

I am holding out. I will not report to spring training until I receive what I'm worth. That's final.
TY COBB, 1913

The great trouble with baseball today is that most players are in the game for the money that's in it—not for the love of it, the excitement and thrill of it.
TY COBB, 1960

Ty Cobb and Negotiation Hardball

Ty Cobb's salary negotiation strategies—fearless and brazen—mirrored his style of play on the baseball field. (National Baseball Hall of Fame Library, Cooperstown, N.Y.)

Long before the advent of free agency and salary arbitration, players negotiated individually with their clubs over salaries, and none was better at it than the incomparable Ty Cobb. Although today's negotiations, at least those involving free agents, are auctions involving many parties, with clubs competing for the services of valued performers, "premodern" negotiations were one-sided affairs with the owners holding the upper hand. Management would inform the player of his salary for the upcoming season, and the player could either accept it or leave organized professional baseball.

Even within this economic environment of a single purchaser for a player's services, a few players were able to obtain remarkably high salary terms from their clubs. Babe Ruth's $80,000 salary for 1931, valued at $781,000 in current dollars, is a well-known example. His purported quip about the amount is as legendary as the Bambino himself. When told by reporters he would be earning more than the president of the United States (who earned $75,000 a year), Ruth retorted, "I had a better year." Indeed, he did, hitting forty-nine home runs in 1930. President Hoover, by comparison, had had a dreadful year, the first full year of the Great Depression. Ruth would have many more "better years" than most presidents throughout his splendid career.

Cobb, Ruth, Honus Wagner, and Rogers Hornsby all were well paid for their services. In 1910, for example, Wagner was paid twenty times the average American worker's wage for working only six (or seven, if you count spring training) months. Club owners enjoyed the success these stars brought to their clubs; they did not pay high salaries out of beneficence or altruism. Baseball is a business, and these stars attracted paying spectators to the ballparks. Owners undoubtedly believed they would suffer the wrath (and nonpatronage) of the paying customers were they not to field a team with these attractive players.

Most baseball players, even at the major league level, are interchangeable and readily substitutable. For players of Hall of Fame caliber, however, the threat to leave baseball is potent. The Yankees could not replace Babe Ruth, who, almost single-handedly, had resuscitated a sport near moral and economic collapse after the Black Sox scandal. He changed the nature of the game from an "inside-baseball" hit-and-run affair to a power explosion of home runs. Fans would come to the stadium to see the Babe swing for the seats. But who would come if the Yankees did not sign Ruth? The Yankees club knew his value and paid for it.

The uniquely skilled but psychologically troubled Ty Cobb was exceptional in using his bargaining power and negotiating ability to achieve salary increases even when there was only a single purchaser for his services—the Detroit Tigers baseball club. Cobb's career is a series of superlatives—highest lifetime batting average (.366), most years leading the league in batting (12), and most runs scored (2,245). Inducted into the Hall of Fame in its first year of existence, Cobb received seven more votes than Babe Ruth.

Al Stump tells Cobb's life story in his compelling 1994 biography of the Georgia Peach. Cobb was a unique character in the history of the national pastime, as foul and irascible a human being who ever sped around the base paths and perhaps the national game's fiercest competitor. In addition to recounting Cobb's well-known exploits on the diamond, Stump relates a number of scenarios that highlight his skill in baseball salary negotiations. An analysis of Cobb's methods will demonstrate bargaining tactics applicable generally in all such transactions.

Spikes Flying at the Negotiating Table

As a bilious but naturally talented teenager, Tyrus Cobb signed his first professional baseball contract with the minor league Tourists club of Augusta, Georgia, a short distance from his hometown of Royston. The Tourists played in the South Atlantic, or "Sally," League. Cobb was the son of a schoolteacher and sometime mayor of his hometown. He was an undisciplined, disputatious, and obnoxious youth with a talent for the game of baseball. He played thirty-four games for the Tourists during the 1904 season at $65 a month. For the 1905 season, Cobb demanded a raise to $125 a month.

Cobb was unsure the Tourists even wanted him back, but, of course, he did not exhibit any doubt in dealing with Andy Roth, the team's field manager, who handled salary matters for his employer. Cobb's negotiation style was "to appear to be unconcerned." Stump relates the Cobb-Roth negotiations as follows:

> Roth stood firm on $65, maybe $75. Ty replied that he wanted to talk to President Bill Croke of the Tourists. Cobb repeated to Roth's boss that southern colleges would be pleased to enroll him. His extreme youth probably influenced Croke's decision; the school threat might not have been believed from a twenty-five-year-old. Croke, thinking of Cobb's age, foot speed, crowd-pleasing steals, room to develop, and the casual interest already shown in him by higher-league scouts, which might lead to a sale or trade upward, settled for between $90 and $125. (Cobb always insisted that he got $125 from Croke; other sources placed it lower.)

This early negotiation scenario demonstrates a number of strategic tactics Cobb would use again in the big leagues to his great financial advantage.

At the threshold of these negotiations, the parties had diametrically opposed interests. Cobb obviously wanted more; the Tourists hoped to hold him at the status quo. Cobb's initial demand started high, at $125 a month. Why would he select that number? Cobb learned this was the amount experienced Tourists players were paid, and thus he could argue he was now "experienced"—or at least contributed to the club's fortunes as much as the experienced players. He was thus basing his argument on the principle of the *inherent equity of being treated as others are treated.* This tactic elevates negotiations beyond a simple demand for more money. The club should pay Cobb that amount, he could argue, because it would be "fair" to do so. It is fair to treat him like everyone else.

Cobb also used the *threat of leaving baseball* to pursue college. Perhaps manager Roth had no idea that Cobb had even considered that option. Frankly, few youngsters from Royston, Georgia, attended college in 1905. Maybe Cobb was bluffing; he never did attend college, but the power of this bargaining ploy depended more on perception than it did on reality.

Roth may have been extremely limited in his flexibility to grant salary increases. He could have told Cobb that he was unable to pay what he demanded. There is, after all, a significant difference between being *unwilling* to grant a player's demand and being *unable* to do so. The latter is a far more powerful bargaining position. Cobb could try to make Roth willing to pay, but if he was genuinely unable to do so, nothing Cobb could do could change the situation. Good bargainers seek to avoid unnecessary impasses. If Roth had been stonewalling and, in fact, had had room to increase his offer, it would have raised the prospect of a standoff in negotiations. Of course, Cobb could always have backed down, but that was not his style.

There is no indication in Stump's recitation of this story whether Cobb was as nasty in interpersonal salary negotiations as he was in running the bases, with his sharpened spikes flashing at defenseless infielders. It was likely he was equally unpleasant, however, because stories about the great player reflect an off-field persona as despicable as his often odious, but awesome, on-field display. He never exhibited a cooperative attitude. It would not have been Cobb's style to "create value" in these salary negotiations by looking for "joint gains," inventing solutions to problems, or engaging in accommodative tactics. He was just interested in "claiming value" for himself.

Cobb hid from Roth the crucial information about his own insecurity. He was unsure whether he had any job, let alone one that would pay him almost twice his previous season's salary. Roth could have used the job security issue effectively, but undoubtedly Cobb's outward arrogance hid his inner self-doubt. Stump's version of the facts, however, suggest that even at this early stage of his professional career, management appreciated Cobb's value to the squad. Unwilling to risk Cobb's departure to another team in another league and recognizing the value of Cobb's services in attracting fans—the gate was a primary source of income to the Tourists—Roth appeared willing to offer Cobb some increase in salary, perhaps to $75 a month.

Cobb then implemented an inspired bargaining strategy. If the party across the table is unwilling or unable to give you more of what you want, switch bargaining partners. Find someone in authority who *will* give you want you want. In this case, Cobb demanded to talk with the owner of the club, Bill Croke. Cobb reiterated his threat to leave baseball and added that he would head off to a southern college that "would be pleased to enroll him." This threat had a greater effect on Croke, who recognized it was at least something Cobb was capable of doing. In this way Cobb changed Croke's perception of his player's alternatives to agreement. Most players have no real options. Cobb made Croke believe that he did.

Even as a novice on the professional stage, Cobb did not have to convince management of the value of his on-field performance, for his promise as a ballplayer was obvious. In addition to his ability to increase ticket sales, Cobb had an even more important value to the club that president Croke understood well, and probably better than manager Roth would have appreciated. A second primary source of income to minor league clubs at that time was selling player contracts to higher minor league clubs and to major league clubs. Long before the advent of the farm system and its blossoming in the 1920s under Branch Rickey of St. Louis, major league clubs relied on independently owned minor league teams to identify and develop baseball talent. Minor league clubs would then sift through their collection of players and market those who had the greatest promise to National and American League clubs. Because Croke knew Cobb would have significant value in such a transaction, he needed to keep him under contract until a major league organization came calling.

Both Cobb and Croke counted on the prospects for the future in order to make a deal for the present—Cobb on his future on the playing field and Croke on his club's future in marketing Cobb. In fact, these salary negotiations created value for both parties, although more for Cobb in the short run, because of the significant immediate value of doubling his salary, and more for Croke in the longer run, because of the potential value of the sale of his contract. In fact, on August 19, 1905, Croke sold Cobb to the Detroit Tigers for $750, more than twice the standard draft price of $350.

It is interesting that Cobb later insisted publicly that he had achieved his initial demand of $125 from the Tourists. His burning need to prevail and, in the process, to embarrass others made him a singular baseball player and an effective negotiator. His game on the field and at the bargaining table knew no limits. As a result, he was capable of making a legitimate, believable commitment in bargaining and stick to it, much in the same way as he would play the game—with complete abandon. As he later said, "I could never stand losing. Second place didn't interest me. I had a fire in my belly."

A Rebel with a Cause: To Win at All Costs

Ty Cobb was soon to become professional baseball's leading hitter and its most despised player, loathed and feared by opponents and teammates alike. He arrived in the major leagues directly from Augusta, and immediately demonstrated the prescience of those who recognized his promise as a player. He was the youngest man ever to win a league batting title, in 1907, just before his twentieth-first birthday. He would win that title the next nine years in a row and twelve out of the next thirteen seasons.

Stump relates the events surrounding the negotiation of his 1913 salary. Once again, Cobb's tactics are instructive in the study of negotiating proficiency. Cobb had earned $9,000 a year for the 1910, 1911, and 1912 campaigns, and demanded from the Tigers a $6,000 raise for 1913. Tigers management—general manager Frank J. Navin and owner William Hoover "Good Times" Yawkey—offered him $10,500. Cobb declined the offer, citing the increased prosperity of the Detroit club. Cobb's two accountants estimated the value of the franchise at $700,000, with Cobb contributing $40,000 per season to team revenues. (It is unclear how these estimates were made, but like much in negotiations, fact and fiction intersect.) Stump reports the interchange between Cobb and management as follows:

> "You know very well they come out to see me," he put it to Yawkey, "and I want $15,000." Navin, as the press reported, retaliated, "You'll play for me at my price or not at all."

For support Cobb called upon such fervid admirers as Grantland Rice of the *New York Evening Mail* and Harry Salsinger of the *[Detroit] News*. The columnists publicized his contributions and salary progress:

1906 — .320 average (led his team), $1,500 salary
1907 — .350 (led league, tied for both leagues' lead), $2,400 salary
1908 — .324 (led his league), $4,500 salary
1909 — .377 (led both leagues), $4,500 salary
1910 — .385 (led both leagues), $9,000 salary
1911 — .420 (led both leagues), $9,000 salary
1912 — .410 (led both leagues), $9,000 salary

These statistics were impressive evidence of Cobb's batting proficiency and his contribution to the club.

The Tigers were not impressed, however, and flatly refused his demand, calling it "unprecedented and outrageous." Its representatives presented the club's list of comparable big league stars and what they earned. Ace hurler Walter Johnson of the Washington Senators earned $8,000 after a 32–12 season in 1912. Big Train already had a career total of 33 shutouts. (He would amass an additional 77 in the remainder of his twenty-one-year career, the most ever by a major leaguer.) Hal Chase, Chicago's star first baseman, earned $7,000. Christy Mathewson of the New York Giants, who won 138 games in the prior five years, earned $9,000. Navin then told the press, "Nobody makes $15,000—Cobb's overimpressed with himself. He'll settle or regret it."

Cobb raised the negotiating ante. He called a press conference and announced: "I am holding out. I will not report to spring training until I receive what I'm worth. That's final." Normally, baseball players were dependent on their salaries for their livelihood, and such a holdout threat was an empty bluff. But Cobb had invested his earnings wisely in Arizona copper mines, Coca-Cola stock, and sporting goods stores; he could afford to make good on his threat. The Tigers' spring training for 1913 began in Gulfport, Mississippi, without Cobb in camp.

One more bargaining ploy by Cobb strengthened the public perception that he could do without baseball: He announced that a Logansport, Indiana, automobile business had offered him $15,000 to serve as its sales agent in Chicago. Cobb wired the car company: "AM READY TO TALK BUSINESS. AWAIT YOUR ORDERS." All these tactics were dutifully reported by the press, often a valuable accessory in negotiations. Frank Navin was furious:

> In the past I have put up with a great deal from Mr. Cobb. It has now reached the point of showdown. It is conceded by everybody that he is the best baseball player in the world. And Mr. Cobb is the best-paid player in the world. But this is not the issue. The issue is discipline. Cobb did not make baseball, baseball made him. A player cannot be bigger than the game which creates him. To give in to Cobb now would be to concede that he is greater than baseball itself, for he has set all its laws at defiance.

Cobb rejoined: "Navin chooses to drag my name through the mud. His statement that discipline and not money is the important issue is enough to queer his whole vicious attack on me. And I wish to deny that I am the best-paid player in the world." (Honus Wagner of the Pittsburgh Pirates actually held that distinction. New York Giants manager John J. McGraw had also just signed a five-year contract at $30,000 a year, making him the highest-paid employee in the game, until Kenesaw Mountain Landis became the first commissioner, earning $50,000 a year.)

The nasty interchange between Cobb and Navin continued in print. Navin offered: "What effect will his I-am-the-law theory have on other players? We might as well turn the club over to Cobb and eventually the League." Cobb than renewed a demand he often made throughout his career: "I'm moveable. Let Detroit sell me elsewhere if they can't meet my demand. I think it likely that some other organization can use me." Frustrated by Cobb's impertinence, the Tigers publicly recapped Cobb's record of insubordination and outrageous behavior in an effort to besmirch his reputation. In an interview given to the New York Times, Tigers management reminded the public of how Cobb had jumped into the stands and punched a disabled fan for heckling him, how he had abandoned the team for a week when he did not like his hotel room, and how he had left in the middle of a pennant race to get married.

Navin called in support from Ban Johnson, the president of the American League, who blasted Cobb by saying that he was an "outlaw. He's always been an outlaw." He then proceeded to recount Cobb's "crimes" in a list that stretched over three pages. Two weeks after the season began, Cobb was still holding out in Georgia, and Johnson formally suspended him for the 1913 season. Cobb seemed cornered, but that was when he was most dangerous. At this point it appeared likely the negotiations would end in a stalemate, unless Cobb were willing to swallow his pride and return to the fold, a most unlikely event. But the great Ty Cobb was not out of negotiating tactics.

As Georgia's favorite son, Cobb had been befriended by two of its legislators, Senator Hoke Smith and Congressman Thomas Gallagher, to whom he had spoken in earlier years about the plight of underpaid professional ballplayers and the collusive actions of the stingy owners. On April 22, 1913, at Cobb's behest, Gallagher introduced a bill in Con-

gress calling upon the Speaker of the House to appoint a special committee "to investigate the operation of the Baseball Trust" and the
attorney general to criminally prosecute team owners who violated the
antitrust laws.

The Tigers surrendered, and the congressional action was dropped.
Cobb's counterattack had won the war. On April 25, he signed a one-
year contract for $12,000, with a $2,000 signing bonus. Detroit owner
Yawkey told Cobb "to be good and take us to another pennant." The
Tigers finished in sixth place at 66–87, although Cobb won another bat-
ting title with a .390 average.

Cobb's 1913 salary negotiations showed the dramatic use of a broad
variety of tactics and strategies. He approached the negotiations with a
simple, announced goal—an annual salary of $15,000. He justified his
demand with performance statistics, dutifully reported to the public by
the press, who appreciated the valuable copy provided by the Cobb-
Navin contretemps. Management responded in the same medium with
contradictory statistics on the salaries of comparable players, which
even in 1913 set the measure of the baseball salary market.

The flaw in the initial strategy of both parties is apparent: Cobb's statistics proved without question that he was a fine hitter, but they do not
make the case for a $6,000 raise. On the other hand, although each name
on Detroit's list of comparable players was an all-star by any standard,
none brought to his team what Cobb delivered. Furthermore, Navin's
parting shot— "He'll settle or regret it"—was gratuitous, and, for a competitor like Cobb, a red flag he could not ignore.

Cobb's next bargaining ploy was the holdout threat. Throughout the
history of professional sports, starting with the New York Giants' Amos
Rusie in the 1890s, withholding services had been the primary cost a
player could impose on his club. The efficacy of such a threat depended
upon the player's perceived ability to carry it out and upon the impact
of his absence on the club. Cobb's holdout imposed a "cost of disagreement" both on himself and on the Tigers.

The efficacy of a *bargaining commitment* such as Cobb's holdout
depended upon whether the Tigers believed he would carry through on
his threat. Here is where Cobb's alternative sources of income played
a significant role. Most teams know that a holdout is costly to the player

whose major source of income comes through his work on the field. Cobb had independent resources, however, and still others waiting in the wings. Because he could hold out, he could make a binding and credible commitment to stop playing baseball, one the Tigers had to recognize as genuine. He was also sufficiently stubborn to stick with a strategy despite economic losses.

At this point in the negotiations, arrogance and hubris played a significant role. Navin said it simply: "The issue is discipline." Cobb had to be taught a lesson in humility, something never previously listed among his personal characteristics. After a series of similar interchanges had not altered the status quo, Navin sought the assistance of league president Ban Johnson to formally banish Cobb from league play for the year. He had called out reinforcements, a strategic commitment on Navin's part equal to Cobb's holdout. After Johnson suspended Cobb, the Tigers would not—because they could not—have Cobb on the squad for the 1913 season. To maintain discipline, the club, not the player, must determine whether Cobb would play. By using Johnson, the club decided that Cobb would sit out the season, whatever the cost to its fortunes.

Stealing Home

The final play in Ty Cobb's 1913 salary negotiations was one of sheer brilliance, not unlike stealing home—a Cobb specialty, by the way, which he accomplished a career record thirty-five times in the regular season and once in the World Series. His strategy outplayed Navin's call to league headquarters for help, for Cobb called Capitol Hill. No mere ballplayer could trigger such a powerful legislative response. It took a legend who was considered the gem of his home state. All the club owners were placed at risk as a result of the legislation introduced in Congress. (Nine years later, the Supreme Court would rule that baseball was exempt from the antitrust laws because the enterprise did not affect interstate commerce. The Cobb-induced legislation would have preempted that decision and would have likely changed the course of baseball history, assuming Justice Oliver Wendell Holmes and his Brethren would have found that Congress had the constitutional authority to enact the Cobb bill.) Although we do not know whether other club owners and league president Johnson contacted Navin about the proposed legislation, it is likely the Tigers were pressured to reach an agreement with their star player and end the threat. Cobb's final tactic produced the favorable settlement he had sought with such tenacity.

Was Ty Cobb worth the $14,000 he received from the Tigers for his 1913 season? He had lead the Detroit club to three consecutive American League pennants in 1907, 1908, and 1909. We do know that Cobb continued to perform for the Tigers at the highest level, but the club did not win another pennant until 1934, a decade after he had ended his playing career. Was he paid too much or too little? His salary was the product of negotiation, and it reflected the economic power and negotiating skills of the parties. It was an efficient exchange. The Tigers club and Cobb decided the player's salary. Both sides used escalating hardball negotiating tactics. They left the negotiations with a deal, but with little respect for one another. (It is not clear whether Cobb had respect for anyone.) They also set a standard for distasteful negotiations that few would ever surpass, but they did reach an agreement.

Cobb approached salary negotiations with the same attitude he showed in the rest of his life. For him, empathy and respect were not only uncomfortable but unthinkable. Cobb and the club fought their battle in the press with indifference to the personal side of the equation. But they reached an agreement, and Cobb continued to star for the Detroit nine.

How do you explain Cobb's success in negotiations when he was bound, as all players then were, to contract with the Tigers and no other team? Cobb obviously possessed bargaining power other players did not. (If they did, they too would have demanded and obtained higher salaries.) Cobb's bargaining power came from his own personal attributes as an athlete who was not averse to risk. There was only one Cobb. Although the Tigers had monopoly power over Cobb, Cobb, in turn, had monopoly power over his unique talents. (Economists refer to this circumstance as one of *bilateral monopolies*.) In the confrontation, the Tigers blinked, because Cobb had superior bargaining strength and political influence.

Ty Cobb's career of excellence as a ballplayer brought him national acclaim and a personal fortune, but it could not bring him contentment. This was not baseball's fault, but his. Although the idol of a generation of young amateur ballplayers, he was despised by his major league peers. Cobb could impose his will on others, including his club's management, but he could not come to terms with his own inner demons. He would, however, leave the game as one of its all-time greats on the field and at the negotiation table.

SEVEN

Every hitter I face is a man trying to take money out of my pocket.

EARLY WYNN

Salary Arbitration in Operation

Always hustling around the base paths and out in center field, Brett Butler achieved success through baseball's salary arbitration process, demonstrating the tenacity that distinguished his fifteen-year career in the majors. (Stephen Dunn/Allsport)

Baseball's salary arbitration process began modestly in 1974. Dick Woodson, a right-handed pitcher with a 10–8 record for Minnesota in 1973, sought a salary of $30,000. His club, the penurious Twins, offered him $23,000. Woodson prevailed, as the salary arbitrator selected his salary demand over the club's offer. His victory was a harbinger of things to come for some players who would prevail in salary arbitration. On May 4, less than three months after winning his case, the Twins traded Woodson to the Yankees for the remainder of his fifth (and final) season in the major leagues.

The salary arbitration process has evolved over twenty-five years, and the numbers have changed considerably. In 1998, Bernie Williams demanded $9,000,000, three hundred times Woodson's submission; the Yankees offered $7,500,000. They settled before the hearing for $8,300,000, an increase of $3,000,000 over his 1997 salary. In 1999, Derek Jeter, the Yankees' classy shortstop, hit the arbitration jackpot on his first visit, when a panel of three arbitrators chose his demand of $5,000,000 over the club's offer of $3,200,000. Jeter scored the first player victory of the 1999 arbitration season after the clubs had swept the first five litigated cases. Management trounced the players in 1999 by a lopsided 9–2 margin.

Even players who proceed to arbitration and lose, leave as multimillionaires. Johnny Damon, the Royals' fine young outfielder, lost his case in 1999 but increased his salary from $460,000 to $2,100,000, the club's final offer. Damon seems a sure bet to join baseball's salary elite if he continues to compile impressive statistics at the plate and in the field, although it will likely be with a club other than the low-revenue Royals. Many other players eligible to file for salary arbitration use that threat to leverage higher pay levels. To avoid arbitration, some clubs have offered their junior star performers multiyear contracts at premium rates.

Over the past quarter-century, some players have won impressive victories in salary arbitration. Bruce Sutter, who won the Cy Young Award in 1979 as an ace reliever for the Chicago Cubs, left arbitration with $700,000 in 1980, when the major league average salary was $146,500. In 1982, Fernando Valenzuela, a tremendous gate attraction for the Dodgers and the leader of its staff, won $1,000,000 in salary arbitration following only his second season in the majors. Sutter and Valenzuela set new levels for junior star pitchers that was soon reflected in salary negotiations for hurlers eligible for both arbitration and free agency.

The salary arbitration process is driven by the numbers, the performance statistics that advocates for the clubs and the players shape into persuasive arguments. When I hear salary arbitration cases, as I have in 1986, 1998, 1999, and 2000, I think of the importance of each game and each at-bat in determining the pay level of players who will be eligible for arbitration. Twenty-five additional hits over a season of five hundred at-bats make the difference between a .250 and a .300 hitter. One hit a week converts a journeyman player into a star and may be worth millions of dollars in salary arbitration. With a few more well-timed safeties with men in scoring position, a player might drive in a hundred runs, a critical production plateau. On the other hand, a starting pitcher who throws just a few more hanging curves might be relegated to the bullpen for long relief or even sent down to the minors. Each event during the long baseball season is later magnified in salary arbitration by representatives of the club and the player.

Early Wynn, the Hall of Fame right-hander for the Senators, Indians, and White Sox who won three hundred games from 1939 to 1963, was perceptive when he said he was involved in a contest for money with the hitters he faced. When asked if he would throw at his own mother if she were at bat, he replied, "It would depend on how well she was hitting."

Brett Butler

Most salary arbitration cases, unlike those involving high-profile players such as Bernie Williams and Derek Jeter, attract little public attention. They may set critical precedents for owners and players, however. For example, Brett Butler filed for salary arbitration in 1986 to prove two important points: First, a run-scoring, splendid-fielding center fielder can earn a salary competitive with that of power-hitting outfielders at similar stages of their careers; and second, low-revenue clubs (in this instance the Cleveland Indians before Jacobs Field) must compensate their players according to the leaguewide salary scale.

Brett Butler's baseball career illustrates the importance of personal commitment to success on the field. Too small to start for his high school team, he played on the junior varsity at Arizona State University and finished his college career out of the limelight at Southeastern Oklahoma University. The Atlanta Braves drafted Butler with their last-round pick in the 1980 amateur draft and signed him to a $1,000 contract. Starting for Atlanta three years later as a regular in center field, Butler enjoyed a long and productive career with the Braves, Indians, Giants, Dodgers, and Mets. When diagnosed with throat cancer in June 1996, Butler called upon his Christian faith and the fellowship of other athletes to fight back. Against all odds, he returned to baseball in September 1996 to a sold-out Dodger Stadium. That day he scored the winning run. After sixteen years in the majors, 1997 would be Butler's final campaign.

After his experiences in salary arbitration, Butler became a strong union adherent, participating on the players association's council as his team's representative. His poster-boy image and hustling play made him a fan favorite wherever he played. Butler is a fine example of an overachieving ballplayer who used the arbitration system to reach salary equity.

The Origins of Salary Arbitration

Salary arbitration traces its origins back a century, to the procedures used to resolve labor-management bargaining disputes in unionized sectors of the American economy. Unlike today's arbitrators, whom employers and unions appoint to resolve grievances under the terms of their collective bargaining agreements, arbitrators then wrote the actual contracts for the parties in, for example, the coal mining, newspaper, and clothing industries.

Baseball first used the expression "board of arbitration" more than a hundred years ago. Before its merger with the American League, the National League called the members of the council of owners that administered league policy its "board of arbitration." This board was not intended to be neutral, but rather the instrument of baseball's collective management. In 1908, Pittsburgh Pirates outfielder Tommy

Leach also used the word "arbitration" to describe the process he proposed to use to settle his contract dispute with club management. He suggested that his salary be set by a panel of three arbitrators fielded from the local business community—one chosen by him, the second appointed by the club, and the third selected by the other two arbitrators. But Pirates owner Barney Dreyfuss declined to participate in this novel procedure because he neither had to nor wanted to. Instead, he offered Leach an ultimatum to accept his terms or leave baseball. Leach signed.

Salary arbitration was first used to settle pay disputes in professional sports in the National Hockey League in 1970. Hockey's process uses a single permanent arbitrator who is not limited to the final choices of the parties in setting a player's salary. In fact, he is almost certain to name a compensation figure between the two extremes presented by each side. In addition, the arbitrator is expected to submit to the parties a written explanation of his reasoning. The hockey collective bargaining agreement specifies the factors the arbitrator must consider, including the player's overall performance, number of games played, length of service in the league and with the club, contribution to the competitive success (or failure) of the club in the preceding season, any special qualities of leadership or public appeal, and the pay of comparable players. Using these criteria, the arbitrator determines the player's market value and orders his club to pay it.

Although hockey's salary arbitration criteria mirror those used in baseball, the procedures are quite different. In fact, under the most recent collective bargaining agreement in hockey, the owners can walk away from a limited number of arbitration awards, an option the Boston Bruins used for the first time in 1999 to reject the $2.8 million awarded to winger Dmitri Khristich. By contrast, in baseball salary arbitration awards are final and binding on the owners and the players.

Arbitration Procedures, Timetable, and Criteria

Baseball's version of salary arbitration is unique in American labor relations. Within twenty-four hours of the hearing, the arbitrators must select *either* the player's demand *or* the club's offer. There can be no compromise, no explanation, and no delay. These fundamental characteristics are designed to drive the parties together to reach a private settlement. In that regard, the process is overwhelmingly successful.

If the parties cannot settle their differences privately, baseball's salary arbitration provides a quick, informal, and, most importantly, final resolution of the dispute. There is no way to appeal the arbitrators' decisions, and the players report to spring training as scheduled under signed one-year contracts. There are no holdouts by players eligible for salary arbitration.

The collective bargaining agreement between the owners and the players association details the procedures, timetable, and criteria to be used to resolve disputes between eligible players and their clubs. We have already explored the contract's permissible and impermissible factors in Chapter 3. The timetable for arbitration begins right after the World Series ends. Each fall the owners' Player Relations Committee (PRC) and the players association jointly select a roster of about two dozen salary arbitrators. These arbitrators are experienced neutrals, typically members of the honorary National Academy of Arbitrators, who have resolved labor grievance cases for decades. Most are also veterans of the baseball salary arbitration process. They have proven they are able to work within the contract's strict protocols. Normally, the parties inform the arbitrators of their selection in early November and request dates each would be willing to reserve to hear cases during the first three weeks of the following February. After eligible players and their clubs invoke arbitration, the PRC and the union inform the arbitrators in late January how many of their offered dates they will need for hearings.

Although they are resolving disputes involving hundreds of thousands (if not millions) of dollars, salary arbitrators are paid a flat fee of $950 for each case scheduled, plus expenses if the arbitrator must travel to the hearing site. In addition, arbitrators are paid up to one day of "study time" for each case actually heard. Typically, more than 80 percent of their cases will settle after they are scheduled but before they are actually heard in February.

Arbitrators have no idea which players' cases they have been assigned. Perhaps this is to keep the neutrals from doing research about specific players before the hearings. On the other hand, the players' agents and the clubs do know who their arbitrators will be. (In my 1999 cases, the names of the arbitrators on the panel were affixed to the parties' written briefs submitted at the hearing but prepared beforehand.)

Following the calendar set out in the collective bargaining agreement, in January the clubs and the eligible players exchange single salary figures for the coming season. The sites for the February hearings alternate annually between the East and West Coasts—one year in Tampa or Orlando, the next in Phoenix or Los Angeles. The cases are presented in arbitration by the player's agent (customarily with vigorous assistance from attorney Michael Weiner of the players association) and the management representative (usually outside counsel, assisted by Frank Coonelley from the commissioner's office). Increasingly, clubs are turning to attorneys from Morgan, Lewis & Bockius in Washington, D.C., to present their cases in arbitration.

The Settlement Dynamic

The final-offer aspect of the arbitration process was designed to insure that the clubs and the players will resolve most cases without arbitrators. Let us use a hypothetical case to see how the settlement imperative operates.

Assume that during salary negotiations a player demands $2,000,000 and his club offers him $1,000,000. The parties know that in arbitration the panel must decide which position—the player's or the club's—is closer to the real market value of the player based on comparisons with other players of similar experience and performance. The midpoint between the parties' positions in our hypothetical case is $1,500,000, and let us assume that this is close to the real market value of the player's services. Arbitrators hearing this case must decide whether the player is worth more or less than this "break point."

It is to the strategic advantage of each party that its final offer be closer to the player's real market value than the other party's, since that is the position that should prevail in arbitration. The club certainly recognizes that the player might be worth more than

$1,000,000, and the player also knows that he may be worth less than $2,000,000. Long before the arbitration hearing, their initial bargaining positions begin to change as each seeks to present the more reasonable final position. The club may offer the player $1,200,000, now only $300,000 away from what we have assumed is the player's real market value. Not to be outdone, the player responds with a demand of $1,700,000, only $200,000 away from the real market value. The club will likely move again closer to the midpoint, as will the player. As the difference between the parties' positions narrows, the opportunity for settlement increases.

There are many advantages to settling a dispute before arbitration. First, as we will discuss below, the arbitration hearing itself imposes costs on the parties by straining the relationship between the player and his club. Second, if they settle, the parties can be creative in designing a compensation package, including bonuses, for example, a no-trade clause, or a multiyear deal. By contrast, the product of salary arbitration is a standard player contract for a single year at a defined salary. Finally, a settlement can build the parties' relationship rather than rupture it. With settlement, both parties win to some degree; with salary arbitration, there is always one winner and one loser.

The settlement dynamic operates in baseball salary arbitration because it is based on the final-offer principle. If the arbitrator could select any salary, as in hockey salary arbitration, he would likely pick some compromise position that he has determined is the actual market value of the player. In that case, it would be best strategically for management to decrease its offer and the player to increase his demand. In this way, the arbitrator would have more room to "compromise" toward one side or the other.

By comparison, in final-offer arbitration the best final position is the more reasonable one, the one closer to the real market value. That value is unlikely to be near the parties' starting positions and more likely to be somewhere near the middle of their positions. Parties move their positions because they want to use salary arbitration to capture the difference between what the player is really worth and what he demands or what the club offers. Winning means being more reasonable, which is the key that unlocks the door to settlement.

Obviously, some cases are not settled and instead are tried in salary arbitration each February. These aberrations may be explained by a number of factors:

1.   Some players enter salary arbitration with distinctly mixed profiles. For example, a player who has had a very good season prior to arbitration—his *platform year*—may have had previous seasons of lesser quality, or he may have spent a considerable amount of time accumulating major league service credit while on the disabled list. The collective bargaining agreement tells the arbitrators to consider both the player's prior year and his entire career, but it does not instruct them on how to weigh these variables. If they point in very different directions, they may offer only confusing indications of the player's real worth. The parties might test the waters of arbitration in these tough cases rather than settle.

2.   Other cases are tried because one party or the other fails to correctly gauge the market value of a player's services. As in all human endeavors, parties in salary arbitration make errors. An offer far below market value or a demand far above market value, what we might call a "numbers mistake," displaces the break point. The settlement dynamic only operates when the break point, equidistant between the parties' positions, is roughly equivalent to the player's market value. Assuming the erring party remains uneducated through the prehearing negotiation process, the case will have to be tried.

3.   Certain cases are not resolved prior to arbitration because the club does not think it has the financial resources to pay anything more than it has offered the player. This is no defense in salary arbitration, however. In fact, a club cannot even mention its inability to pay at the hearing. Yet, the opportunity to prevail in arbitration at a more affordable salary can encourage management to take a chance and role the dice. If it loses, it can trade the player, and it often does.

4.   Even if management has the resources to pay a particularly accomplished junior player, a generous voluntary agreement between the club and the player has horizontal impacts beyond the case at hand, and will encourage others on the roster to demand more. On the other hand, if the club is *ordered* to pay a player a high salary as a result of arbitration, management can argue to its other players that this figure was imposed, and that it is not to be seen as either club policy or a precedent.

5. Finally, and perhaps most importantly, some cases are not settled without a salary arbitration hearing because of the personalities and egos of the participants. A particularly irascible agent may make settlement discussions distasteful and may stretch a salary demand beyond market norms. A general manager may refuse to pay an uncooperative player what he is really worth. Some obstinate owners will simply refuse to recognize the true market value of their arbitration-eligible players on "principle." Personal chemistry (or lack thereof) at the negotiation table may also make a voluntary settlement impossible.

The Scorecard

Management has done extremely well in the salary arbitration forum, although it regularly complains about the results of the process. There has been a total of 417 cases heard in salary arbitration since 1974. The clubs have prevailed in 236, the players in 181. As the following table shows, in only six years (1980, 1981, 1989, 1990, and 1996) did players prevail in more cases than their clubs:

Year	Owners	Players
1974	16	13
1975	9	6
1978*	7	2
1979	6	8
1980	11	15
1981	10	11
1982	14	8
1983	17	13
1984	6	4
1985	7	6
1986	20	15
1987	16	10
1988	11	7
1989	5	7
1990	10	14

Year	Owners	Players	
1991	11	6	
1992	11	9	
1993	12	6	
1994	10	6	
1995	6	2	
1996	3	7	
1997	4	1	
1998	5	3	
1999	9	2	
Total	236	181	*There was no arbitration in 1976–77.

These figures may indicate that some player agents misread the market more often than club representatives. Alternatively, it may show that some salary arbitrators are reluctant to award increasingly high player salaries. In addition, the outcome of cases heard during the three-week salary arbitration "season" affects cases heard later in the period. A club may prevail in the case of a light-hitting infielder if a similar player lost his case the prior week. Each victory or loss thus has precedential value under a system that focuses on comparables as the measure of player value.

One Arbitrator's Experience

In February 1986, I traveled to New York City to arbitrate my first player salary dispute. Arriving at the New York Hilton the night before my cases were scheduled to be heard, I was stunned when the desk clerk told me that they did not have my reserved room. My daze lasted only a moment. "Professor Abrams," he said, "I am afraid we will have to put you in one of our luxury suites." My room, including a wet bar and sculpture, was quite a change from a labor arbitrator's usual digs at a small-town Holiday Inn. I knew then this would be a memorable trip.

Salary arbitrations in 1986 were held in New York, Chicago, and Los Angeles, whichever site was closer to the club and the player. Only later did the parties realize that the climate in Tampa and Phoenix was far more appealing during the first three weeks of February and that air connections made centralizing the hearings convenient. The hearings in New York in 1986 were held at the sterile midtown offices of the American Arbitration Association. (By comparison, the 1999 hearings were held in the lovely *casitas* at the Hyatt in Tampa.)

I arrived at the New York City hearing site early, carrying my luggage and attaché case filled with pens and paper. I found the parties already awaiting my arrival in a small hearing room. I had been assigned the salary dispute between Brett Butler and the Cleveland Indians. As chance would have it, I knew about Butler's fielding exploits roaming the vast expanse of the Municipal Stadium outfield. A pile of important-looking papers awaited me at the end of the table. I walked around the table, introducing myself to the assembled group, meeting Butler for the first time. I always knew he was diminutive, but at 5 feet, 10 inches, I towered over him. Sitting next to Butler was one of the game's great power hitters and the American League's Most Valuable Player in 1979, Don Baylor, then a New York Yankee. I was not sure why Baylor was there, but I would soon find out.

As the room continued to flood with additional representatives from the commissioner's office and the players association, I realized we were too cramped in that small space. At my request, someone located a larger conference room, and the spectators caravanned down the hallway. I assembled the case papers that had been left for me, a stack of joint exhibits over a foot high. Hoisting the exhibits under one arm, with my luggage in the other and my attaché case in search of a third, I stood there for a moment. Don Baylor was the only person left in the room. He asked, "Professor, could I help you?" So MVP Don Baylor carried my luggage down the hallway. It was indeed a memorable day.

During the hearing, Butler's agents, Dick Moss, the former general counsel of the players association, and Steve Fehr, the brother of the union's executive director Donald Fehr, presented arguments in support of the player's demand for an $850,000 salary for the 1986 season. Butler had had an excellent 1985 campaign, ranking sixth in the league in batting and in the top ten in six offensive categories. He scored 108 runs, the most by an Indians player in forty-five years. As the lead-off hitter, Butler's role in the offense was to get on base and move into scoring position. His exemplary defensive prowess in the outfield ranked him first in the league in fielding percentage.

Tal Smith, the former general manager of the Houston Astros, represented the club. Smith had amassed great credibility in the game, and his consulting firm represented many clubs in the salary arbitration process. In support of the club's offer of $600,000, Smith explained that Butler's .311 batting average produced few runs and that he was always among the league leaders in unsuccessful steals. Most importantly, Smith argued that center fielders were expected to drive in runs, which Butler did not do. With regard to Butler's fielding, Smith reminded me that since a fielder can only be charged with an error if he reaches the ball, Butler's almost perfect fielding percentage was an unreliable measure.

It was time for Don Baylor to play his role on the arbitration stage. Testifying in response to the club's contention that Butler lacked range in the outfield, he said: "To see him play day-in and day-out, to make those plays tremendously against our ball club was awesome. He plays a shallow center field and then goes back and makes the plays. He is among the best in the American League." Baylor acknowledged that his former Orioles teammate Paul Blair was a better center fielder, but believed that Brett Butler was "in that category." Baylor also said he hated to play against the Indians, because Butler "gets everything I hit."

Resolving the Butler salary dispute involved comparing his performance—both in the platform year and over his career—with other players in his service class. My task was to determine whether Butler deserved more or less than $725,000, the midpoint between his demand and the club's offer. If his fair market value was $1 more than $725,000, he must receive his demand; if it was $1 less, then the club's offer would be his salary. I would have twenty-four hours to make the decision.

A salary arbitrator cannot be concerned with how high a salary the player demands or how low a salary the club offers; the focus instead must be on the break point. The parties have ordained in their contract what the arbitrators must do after they decide on which side of the break point the player should be slotted.

After a quick New York deli sandwich, the afternoon case commenced. It was hardly an anticlimax, for now I was assigned to resolve the dispute between the New York Mets and Ron Darling, their number-two pitcher, behind Dwight Gooden. Darling had enjoyed a spectacular 1985 season, with a 16–6 record, a 2.90 ERA, and an All-Star team appearance. His Achilles' heel was walking batters; his redeeming virtue, however, was a minuscule opponents batting average (OBA) with men on base. Darling sought $615,000, while the Mets had offered $440,000. The case turned on the comparables as well. Was the player more like Dwight Gooden, Fernando Valenzuela, and Bret Saberhagen, as he claimed, than Storm Davis, Bud Black, and Danny Cox, as the club maintained?

I started reviewing the data submitted by the two players and their clubs in the taxi on the way to La Guardia Airport. By late the next morning I had decided in favor of Butler, but against Darling. Both cases were close calls, as are most of those that reach arbitration. In retrospect, I would not change either decision, but I would not have been unhappy had I gone the other way. The saving grace of my experience in salary arbitration is in knowing that I decided the cases based on the criteria and procedures set forth in the parties' own collective bargaining agreement.

Assuming a player's true market value lies somewhere in between the final demand and the final offer, players who proceed through the salary arbitration process are always paid too much if they win or too little if they lose. The next year both Butler and Darling returned to arbitration. This time Butler lost and Darling won.

Arbitration Panels

Under their current collective bargaining agreement, the parties agreed to phase in a new system using panels of three arbitrators rather than single arbitrators. In 1998 half of the cases were heard by panels, which increased to three-quarters of the cases in 1999 and all cases in 2000. Management had pressed for this change during the tumultuous 1994–96 labor dispute, believing that three-member panels were less likely to produce clearly wrong decisions. However, the results from the first two years of panel implementation show no significant difference in outcomes between panels and single arbitrators.

I served as a member of these new three-arbitrator panels in February 1998, 1999, and 2000. Comparing the experience with my single arbitrator cases, I found no real difference other than in the increased time requirements imposed on the arbitrators, who must meet after the hearing and review all the evidence together. In each instance, the arbitrators met for hours, reviewing the arguments made by the parties and analyzing the copious data. Sometimes, we reached the same conclusion we had all thought was appropriate at the outset. In other cases, we changed our minds. Although the evidence to date suggests there is no difference in outcomes between panels and single arbitrators, there may be instances in which the three-member approach will keep an arbitrator from deciding the dispute based on a misreading of the submitted materials. In any case, by 2000 the single arbitrator option was history.

Presenting a Case

The owners and the players association designed the salary arbitration process to set the compensation for players who have already demonstrated their ability to play at the major league level. Club management retains the exclusive right to the player's services under the vestige of the reserve system, but the player's salary is set by the major league scale. In salary arbitration, the clubs and the players, through their agents, have the opportunity to demonstrate to the arbitrators where the player should be situated in the established salary market of major league baseball.

The final-offer protocol of salary arbitration not only avoids compromise decisions by the neutrals but also focuses the parties' presentations. Each side must explain to the tribunal why the player is worth more or less than the midpoint between the club's final offer and the player's final demand. Although the presentations of the parties are based on the same statistical data, their perceptions of the player's value to his club differ fundamentally. At times, the arbitrators may wonder whether the club and the agent are talking about the same ballplayer.

With the ready availability of computer databases, salary arbitration has become a furious battle of statistics. Baseball has always been a game of creative statistics, but now they convert directly into dollars.

Parties in salary arbitration have customized these data to meet their partisan needs. Aficionados of the game, in particular Bill James, have devised complex formulae within the new science of "sabermetrics" to describe a player's contribution to his club's success, but parties in salary arbitration devise their own statistical measures to help their case, even if they do not make much baseball sense.

Today's salary arbitration hearing room table is adorned with laptop computers capable of generating any needed comparison at a moment's notice. Every claim is met with a counterclaim, until the arbitrators are left with a huge pile of numbers. At times, the litigation seems to have more in common with rotisserie baseball leagues than with normal grievance arbitration. Player performance is particularized, dissected, chopped, and diced. Anything that cannot be converted into numerical terms, such as team leadership, hustle, and courage in the face of debilitating injury, seems to play no role.

The time limits for the arbitration hearing are set forth in the agreement—one hour for each side, followed by a half-hour rebuttal. In recent years, these limits have been stretched in practice so that each party has a full opportunity to rebut and clarify the data. With millions of dollars at stake, arbitrators are understandably loath to make a judgment based on an incomplete understanding of the facts. Even so, the skilled advocates of the parties seem determined to present their whole case without taking a breath. Lest they leave out some salient fact an arbitrator might find probative later that night, the parties err on the side of overkill.

Some salary arbitrators are so overwhelmed by the numbers that they would urge the parties to supply the data long before the hearing so it might be digested. Alternatively, they would want more time after the hearing to review the submissions. Neither alternative seems likely to be adopted.

The Relevant Statistics

There is a story told about a salary arbitration hearing involving a relief pitcher in the 1970s, when, after hours of statistical presentation, the neutral asked, "Now, what is a save?" Both sides were dismayed to discover that their presentation of sophisticated statistics had been wasted time and energy.

Today, virtually all salary arbitrators are veterans of the process and have been schooled in the game's parameters and statistics. The parties in salary arbitration traditionally have followed the assumption that there must be something in their submissions that will catch the arbitrator's eye, but they do not know exactly what that is. Thus, they supply an enormous amount of information, reams of data and fancy calculations. The parties seem to ignore the fact that the arbitrators have but twenty-four hours in which to resolve the matter. No one can penetrate all of the data in that period of time.

Parties would be far better off using a pinpoint approach rather than a scattergun to deliver statistics. Branch Rickey used to call his players who were all statistics and little performance, his "anesthetic players":

> You watch them all year, and you say they are not contributing much to the team. Then they show you a lot of impressive statistics. They put you to sleep with statistics that don't win games.

At times it seems as if salary arbitration is swamped with those same "statistics that don't win games." But what then should the parties focus on? Which statistics should be presented and massaged?

The winning strategy in salary arbitration should be to present in simple, straightforward terms the right class of comparables. An agent who does well in salary arbitration focuses on the core characteristics of his player. A team wins games by scoring runs. Run production—runs scored and RBIs—is the key offensive statistic. While batting average is interesting, it does not tell you very much about a player's contribution to team success. Slugging percentage—total bases divided by times at bat—is a much more important measure, although not as useful as total run production. It might be helpful to use more targeted statistics, such as run production in key game situations or slugging average with men on base. There are also significant differences between the two leagues and between playing in Coors Field in mile-high Denver versus every other ballpark. Again, the core issue is not how well the player performed, but how well he performed *compared to other players.*

For pitchers, the vital statistic in salary arbitration is not wins and loses, because pitchers cannot control their clubs' run production. A very good pitcher on a bad club should be considered roughly compa-rable to a very good pitcher on a great club, although the latter is likely to have a much better winning percentage. Earned run average is a use-ful measure, remembering, of course, that ERA is a half-point higher in the American League than in the National because of the designated hitter. Opponents' batting average may be an interesting statistic, but it is far more telling when pinpointed to OBA with men on base or in scoring position. Walks can hurt, and strikeouts can help, but neither is as important as stopping run production.

Baseball people (as opposed to baseball lawyers) know what wins or loses games. They know, for example, that a critical event in an inning is whether the lead-off hitter gets on base, because, if he does, he is likely to score. They know that the pitcher's primary responsibility is to keep that first batter off the base paths. The timely hit or strikeout also is vitally important. The focus of the statistics offered in salary arbitration should be on these types of game-winning (or game-losing) events. A batting average padded with meaningless at-bats is not as important as the ability to produce in run-scoring situations when a game is on the line.

Arbitrators can understand why either the club's representatives or the player's agent might shy away from using these targeted statistics, since they might not present what the partisans see as their best case. Nonetheless, these are the important statistics, and the salary arbitra-tors should not allow other, less meaningful numbers affect their delib-erations. All statistics are not equal in the arbitration calculus.

It is possible that some of the data submitted by the parties in salary arbitration are based on incorrect or questionable assumptions, but there is no way the salary arbitrators can independently evaluate the accuracy of the figures. We must instead leave it to the opposing par-ties to analyze the submissions and make the necessary corrections known to the panel at the hearing.

A Strategy of Effective Presentation

Parties in salary arbitration must develop a theory of their case. This is not rocket science but rather common sense, always a valuable asset in the business of baseball. Instead of focusing on some cohesive approach, parties now spend half of their first allotted hour statistically glorifying or demonizing the player. It would be better were an agent to say simply: "This is a case about a shortstop with great range and play-making abilities. His contribution to the club at the plate is not as important as his play in the field. We will compare his performance to the other premier shortstops in the league and that will justify a salary figure above the midpoint between his demand and the club's offer." In return, the club might say: "This is a case about a good shortstop who is not yet in the class of premier middle infielders. While we appreciate his fielding abilities, his failure to perform at the plate has diminished his overall contribution to the club."

When I start a salary arbitration hearing, I ask myself: "What kind of player is this? What job was he hired to perform?" Pitchers, for example, fall into one of five categories—starters, closers, set-up men, lefty specialists, and mop-up men. Some players, such as middle infielders and catchers, may be valued primarily for their defensive performances. Others, while adequate fielders, are prized for their power and clutch hitting or their ability to get on base. Comparing the salaries of players who perform different roles for a baseball team is like comparing apples and oranges.

By starting with these different categories of players who make up a major league team, I have a fairly good idea whether the parties' comparables are, in fact, comparable. I then ask myself, "How well did this player perform the job he was asked to do?" Within each of these categories there are different levels of performance, of course. There are truly outstanding starting pitchers and quite ordinary starting pitchers. My job is to ask, "Into which classification does this player fall?"

For over two decades, the parties in salary arbitration parties have put a premium on glossy presentations of charts and analysis. If they cannot convince the arbitrators on the statistical merits, perhaps they can dazzle them with their fancy reproductions and bright colors. An organized presentation is admittedly useful, however. Handing the panel one document at a time is likely to mean that key papers become mixed up in the arbitrators' briefcases. A loose-leaf binder with tabs and an index is particularly helpful in avoiding such problems.

Current Issues in Salary Arbitration

Salary arbitration is a battleground of statistics. The party that constructs the better argument with the numbers wins the case, and perhaps this is how it should be. Although owners and players have had over twenty-five years of experience with the process, a collection of important issues, which the parties have left to their neutrals to handle on a case-by-case basis, remains unresolved. The way arbitrators decide these matters will determine the outcome of many cases.

The critical variable in every salary arbitration case is the comparables presented by each side. A player would prefer to be compared with players who have more major league service than he does, because it is quite likely they will be earning a higher salary. The club, on the other hand, would prefer the arbitrators to compare the player with others in his "service group," that is, with players with the same number of years of major league service. The relevant language in the salary arbitration provision of the collective bargaining agreement is particularly unhelpful about what the arbitrator should do about this issue:

> The arbitrator or arbitration panel shall, except for a Player with five or more years of Major League service, give particular attention, for comparative salary purposes, to the contracts of Players with Major League service not exceeding one annual service group above the Player's annual service group. This shall not limit the ability of a Player or his representative, because of special accomplishment, to argue the equal relevance of salaries of Players without regard to service, and the arbitrator or arbitration panel shall give whatever weight to such argument as is deemed appropriate.

The paragraph is filled with ambiguities over the use of comparables that can make an arbitration hearing a free-for-all. On one hand, arbitrators are directed to give "particular attention" to the player's service group and one service group above that group. But just what does "particular attention" mean? There is also escape language in the provision that allows for comparisons without any regard to service because of a player's "special accomplishment." And what does this mean?

The service group issue is important because there is a marked difference in compensation between players with different amounts of service. The average salary of players with three years of service is $1,052,483. This average rises to $1,626,893 for players in the four-year service group and $2,476,495 for those in the five-year service group. Unless player compensation correlates perfectly with player performance (a claim no one makes), it is likely that two players with about the same level of performance but with different years of service will be earning different salaries. When arbitrators reach upward in service groups to identify comparable players—something the collective bargaining agreement clearly authorizes but does not mandate—the result is to inflate salaries and discount the importance of service. But if arbitrators stick within a player's service group, particularly good players are penalized.

Players included in the three-year service group include all those with at least three years but less than the additional 172 days on a major league roster needed to move them up to the four-year category. It makes perfect sense to compare a player with almost four years of service to those in the four-year service group. The obverse is also true: It is less appropriate (although clearly permissible under the collective bargaining agreement) to compare a player with barely three years actual playing time to players well into the next higher service group.

Another live issue in salary arbitration involves the use of what the parties call *look-back comparables*. Assume the player in arbitration is a middle-relief pitcher with three or four years of service. The critical statistic for such a set-up man is a "hold," defined in general terms as when the pitcher maintains a club's lead so a closer can obtain a save. At the hearing, either side may introduce as comparables set-up men who now have much more seniority in the league, but then "look back" to the years when they had only three or four years of service. What was their performance then, and what was their compensation?

Look-back comparables must be used with caution. If all players are paid more now than those look-back comparables were when they had three or four years of service, the comparison is unfair. One way to investigate this aspect of the issue is to examine the inflation of player salaries. The average annual salaries of three- and four-year players are as follows:

Year	Annual Salary of Three-Year Players	Annual Salary of Four-Year Players
1991	$670,930	$1,194,205
1992	$855,880	$1,275,992

Year	Annual Salary of Three-Year Players	Annual Salary of Four-Year Players
1993	$906,198	$1,667,404
1994	$1,092,179	$1,539,654
1995	$1,082,092	$1,999,746
1996	$1,042,118	$1,609,511
1997	$926,033	$1,666,583
1998	$1,041,025	$1,601,351

As these figures show, average compensation for players with three and four years of major league service has *not* increased since 1995. Although the averages increase and decrease over time, there has not been salary inflation in recent years among players eligible for salary arbitration. Look-back comparables do have validity, but they must be based on an assumption of parity of player performance.

A third unresolved issue deals with how to value noncompensation provisions typically included in a negotiated contract but not in the standard uniform contract a player receives after salary arbitration. Comparing compensation figures is easy, but how do you value a no-trade clause, or a bonus provision, or a guarantee of payment for the full term of the contract? The collective bargaining agreement offers arbitrators no guidance in this area.

As with all matters in dispute between labor and management, these issues could be resolved through collective bargaining or by interim agreements during the term of the contract. In their current collective bargaining agreement, the parties did address one issue that had divided them for years: how to account for a contract-signing bonus. The parties have decided it should be allocated evenly across the entire length of a contract rather than only in the year the bonus is received.

One procedural issue the parties resolved in 1999 was the order of presentation at the salary arbitration hearing. The collective bargaining agreement states that each side has one hour to present its case, followed by a half-hour for each party's rebuttal. However, it says nothing about who goes first. Normally it would be to a party's advantage to have the last say and let his opponent go first. The practice in salary arbitration has always been for the player's side to present first. During some of the 1998 salary arbitration hearings, however, player agents—in particular, the articulate Dick Moss—strongly objected to the practice.

Before the 1999 arbitrations, the players association and the commissioner's office reached a compromise on this issue. The parties must now exchange all written materials they intend to present in arbitration before the hearing begins, thus affording the player's agent the opportunity to anticipate the club's arguments and address them during his case in chief. In return for the prehearing document exchange, the players association agreed that the player's agent would be the first to present the case.

The Player's Role

The ballplayer always attends his salary arbitration hearing, sitting quietly next to his agent. In about half the cases, the player says a few words at his hearing. The player's participation adds a nice touch to the hearing, humanizing what has become a sterile statistical battle. In other hearings, however, the players just sit, even appearing bored at times, as their agents extol their virtues and their clubs present a litany of their failures.

The risks of injury to the relationship between the club and its player from a salary arbitration hearing are immense. It would not hurt a club's chances for success if its spokesperson explained that the player was valuable to the club even if he isn't perfect. After all, no one is perfect.

Judgment Day

The arbitrators must reach a judgment on their case within twenty-four hours of the hearing. The panel chair then has two ministerial tasks—first, to telephone the representatives of the owners and the union to report the outcome, and second, to fill in the salary amount in the blank in paragraph two of the already-signed player contracts and mail them to the parties. Under the new tripartite panel system, in March the chair also informs the parties of the vote in the case.

Baseball management has criticized salary arbitration since its inception for inflating player salaries. There is no doubt that players eligible for arbitration earn more than those who have not accumulated the necessary major league service to participate in the process, but few could have thought it would be otherwise. Compensation for players eligible for salary arbitration, however, has remained virtually stable over the past six years, while free agent salaries have ballooned in the competitive free market. It might be argued that salary arbitration has controlled salary inflation in a way the owners are unable to do themselves.

Unlike the experience in other professional sports, there are no holdouts in baseball among players eligible for salary arbitration. Each case is resolved within twenty-four hours of the hearing, and the player reports to spring training under a signed contract with his club. The defining characteristic of baseball's salary arbitration is its finality. Management's understandable concerns about the outcomes of some of the arbitration cases must be balanced against the value of this certainty. The clubs know they will have their best talent on the field for the coming season.

Salary arbitration has changed as the parties have learned to work within the system to achieve their goals. Perhaps the most important recent development is the aggressive effort by the commissioner's office to avoid management losses in arbitration. In 1999, baseball officials privately urged clubs to settle cases that they thought might be decided in the player's favor in arbitration. In addition, the commissioner's office has stepped up its technical support efforts. As Rob Manfred, baseball's vice president for labor relations, told the press: "We set out at the beginning of the year to try and improve the clubs' level of preparation. We were pleased with the results." The strategy proved brilliant, at least in terms of the 1999 results in arbitration.

In 1999, the clubs won nine cases against two losses, its highest winning percentage ever. In fairness, however, these outcomes must be considered within the context of the overall pool of players eligible for salary arbitration that year. Did management's increased effort to settle cases without hearings mean those players received higher salaries than they would have had they gone to arbitration?

What does management's resounding triumph in the cases actually heard in 1999 indicate? Over the quarter-century of experience with the process, management has won more cases in arbitration than it has lost. The 1999 scorecard—nine wins for the owners versus two for the players—was the most lopsided in the history of salary arbitration, however. These results may show that player agents were reaching too high, but why should that have been any different in 1999 then in any previous year? If it is not an aberration and is followed by similar club successes in 2000, it may signal to eligible players that the salary arbitration process is no longer a friendly field on which to play. This, in turn, may result in even more settlements and far fewer, if any, cases actually tried. Like the state under Marxist theory, hearings in salary arbitration may just "wither away." That, of course, was the parties' intention when they created a process designed to end holdouts by eligible players and produce settlements, not litigation.

EIGHT

We count on our fingers the number of years that we'll be able to play. That makes it plain that we must make all the money we can during the short period we may be said to be star players.

WEE WILLIE KEELER, 1898

The Free Agency Auction

Soft-spoken and steady at the plate, Bernie Williams, the Yankees' noble center fielder, achieved economic prominence in the 1998 free agency auction. (Scott Halleran/Allsport)

The World Champion Yankees of 1996, 1998, and 1999 were led by a gentle man who played classical guitar and impressed his teammates and opponents alike with his grace and dedication to his profession. It is too early to know whether Bernie Williams will be remembered as one of the great Yankees, along with Ruth and Gehrig, DiMaggio and Mantle. But it is not too early to know that his elegance and poise will be remembered in an age when too many entertainers equate style with garish pretense. Williams is representative of those players who have played and won big at baseball's "free agent auction."

Williams was the league batting champion in 1998 at .338 with ninety-seven RBIs, although he missed thirty-one games midseason with a sprained right knee. He had mastered the key to batting success expressed by Wee Willie Keeler of the old Baltimore Orioles by learning to "hit 'em where they ain't." As the Yankees' highest paid player, his 1998 salary was $8,250,000, the amount negotiated in settlement of his salary arbitration case shortly before it was to be heard in Phoenix in February 1998. The Yankees had acquired Williams, a native of Puerto Rico, as a nondrafted free agent in 1985. He had always been a Yankee. The 1998 postseason free agency auction would determine if he would remain a Yankee.

As his agent Scott Boras boasted to potential purchasers of his services, in 1998 Williams became the first player to win a league batting title, a Gold Glove, and the World Championship in the same season. He was one of a handful of players in the history of the sport to score 100 runs and drive in 100 runs for three years in a row. Among the Yankee greats, only Mickey Mantle and Joe DiMaggio had accomplished that feat. Boras's selection of the 100/100 mark as a measure of Williams's value to the club was arbitrary, of course, much like the 40/40 measure of home runs and stolen bases often used to describe a player with power and speed. But the 100/100 figure does show that Williams was responsible for run production, and, without runs, no team wins.

Reviewing the Rules

The free agent auction is the penultimate stage of the salary-setting process. A player with fewer than six years of major league service has one potential purchaser for his services, the club that holds the rights to his contract. That may be the club with which he first signs or the club to which he is traded, either in the minor leagues or at the major league level. Salaries for players not eligible for free agency or salary arbitration only need to be sufficient to keep them from quitting the game to pursue employment alternatives, although, as we have seen, some truly unique performers, like Ty Cobb and Babe Ruth, used their considerable bargaining power to obtain significant salaries even in a one-on-one market. Salary arbitration creates a substitute market for experienced eligible players by providing an enterprise-wide salary scale based on player performance. Once a player achieves free agent status, however, the bargaining relationship changes dramatically, and the free agent negotiations become an auction, with the player signing with the highest bidder. The highest bidder, however, is not necessarily the club offering the most cash, because a player may value other factors, such as location and club prospects, equally, or even more. Some, like Bernie Williams, may value team loyalty.

The operation of the free agency auction is not unlike the competitive bidding between major league clubs over the best minor league prospects that went on before the advent of the farm system. In those auctions, of course, the minor league team would pocket the sale price, whereas under modern free agency, the ballplayer reaps the full value of his projected services.

In 1897, the major league clubs bid for the services of Honus Wagner, then under contract with the Silk City club of Paterson, New Jersey, owned by future major league magnate Ed Barrow. Pittsburgh offered Barrow $1,500 for Wagner's contract, which Barrow immediately rejected. Harry C. Pulliam, president of the National League's Louisville Colonels and later president of baseball's National Commission, next offered Paterson $2,000 for Wagner. Barrow, who had earlier promised Pittsburgh the opportunity to beat any bid, wired the Pirates with this information and received a matching offer. Pulliam then increased his offer to $2,100, which Pittsburgh would not match. Wagner therefore became a Louisville Colonel and was paid $250 a month. (When the Colonels folded after the 1899 season, the Pirates purchased the rights to fourteen Louisville players, including Wagner, for $25,000.)

The First Free Agent Auction

Jerry Kapstein was one of baseball's first superagents. It was his good fortune to participate in the "Gold Rush" of 1976, the first year of free agency under procedures negotiated by the players association and the owners in the aftermath of the Andy Messersmith arbitration, which ended the restrictive reserve system. John Helyar, in his exceptional book *Lords of the Realm*, explains how Kapstein auctioned off his clients' services.

In the fall of 1976, Kapstein represented ten of the twenty-two available free agent ballplayers. He rented Room 4B in the downtown bank building in Providence, Rhode Island, Kapstein's hometown. There he entertained club representatives who brought contract offers for some of the game's brightest stars. Kapstein did little negotiating; he conducted the auction and then offered his clients a choice among the escalating alternative offers.

One of Kapstein's clients was the Baltimore Orioles' stellar second baseman, Bobby Grich. For years, Grich's performance in the field had been at record levels—for example, in 1973 he made five errors on a thousand chances at second base. He was a solid contributor at the plate as well and would have been a significant acquisition for any ball club. The Yankees' George Steinbrenner, who certainly appreciated Grich's potential value to his Bronx club, told Kapstein that he wanted the last play in the auction and promised to top all other offers. Grich, however, told Kapstein he was interested in returning home to play in southern California, and California Angels general manager Harry Dalton had made a very acceptable offer for Grich's services. Across Kapstein's auction table in Room 4B, Steinbrenner made his pitch directly to Grich. Grich, he said, was the person who would "guarantee" the Yankees would be World Champions once again. He then disparaged the Angels as perennial losers.

The Angels' Dalton had just returned to California after buying Joe Rudi in Kapstein's auction. Kapstein contacted Dalton, who immedi-

ately returned to the East Coast, met with Grich, and denounced Steinbrenner. Grich knew that his old friend from the Baltimore Orioles,
Don Baylor, had also signed to play for the Angels. Convinced that he
would be better off playing for that club, Grich signed a five-year contract with them for $1,550,000.

Steinbrenner had promised Kapstein that he would outbid the highest offer because he knew he was involved in an auction negotiation. As
he said repeatedly: "I hate to lose. Hate, hate, *hate* to lose." He assumed,
incorrectly, that the players would select the highest number. It was to
Kapstein's and his client's advantage to obtain competing legitimate
offers that Steinbrenner could top.

Unlike a simplified economic model, however, where price may be
the only variable, a ballplayer's decision about where to play is informed
by a number of factors, some of which may not be directly financial.
Playing for a winning ball club, joining a club with old friends, returning home, staying away from George Steinbrenner—these factors may
not have headline value in the sports pages when the media reports
salaries, but they do influence individual decision-making. Some players may be drawn to New York City, the country's economic and entertainment capital; others may be scared away by its media attention.
(One way an economist could translate these real benefits or detriments
into monetary units would be to ask a player how much he would be
willing to pay to obtain them or to avoid them.)

Grich wanted to go home, and he did. He played for the Angels from
1977 through 1986, completing a seventeen-year professional career. As
Steinbrenner predicted, however, Grich would never appear in a World
Series.

One player who found New York City to be attractive was the Oakland A's slugger Reggie Jackson. After Steinbrenner was burned in the
Grich contest, he set his eyes on Reggie. Reggie had a series of lucrative offers on the table—almost $5,000,000 over five years from Mon-
treal, $3,400,000 over five years from San Diego, $3,000,000 over five
years from Baltimore, and the same from the Yankees. Steinbrenner,
the consummate salesman, went to work, believing that his "personal
touch" might speak louder than his checkbook. Over Thanksgiving
1976, Steinbrenner escorted Jackson on a tour of the town in the

owner's chauffeured limousine. Jackson later said, "He hustled me like a broad."

Jackson was impressed with the city, and he counteroffered: He would sign if Steinbrenner would throw in $63,000 for a new Rolls-Royce Corniche. The Boss agreed, and Reggie went on to become the Yankees' "Mr. October," perhaps the best free agent Steinbrenner ever signed. He established his reputation during the 1977 World Series, hitting 5 home runs in 20 at-bats against the Dodgers. In game six, Jackson hit 3 successive homers, each on the first pitch, and each against a different pitcher. The Hall of Famer hit 144 homers in five seasons in Yankees pinstripes.

Jackson's choice to become a Yankee was not based solely on monetary comparisons, as personal factors came to the fore once more. Steinbrenner had shown Reggie how much he wanted him to be a Yankee, but he never showed Jackson that kind of personal attention again. Thus, after the 1982 season, Jackson left New York City to join Grich with the California Angels.

The auction of free agents proved particularly profitable for agent Kapstein. His ten clients in 1976 signed for a total of $16,000,000. Kapstein's cut was $1,000,000. Kapstein and the other player agents helped triple the average baseball player's salary from 1976 to 1980. At the same time, baseball attendance, fueled by the excitement of new heroes on many clubs, increased almost 40 percent.

The average 1976 salary for free agents was over $1,000,000. It rose in 1977 to $1,730,000 for the fourteen free agents, but then dropped to $1,560,000 for a less attractive group of ten free agents in 1978. It soon became apparent that the owners could not control the free agent auction process, because they could not control themselves or each other. This auction of proven stars, with its promise of quick success on the field, was seductive. Some owners made what turned out to be foolish decisions, purchasing players who failed miserably. The Cleveland Indians, for example, signed Baltimore star pitcher Wayne Garland to a $1,800,000 deal, paid out over ten years. Garland had won twenty games for the Orioles in 1976, but he would lead the American League in losses for the Tribe in 1977 with a 13–19 record.

He only played four more years in Cleveland, winning a total of fifteen games and losing twenty-nine with an earned run average of 5.4. (By comparison, during his three full years in Baltimore he had an ERA of 3.0.) Garland started only fifty games for Cleveland in five years and was often on the disabled list. (While on the disabled list, he would pump gas at the filling station he owned in suburban Shaker Heights, Ohio.)

Many other free agents also proved a disappointment. The Braves in 1984 inked a five-year, $4,500,000 deal with pitcher Len Barker, who went 9–17 the next two years and then left baseball; the Texas Rangers signed outfielder Richie Zisk in 1978 to a ten-year, $3,000,000 deal. Three years later, Zisk was shipped out in a trade.

For every bad free agent acquisition, however, there was a balancing good one. Richard "Goose" Gossage, the Yankees' powerful right-handed closer, agreed to a modest $2,750,000, six-year contract in 1978. He accumulated 150 saves for the Yankees over that period, adding 8 more in postseason play.

Seemingly addicted to this interclub competition that drove up prices, the owners sought to change the rules of the free agency auction through collective bargaining with the players association. Under the owners' proposal in 1980, free agency would remain, but a club signing a free agent would have to compensate the team that lost a free agent with a major league player. Although it sounded like a "fair" system (and was played that way in the press by club owners and sportswriters), the intended effect of the compensation was to increase the cost of signing a free agent and thus dampen the marketplace. The signing club would pay twice—once to sign the free agent and again to com-pensate the club that lost him with a substitute player. Thus, requiring player compensation would in effect turn free agency into a forced trade of ballplayers.

But the players association would not accept this alteration in the rules. After protracted negotiations, the players struck on June 12, 1981. The strike was settled on August 8 after the owners' strike insurance payments ran out. Under the new contract, a club that lost a free agent would not receive compensation in the form of another major league player, and the free agency system remained otherwise fundamentally unchanged, as did the owners' anger at the system and, presumably, at themselves.

In the mid-1980s, the owners tried an alternate strategy for dealing with the free agent system that proved more effective but eventually quite costly. The evidence indicates that they decided to cooperate among themselves, agreeing not to bid on a free agent as long as that player's club continued to show interest in signing him. It was a remarkably successful tactic. Salaries for free agents tumbled. The only flaw with this strategy, and it was a quite significant one, was that the owners' secret agreement violated the provision in the collective bargaining agreement that prohibited collusion, as baseball's arbitrators Tom Roberts and George Nicolau later ruled. In December 1990, management paid the players $280,000,000 to settle outstanding damage claims that arose from the collusion. After this strategy was banned, unconstrained owners once again made some baseball free agents very wealthy.

Auction Theory

Game theorists and economists have used econometric principles and models to analyze the auction, a "game" of multilateral trading where there is more than one potential buyer or seller. The participants interact, outbidding each other to determine the terms of the trade, that is, the price of the commodity. For example, prospective sellers in a sealed bid process to obtain a construction job will set the lowest price for their work that still covers their costs and reaps a profit. Owners of major league ball clubs compete to sign free agents by raising the price they are willing to pay only when a rival offer is on the table, but capping increases at the point where the player's services no longer justify his cost to the club. Clubs have different needs and different resources, which affect their ability and willingness to participate in the auction and the marginal utility of acquiring the free agent. Assuming perfect knowledge and rational behavior—major assumptions in discussing baseball free agency—exchanges reached through auctions achieve efficient outcomes.

In many auctions, the rules of play are precise and clearly expressed. They may even be mandated by public law, as with bidding procedures for government contracts. Baseball's version of the auction game, however, is not publicly regulated, and the only private regulations are the procedures and timetables set forth in the collective bargaining agreement. Every agent can create subsidiary rules, bounded only by the need to maintain legitimacy by treating all potential purchasers equally. Pernicious dealings will undermine, and eventually destroy, an agent's ability to participate in the negotiation games of baseball.

The paradigm of the good first move in one-on-one negotiations—a high initial demand or low initial offer—may not apply in the auction game. In a single-offer, closed-bid auction, the purchaser or seller wants to set the price at a level likely to win the game. But in a multiperson, multimove auction—baseball free agency, for example—the initial move may be made to smoke out competitors. Each buyer wants to start low enough to be able to raise its offer later, but not so low that the seller discounts the buyer as a potential player. (Offering the contract minimum for an experienced free agent, for example, would send the wrong signal about a club owner's intentions.) The most effective strategy depends upon the particular context and circumstances.

The baseball free agent auction normally follows the rules of a silent, but not sealed-bid, auction. Unlike the English auction used to sell art and antiques at Sotheby's, the baseball owners or their representatives are not in the same room at the same time, bidding against one another until only one bidder, the one with the highest offer, remains. Instead, the player's agent, seeking to maximize the price but retain credibility, solicits bids, normally in writing. He will inform each bidder what others have already bid. If more than one owner wants the player and is willing to bid higher to obtain his services, the English auction works in the player's favor. On the other hand, if there is only one real bidder, the English auction can be disastrous for the baseball player, for that bidder will stop raising his offer as soon as competition disappears from the game.

In the baseball free agent auction, ballplayers sometimes compete against each other, for there may be more than one available free agent who meets a particular club's needs. With the leverage reversed, the competing ballplayers might moderate their salary demands to reach a contract price, especially if the buyer club is a pennant contender.

Ballplayers are competitive people on and off the field. They compete with one another to be the highest priced talent. Roger Clemens's contract with Boston on February 15, 1989, set an annual salary record of $2,500,000. It was topped the next day, however, by Orel Hershiser's contract with Los Angeles at $2,633,333 per season. Both players were then bested after the 1989 season by pitchers Bret Saberhagen ($2,966,667) with Kansas City, Mark Langston ($3,250,000) with California, Mark Davis ($3,250,000) with Kansas City, and Dave Stewart ($3,550,000) with Oakland. Albert Belle's 1996 free agent contract with the White Sox allowed him to test the free agent market during a one-month window period after the 1998 season, but only if he were no longer among the highest paid players in the game. Belle took advantage of this option, as we will see.

Clubs and fans are often disappointed with the performance of the free agents whose services are purchased at auction. Steven E. Landsburg, in *The Armchair Economist: Economics and Everyday Life*, offers an explanation of why buyers at auction may be dissatisfied with their purchases: "Most things in life don't turn out as well as you thought they would." Club owners do not court free agents at random. Based on their experience (or the experience of their "baseball people"), they seek to acquire someone they expect to be among the very best, or certainly among the best available at a certain pay level, at doing what the owner needs—pitching, hitting, catching, and fielding. A team signs the free agent with inflated expectations about his future performance. Since the owner expects only excellence, and since ballplayers, like everyone else, are sometimes excellent and sometimes not, the owner is likely to be disappointed. The fans expect miracles from high-priced talent, but only one club can win the World Series each year, and many clubs acquire free agents each year. As with choosing a partner in marriage, Landsburg reminds us, "the one who seems the perfect match is the one whose flaws you are most likely to have overlooked."

The 1998 Auction Season

In the weeks following the close of the 1998 season, fans were provided with a public display of the free agent auction unparalleled in major league baseball history. Major stars were in the marketplace, including three of the game's premier hitters—the Yankees' Bernie Williams, the Red Sox' Mo Vaughn, the White Sox' Albert Belle—and two of baseball's finest starting pitchers—the Padres' Kevin Brown and the Astros' Randy Johnson. The hitters were the first to take center stage.

We have described the Red Sox soap opera starring Mo Vaughn in Chapter 5. Although not a disaster of Ruthian proportions, the Sox' inept handling of negotiations with its prized first baseman, the best player at his position in the game, drove him to Anaheim and a huge payday—$80,000,000 over six years. The Sox' last act in its aborted dance with Tom Reich, Vaughn's talented agent, was to refuse the player's request for a no-trade provision. Although the club wanted Vaughn to accept less money than he could obtain elsewhere, it was unwilling to assure him that the club would keep him in a Red Sox uniform at that lower price. This was either remarkably incompetent bargaining or, more likely, a deliberate design to remove Mo Vaughn's salary from the Boston payroll.

The Yankees followed a similar negotiating approach with their center fielder, Bernie Williams, who had impressed jaded New York fans and opposing pitchers with his cool reserve, sure-handed fielding, and steady bat. The Yankees front office scoffed at the demands made by Williams's bright and brash agent, Scott Boras. In mid-November 1998, the club offered Williams a five-year, $60,000,000 contract. The Yankees seemed destined to lose its treasured center fielder.

Nineteen ninety-eight would turn out to be a "career year" for agent Scott Boras. It began before spring training, when the Cardinals signed Boras's rookie client, J. D. Drew. It would end in early December, when he negotiated baseball's first $100,000,000 contract. Boras had predicted that Bernie Williams would be this premier nine-figure ballplayer, and, as was his customary tactic, he declined the Yankees' $60,000,000 offer. At the close of the regular baseball season and the commencement of the baseball free agent season, Boras went shopping for another buyer for Williams's services. He eventually found two clubs willing to offer Williams guaranteed money and a seven-year contract.

With almost a quarter-century of experience in the free agent market, the Yankees were not going to let a sports agent embarrass the club into upping its offer to Williams. Seeking a viable "no-agreement alterna-tive," the New York club went shopping for a potential replacement for Williams. Albert Belle could provide power in the middle of the Yan-kees' batting order, replacing Williams, although many had raised con-cerns about his temperament. And while Belle's fielding had improved, it paled in comparison to Williams's Gold Glove performance.

Yankees manager Joe Torre played golf with Belle on November 16, 1998, and ceremoniously announced to the press that he would wel-come him as a very acceptable addition to the Yankees family. George Steinbrenner seemed amenable to Belle's salary demands, and Brian Cashman, the Yankees' general manager, was impressed with Belle's demeanor. The Yankees were prepared to offer Belle a four-year, $52,000,000 deal, a 30 percent increase over his contract with the White Sox. Yankee management also inquired about lesser (and cheaper) stars who could fill the center field gap, including Montreal's Rondell White and Anaheim's Jim Edmonds, both of whom might be acquired by trade, and the Cardinals' Brian Jordan, an unsigned free agent. Now the Yankees believed they had others options in dealing with Bernie Williams.

Boras would not be deterred, however. He bragged that he had mul-tiple bids in hand for Williams that exceeded the Yankees' bid. The Ari-zona Diamondbacks, managed by Williams's former Yankees mentor, Buck Showalter, showed interest. On November 11, Boras and Dia-mondbacks' owner Jerry Colangelo reached an understanding that it would take an eight-year, $100,000,000 deal to sign Williams, but no for-mal offer was made. (The Diamondbacks later landed Randy Johnson, the "Big Unit," a fearsome left-hander, with a $52,400,000 contract cov-ering four years. Johnson, who might have earned more elsewhere, chose the Arizona offer to be near his Phoenix-area home. The Dia-mondbacks also gave Johnson use of a luxury box and two season tick-ets for the Colangelo-owned Phoenix Suns.)

Steinbrenner thought Boras was bluffing and challenged him to pro-duce the details of any rival offers. Boras produced more than details; late in the negotiating game, he played his trump card. The eager, often-burned Boston Red Sox, resigned to the loss of Mo Vaughn, were salivating at the thought of Williams patrolling center field in Fenway

Park against the club's historic rival, the Yankees. The Red Sox were serious, and this time they would not be labeled inept. On November 23, 1998, they offered Williams a seven-year, $91,500,000 deal.

The Yankees' other no-agreement options then began to disappear. The woebegone Montreal Expos demanded four top Yankees minor league prospects in a trade for Rondell White, too much talent in the Yankees' estimation. Free agent Brian Jordan signed with the Atlanta Braves, and the Angels demanded Yankees pitcher Andy Pettitte for Jim Edmonds, again too high a price for the New Yorkers to pay. The Yankees were left with Albert Belle as their only real alternative to Williams.

The 1998 free agent auction ended with fireworks. Although willing to play the auction game, Bernie Williams did not want to desert the Yankees, his employer throughout his professional career. His image as a steadfast and loyal chevalier proved genuine. After receiving Boston's offer, he asked to meet with George Steinbrenner for one last discussion and did so in Tampa on November 24, 1998. That afternoon, during the meeting with Boras and Williams, Cashman's beeper went off. It reported bad news. The Baltimore Orioles, another avid division rival, were showing serious interest in signing Albert Belle, the Yankees' only remaining alternative to Williams. Around midnight, Cashman called Belle's agent, Arn Tellem, and offered to sign his client to a five-year, $60,000,000 deal.

The next morning at around 11 A.M., Cashman and Belle spoke. Belle said he would sign with New York if they altered their offer from $12,000,000 a year for five years to $13,000,000 a year for four years. Cashman thought this would work and consulted with Steinbrenner, who agreed. Cashman called Belle's agent, but he could tell that Tellem was having second thoughts. Something was going on.

At 1 P.M. on the afternoon of November 25, 1998, Williams telephoned Cashman to see whether Steinbrenner's position had changed. It had not, but it soon would. By 2 P.M. the Yankees had learned that the Orioles, in fact, had offered Belle a five-year, $65,000,000 contract, which matched the Yankees' annual salary figure offer, but extended it for another guaranteed year. The Yankees quickly made a prospect-filled offer to Montreal for Rondell White, but sensing they were in a strong bargaining position, the Expos demanded even more in exchange. The Yankees had lost all of their no-agreement alternatives.

It was time for the Yankees to make a deal for their center fielder. Williams had made it plain to Cashman that he "just wanted to be a Yankee." At this point in the auction, the Yankees just wanted him. Three hours after learning of the Orioles' offer to Belle, the Yankees offered Williams a seven-year, $87,500,000 contract, an 46 percent increase in the club's initial offer. The deal contained an eighth-year option that, if exercised by the Yankees, would bring the value of the entire contract to $99,000,000. In the end, it took twenty minutes to negotiate the final contract. Steinbrenner had capitulated, but agent Boras had not quite lifted his client to the $100,000,000 plateau.

It seems that at first the Red Sox had ended up the big losers in the 1998 auction. They lost Mo Vaughn and failed to sign Bernie Williams. It was the latest in a long series of Boston marketplace fiascoes. In earlier years, they had lost Carlton Fisk, Fred Lynn, and Roger Clemens. The media scoffed at the Red Sox' claims that free agent Jose Offerman would provide the punch needed to propel the Bosox back into the playoffs. Whether a matter of luck or design, however, the Red Sox club stayed in contention.

The Yankees' delay in signing Williams had proven costly. In the 1997–98 off-season, they had offered him a five-year, $37,500,000 deal, but he wanted a seven-year, $70,000,000 deal. Had the Yankees met this salary request before the free agency auction began, they could have secured their finest player at a much lower annual price without the Sturm und Drang of the 1998 auction. The 1998 free agent auction of Bernie Williams cost the Yankees $17,500,000 over Williams's earlier demand. In the end, however, the Yankees retained, although at a higher cost, all the stars who made the 1998 championship season so memorable and once again prevailed in the World Series.

Scott Boras was not done, however, and his final deal would set free agency records for 1998. He represented the Padres' thirty-three-year-old pitching star Kevin Brown. Brown had led the Florida Marlins with a 16–8 record and a 2.69 ERA in the club's 1997 World Series championship campaign. The following season, Brown led the San Diego Padres to the National League pennant with an 18–7 record and a 2.38

ERA. On December 12, 1998, he agreed to a seven-year, $105,000,000 contract with the Los Angeles Dodgers. His $15,000,000 average annual salary topped the 1998 auction price list.

Rupert Murdoch's Dodgers will pay Kevin Brown more money than it would cost to purchase many major league franchises. Brown earns over $400,000 per game. Over 17,000 fans will have to show up at Dodger Stadium every time he pitches just to pay his salary. The Dodgers had to outbid the Rockies, Cardinals, Orioles and Padres to sign Brown, and it sweetened the deal with a no-trade clause and twelve round-trip flights a year between Macon, Georgia, and Burbank Airport, aboard the Dodgers' private jet, for his family.

Sandy Alderson, baseball's vice president of operations, castigated the Dodgers for the Brown signing: "This is an affront to baseball. This just accentuates the problems we've been talking about, the disparity between small-market and large-market teams. Now everyone can see [it] in vivid color." Although Alderson's assessment may have been correct, the Dodgers' deal reflected the economic realities of the free agent auction. George Steinbrenner did not share Alderson's concerns, however: "The last time I checked," he commented, "we were still operating under a democracy, a free-market system. We aren't socialists in baseball, and I won't be the one to recommend that we become socialists." Steinbrenner said he was "not convinced baseball fans want parity."

An Analysis of the 1998 Auction

In 1998 Mets catcher Mike Piazza's multiyear contract at $13,000,000 a season set a record—but it lasted less than two months. Mo Vaughn replaced it at $13,300,000 a year, but that record was short-lived as well. Rupert Murdoch, the Dodgers' new owner, thought he had bought a pennant for Dodger blue with his acquisition of Kevin Brown at $15,000,000 a year. For sure, he had agreed to pay his new number-one pitcher at a record level.

The 1998 free agent auction was baseball's largest bender since Candy Cummings invented the curve ball in the nineteenth century. Club owners proved beyond any doubt that competition would drive up the price of valuable, unique personnel. Club after club had misjudged the upward trend in the marketplace, and it cost them in terms of either the talent they lost or the salaries of players they signed. Within one ten-day period, baseball clubs that played in the free agent auction had committed themselves to more than a half-billion dollars in guaranteed player contracts.

Although the 1998 free agency auction commanded much public attention, it was merely the preamble to the 1999 and 2000 free agent spectacle. The Class of 2000 is particularly notable: Ken Griffey, Jr., and Alex Rodriquez are likely to top the $20,000,000 a year mark. Other potential free agents stars include Chipper Jones, Craig Biggio, Mike Mussina, Andy Pettitte, and Mark McGwire. In retrospect, the high-priced deals of the 1998 auction may look more like steals.

The Impact of Free Agency

There can be little question that the advent of free agency has dramatically increased the salaries these premier young athletes can demand for their services. It has benefited both the stars of the game and the day-to-day players, and has affected the salaries of players not yet eligible for free agency. Free agent salaries also have an impact on salary arbitration awards, especially for players with four or five years of major league service.

Economists insist that a change in price is neither good nor bad; the only issue, they argue, is whether it is efficient. The price for a ballplayer's services has certainly changed. That in itself is neither good nor bad, but is it efficient? The change in negotiating rules resulted from the unionization of the players and the efforts of their relentless leadership to bring equity to the game—at least in terms of sharing the wealth the enterprise produced. Free agency resulted from a labor arbitration decision followed by collective bargaining between the owners and the players association. The price escalation for premier free agents, however, came from the conduct of the owners themselves. If they complain about the salaries of the elite ballplayers—and they do—they have no one to blame but themselves.

Since 1976, club owners' bids for eligible free agents have continued to climb. Unless proven otherwise, we must assume the amounts the owners pay reflect their individual preferences. They are willing to pay, and the players are willing to receive the pay. Economists would conclude that these are efficient bargains.

Are free agents profitable for management? Some are; others are not. In either case, we should not care, since all businesses involve risk. Nothing is a sure thing. Even Sandy Koufax got knocked out of the box on some occasions, albeit few. We have to assume that owners are rational economic actors, even if they have lost the absolute power they used to exercise.

A much better question to ask is whether free agent signings make the participants happier. Presumably, the players are thrilled to accept the largesse, and the owners are pleased with their new "possessions." But would the owners be happier if they had to pay less money? Certainly, and the players would be less happy with less money, but that does not mean that the deals that are made do not produce mutual happiness. When individuals act rationally within a competitive free market, outcomes are efficient and maximize happiness. In other words, there are no "unexploited opportunities" that could improve everybody's level of satisfaction.

And what about the fans? We are not pleased to pay higher prices for admission to the games, and management is quick to blame the players for these increases, although the empirical evidence is to the contrary. Player salaries escalate after ticket prices increase, not before. A day at the ballpark remains the least expensive form of sports entertainment, and the major leagues continue to set attendance records. More than 70,000,000 fans attend major league games each year. The clubs that sign the better ballplayers attract the most fans. There are few complaints raised about the money spent by winning ball clubs to bring better performers to town.

Is free agency desirable? We can list its benefits, both proven and assumed. Baseball is no longer the province of one-team dynasties. Clubs ready to commit the financial resources needed to play in the free agent auction can compete for the championship. Free agency has produced winners and losers based on baseball acumen and skillful bargaining. For those who have prevailed, the modern business of baseball has proven to be a bonanza. For those who have struck out, the game remains, as always, a frustrating experience.

Loyalty is a two-way street.

TONY GWYNN

Player Attitude and Disloyalty

Mark McGwire's home run power, genuine humility, and personal flaws made him the quintessential modern baseball hero at the turn of the millennium. (Eliot Schecter/Allsport)

After more than two decades of stunning salary increases for star base-ball players, fans may have become numb to the titanic numbers. After a while, a fan who might earn $35,000 a year remains unaffected by an extra million here, an extra two million there. He or she does care, how-ever, when each year there are different players suited up in the home team jerseys. What happened to last year's heroes? What happened to team loyalty?

Tony Gwynn, the San Diego Padres center fielder, is the notable exception to the rule of player mobility, for he has spent his entire eighteen-year career with a single club. Gwynn surpassed the 3,000-hit milestone during the 1999 season, the first player in the National League to do so since Lou Brock in 1979. When asked whether he intended to finish his career with San Diego, Gwynn responded that it all depended on the club's wishes: "They got to want you. You got to want to stay. I think they know where I'm coming from. I'm not sure where they're coming from." Life in the major leagues is always uncer-tain, even for true superstars like Tony Gwynn.

Tony Gwynn has served as a fine role model for American youngsters, but not all his fellow ballplayers have followed his lead. Baseball fans are peeved by what they perceive as the ungrateful attitudes of some of these well-paid athletes. Churlish behavior by players on and off the field is disgraceful. Fans wonder why these selfish, wealthy young men do not seem appreciative of the opportunity given them. They spit at umpires, ignore young fans' requests for autographs, and fill the criminal blotters with arrests for disorderly conduct or drug abuse. Then, to add insult to the abundant injury suffered by the fans, when players become free agents, they leave town. They may consent to stay with their home clubs, but only if they meet their salary demands. If other teams make a better offer, they pack up and leave their teammates and loyal devotees. Even if the marketplace justifies the players' high salaries, fans see player atti-tude and demeanor as atrocious and unacceptable. Whatever happened to the baseball heroes who were our champions?

The facts belie the public perception, however. In many ways, more ballplayers are involved in public service today than ever in the history of the sport. The great modern baseball role model is a telegenic, red-haired All-American hero—Mark McGwire. He donates $1,000,000 a year to his Foundation for Children, which provides assistance for abused children. He says, "I'd rather be associated with something I'm doing for my foundation than as a baseball player." At times, Big Mac seems to be just a happy kid enjoying a great game of ball. A divorced dad who has gone through counseling, he has provided therapy for the American spirit. He and the equally magnetic Dominican, the Cubs' Sammy Sosa, held the sporting public transfixed through the 1998 season as they assaulted the major league home run mark.

Mark McGwire grew up in California, and, legend has it, he hit a home run in his first plate appearance in Little League. He attended the University of Southern California for three years. After two years in the minors, McGwire exploded on the major league scene in 1987, becoming the first player in history to hit thirty or more home runs in each of his first four seasons. After a slump in the early 1990s, McGwire returned to form and became the first player to hit more than fifty home runs in three consecutive seasons. A reluctant hero, McGwire has a genuineness that shines through each public appearance.

McGwire's 1998 performance was awesome. Surpassing Roger Maris's mark of sixty-one home runs set in 1961—a record that had lasted longer than the Babe's sixty home run mark set in 1927—McGwire electrified America's baseball audience. Commissioner Bart Giamatti wrote, "Baseball is about going home and how hard it is to get there." We found in Mark McGwire a hero for our times, who brought us home with every blast.

Divorced in 1991, McGwire almost lost his game that season, batting .201. But he recovered from the trauma and stayed close to his son Matt, who followed his father around the league as the Cardinals' bat boy. At six-foot five, 250 pounds, McGwire is an authentic figure of power. Roger Angell aptly described his "massive, gauntleted arms . . . opening eloquently after his swing and the bat dropping from his left hand and his gaze tilted upward toward the rising and departing ball."

McGwire charmed us all with his honesty and humility. He could say, after he achieved the unthinkable mark of seventy home runs on the last day of the season, "I am in awe of myself." We bought his comments as a candid self-evaluation by a man who carries on the great traditions of the game.

In 1997, Oakland shipped McGwire to St. Louis. Did that hurt the sport? For his 1998 efforts for the Cardinals, he was paid almost $9,000,000, including a significant attendance bonus for bringing fans into Busch Stadium. Obviously, one club's loss was another's distinct gain. McGwire acknowledged that he used a dietary supplement, androstenedione, allowed under major league rules but banned in some other sports. Did that make him a miscreant worthy of public scorn? Flawed yet talented, McGwire presents the paradigm of the human side of modern professional baseball, of those players who play for pay.

McGwire's performance on the economic diamond and the prospect that he will reap even greater financial rewards when his contract expires in 2000 (if he does not exercise his option for an additional year) make him an appropriate subject in our study of baseball's economics. He will join other baseball superstars for the next round of the free agent auction at a time when it is likely that a $100,000,000 contract will seem like a bargain. With the infusion of seemingly limitless financial resources into the national game by cash-rich corporate conglomerates, there appears to be no end in sight, much like a McGwire home run that heads out over the outfield wall, disappearing from view.

Angels Dancing on the Head of a Pinstripe

Although we like to think otherwise, baseball players have never been saints. During the first hundred years of the professional game, ball clubs were filled with sinners and knaves, nasty, dirty players, and low-life characters who happened to have the talent to play baseball. Players drank, smoked, caroused, and overindulged in alcohol, not milk. Some reported to play while still intoxicated. In 1889 A. G. Spalding's *Guide* declared that "the two great obstacles in the way of success of the majority of professional ballplayers" were the saloon and the brothel. The off-field escapades of ballplayers are legendary. A *Sporting Life* editorial in 1911 bemoaned the "demoralization" of the game, saying that players have

> too much idle time, too much hero worship, too much automobiling, too
> much "joy-riding," too much high living—all the result of the exceeding
> prosperity that has favored base ball in recent years to the great financial

benefit of the player; a small, but potential, minority of whom have lacked the character and disposition to bear their honors meekly and to accept their good fortune with gratitude and discretion.

On the field, contemptible players like Ty Cobb would just as soon cut an opponent with a spikes-high slide as make it safely home. To Cobb, sportsmanship was a noble virtue displayed only by losers. True Christian athletes, like the New York Giants' divine Christy Mathewson, and gentlemen, like the Pirates' Honus Wagner, were notable because they were the exceptions.

Yet despite the reality of the sport's unseemliness, Americans have always idolized their baseball heroes as the embodiment of national values. Spalding extolled the virtues promoted by the commercial amusement and those who played the game:

> I claim that Base Ball owes its prestige as our National Game to the fact that as no other form of sport it is the exponent of American Courage, Confidence, Combativeness; American Dash, Discipline, Determination; American Energy, Eagerness, Enthusiasm; American Pluck, Persistence, Performance; American Spirit, Sagacity, Success; American Vim, Vigor, Virility.

At the opening of the Hall of Fame Museum in Cooperstown, Commissioner Kenesaw Mountain Landis declared that the shrine was dedicated to "lovers of good sportsmanship, healthy bodies, [and] clean minds." He was only expressing what people believed to be the case, which is why the Black Sox scandal of 1919 had presented such a threat to the baseball enterprise. It seemed as though the American trinity of baseball, apple pie, and motherhood would be corrupted into bedlam, sour mash, and prostitution. To maintain its public legitimacy, the magnates willingly ceded absolute authority over the operation of their business venture to the officious Landis, who would rule with an iron fist for decades until his death.

The Seamy Underbelly

New York Yankees pitcher Jim Bouton, in his memorable exposé *Ball Four*, revealed what the insiders already knew well—that baseball players are not choir boys. Bouton's disclosures about Mickey Mantle and

Billy Martin (both of whom later died as a result of damage caused by their alcohol addiction) provoked real consternation among the old guard of the game. Bouton was banned from the Yankees' old-timers' games for twenty-five years. The truth was out of the beer bottle, however.

The fans have good reason to conclude that some of today's ballplayers lack the basic moral virtues that Landis claimed for the sport. In *Legal Bases*, I documented stories of the use of illegal drugs by young men suddenly enriched by baseball's new salary structure. The media regularly reports the off-field antics of players. It is the on-field behavior, however, that seems more troubling. The 1996 Robby Alomar–John Hirschbeck spitting incident provides a perfect case study.

Near the close of the 1996 regular season, the Baltimore Orioles' outstanding second baseman, Roberto Alomar, protested vehemently when umpire John Hirschbeck rang him up on a called third strike. Hirschbeck apparently said something that Alomar found offensive, and the All-Star spit in his face. Alomar then added insult to injury, accusing the umpire of being unbalanced since the death of his eight-year-old son, who had suffered from a brain disease. Fans may forget the aftermath—an apology from the player and his significant donation to the foundation that supports the fight to cure the disease that claimed Hirschbeck's son. They will not forget Alomar's disgusting display, however, what Hall of Famer Joe Morgan called "the most despicable act by a baseball player ever." (Harvard law professor Paul Weiler suggests quite correctly, however, that the Black Sox' fixing of the 1919 World Series was certainly more despicable.)

Professional athletes are now quite wealthy. They have the cash to purchase mind-altering substances more damaging than a mug of beer after a game. Illegal drugs—a scourge across all of American society—have destroyed some wonderful baseball careers. Steve Howe, Dwight Gooden, Darryl Strawberry, and many others sacrificed true greatness on the altar of cocaine.

Throughout the history of the game, some ballplayers have carefully protected their squeaky clean images. In his *Historical Baseball Abstract*, Bill James lists his gentlemen of the game—Honus Wagner, Stan Musial, Christy Mathewson, Lou Gehrig, Walter Johnson, and Mike Schmidt. I would add one more: Cal Ripken, Jr., a ballplayer who does drink milk "straight up" and who showed up to play for the Orioles every day for sixteen straight years. Ripken's foundation underwrites the Learning Center, providing free services to Baltimore residents in reading, writing, and job hunting.

Loyalty

Baseball's special charm comes, in part, from its continuity. The National League has operated continuously (except for labor stoppages) since 1876; the American League since 1901. Today's heroes can be measured against yesterday's giants by comparing their performance statistics. They play basically the same game by the same rules, and they have done so for over a century. Everyone recalls a childhood filled with baseball memories, rooting for their team and for the players who spent their entire careers with that home club. But today's sports pages reveal the sorrowful news of defections—many hometown favorites will don another club's uniform next season in exchange for a large pile of cash. As the Cincinnati Reds' general manager Jim Bowden said: "Given a choice between making a nice living in Cincinnati and a fortune in New York, a baseball player will go after the money every time. Who wouldn't?"

Does the popular belief that players are disloyal reflect the reality of the baseball business? Has loyalty waned in the era of free agency?

Before A. G. Spalding and his fellow magnates installed baseball's reserve system in the late 1870s, ballplayers moved from team to team as their annual contracts expired and sometimes even within the course of a single season. These "revolvers" would change uniforms for a few extra hundred dollars. Despite rules that banned midseason tampering with players under contract, Spalding himself signed a lucrative contract to play the 1876 season with the Chicago club in the middle of his 1875 season with Boston. Player services were for sale until the magnates secured their players within a collusive reserve system and jealously guarded their exclusive right to assign players to other clubs in exchange for players or cash. Under the reserve system, players stayed with their clubs for their entire careers until traded, sold, or released at management's discretion.

The mobility of modern baseball players can be measured statistically, and it does show an increased movement of players between clubs compared with the pre–free agency era. Of the 838 players on the 1998 opening day rosters (which included players on the disabled list), only 111 had been on the same team four years earlier. The 87 percent of players who had changed teams included those who had retired or been released by their clubs, as well as those who had left voluntarily as free agents or had been assigned to another club by way of a trade. By 1998, the Detroit Tigers had no players remaining from their 1994 roster; the Giants, Marlins, and Expos each had but one. For every player who has spent his entire career with a single club—the Orioles' Cal Ripken, Jr., the Twins' Kirby Puckett, and the Padres' Tony Gwynn, are good examples—there are dozens who have moved from team to team, either by choice or by trade. Some are superb talents, such as Rickey Henderson, who has moved between clubs ten times, including four tours with the Oakland A's.

For the 1998 season, there were sixty-one major league players who had moved so often that they had played for the same club on more than one occasion. Mike Morgan, a Twins pitcher for the 1998 campaign, had played for ten teams in seventeen seasons. In moving to the Rangers in 1999, he set a new major league record by playing for his eleventh club. An analysis of the 1998 opening day rosters by *USA Today* showed that a player moved on average every 3.3 seasons, that 60 percent of the players were not with their original teams, and that only half of the players were with their 1997 clubs for the 1998 season.

As noted, there have been player movements between clubs throughout baseball history. However, with the exception of players who took advantage of the rise of rival circuits in 1890 (Players League), 1901–2 (American League), and 1914–15 (Federal League), these moves were all generated by the club owners, who traded or sold the rights to their players. Branch Rickey explained the process:

> With the [Cardinals] always finishing at the bottom of the pennant race, it was not to our advantage to sell the one or two stars on the team. The headliners were about the only incentive for the handful of fans to turn out to see a Cardinals game. Nevertheless, when you have something that the other fellow wants, you are broke, and he tantalizingly dangles a gigantic roll

of folding money before your eyes, offering the sum for what you have—
well, you are first tempted, and then you finally relent and sell.

Connie Mack's periodic dismantling of the Philadelphia Athletics for
purely financial reasons was only the most extreme example of owner
infidelity: In 1914, he sold Eddie Collins to the White Sox for $50,000;
in 1916, he sold Frank "Home Run" Baker to the Yankees for $35,000;
in 1932, he sold Al Simmons to the White Sox for $150,000; in 1933, he
sold Lefty Grove to the Red Sox for $125,000 and Mickey Cochrane to
the Tigers for $100,000; and in 1935, he sold Jimmy Foxx to the Red
Sox for $150,000.

The most infamous of player trades and sales continue to haunt the
psyches of loyal fans decades later. In 1920, the Boston Red Sox sold
Babe Ruth, already the game's greatest slugger, to the hated New York
Yankees for $125,000 and a $300,000 loan secured by a mortgage on
Fenway Park. The "Curse of the Bambino" followed Red Sox loyalists
for the remainder of the century; the club has not won another World
Series. Some trades were even more heartless. In 1934, Washington
Senators owner Clark Griffith sold his manager and star shortstop, Joe
Cronin, who was also his son-in-law, to the Boston Red Sox for
$225,000.

Perhaps the most famous baseball trade took place in 1926, when the
Cardinals traded Rogers Hornsby to the Giants for Frankie Frisch.
Frisch had challenged the authority of Giants manager John J.
McGraw, and Hornsby, the Cardinals' player-manager who had just
guided the club to a World Series victory, had a feud with club owner
Sam Breadon. Hornsby, who was the National League's biggest star
since Honus Wagner, stayed only a year in New York, moving on to the
Boston Braves for a year and then to the Chicago Cubs, but Frisch com-
pleted his Hall of Fame career with the Cardinals.

The Yankees franchise has always been particularly adept at acquiring players of stellar caliber to staff its pennant-winning clubs. As a
wealthy team, it has also had the funds to make the purchases. In addition to "Home Run" Baker and Babe Ruth, the Yankees acquired brilliant Hall of Fame pitchers through trade and purchase: Waite Hoyt in
1920, Herb Pennock in 1923, Lefty Gomez in 1929, and Red Ruffing
in 1930.

Perhaps the worst trade ever made occurred in 1900, when the New York Giants exchanged fading star pitcher Amos Rusie for Cincinnati's untested Christy Mathewson. Rusie, "the Hoosier Thunderbolt," had won 246 games as the game's premier hurler in the 1890s, but he would not win another major league game. Mathewson, on the other hand, would go on to win 373 games for the New Yorkers over a seventeen-year, Hall of Fame career.

Some baseball clubs have developed what Eric Leifer calls a "transaction relation," exchanging players annually. For example, starting in 1971, the Chicago Cubs and the Oakland Athletics made nineteen trades, at least one a year for nine consecutive years. Beginning in 1969, the St. Louis Cardinals and the San Diego Padres made fifteen trades, at least one a year for ten years. By comparison, other clubs maintain an "avoidance relation." For example, although the Yankees organization acquired players by purchase and trade with most clubs, it did not deal with the Detroit Tigers, the Cleveland Indians, or the Chicago White Sox for most of the century. Similarly, the Chicago Cubs and the New York Giants avoided transactions.

The career of Charlie Hayes, a journeyman infielder best remembered for catching the final out in the Yankees' 1996 World Series victory, offers a perfect example of how a solid, but not superstar, player may move between clubs. Drafted originally by the San Francisco Giants, Hayes moved between major league clubs four times by trade, twice as a free agent, and once in an expansion draft. He has played for the Giants twice, the Phillies twice, and the Yankees three times. Only two of the reassignments were at his behest. Hayes was not disloyal; rather, he was good enough to be traded, but not good enough to keep.

Bill Veeck, perhaps the most "pro-player" owner in the history of the game, explained the "kick" he received from a trade's "back-scene, front-office maneuvering." He professed to like ballplayers as friends and heroes, yet when it came to making trades, he found himself "depersonalizing them, maybe even dehumanizing them. I find myself looking upon them, of necessity, as currency, as a means of exchange." However, although he wanted to, even Veeck could not trade Cleveland's favorite, his player-manager Lou Boudreau. After the 1947 season, the Cleveland press accurately reported that Veeck was discussing a major trade, including Boudreau, with the St. Louis Browns. The Cleveland fans erupted in public demonstrations. The *Cleveland News* printed a ballot on its front page, and 100,000 fans voted 9–1 in favor of extending Boudreau's managerial tenure. Veeck relented, signed Boudreau to a two-year contract, and looked like a genius when Boudreau led the Tribe to the 1948 World Championship, its last World Series victory.

George Steinbrenner has compared the current state of baseball free agency to college sports, and it is not a far-fetched analogy. Amateur student-athletes are eligible for only four years of college play. Many premier basketball players turn professional after one or two seasons of college ball, yet despite this built-in turnover in team personnel, college sports continue to thrive. According to Steinbrenner, baseball can prosper as well with similar player turnover.

When an owner trades a player, fans are told the decision was motivated by a desire to improve the club. This may be the case when the team receives valuable players in return; sometimes promises come true. But this would not justify the sale of a player's contract rights for cash, however, which enriches the owner (or help him pay his bills) and provides no benefit to the fans unless the funds are used to acquire or retain other talent. Traditionally, small-market or poorly operated franchises would market their players in this way to reduce their payrolls and enhance their profits.

The crux of the problem with modern player-initiated player movement is that it is motivated by a desire to benefit not the home club but the personal circumstances of the free agent, although not necessarily just his salary. He may be fleeing an intolerable employment situation, for example, or his club may have no interest in re-signing him. Unaware of all the factors involved, fans might see a player's desire to move as simply the product of his selfish disloyalty to his team and its fans.

Many things have changed since Honus Wagner turned down Clark Griffith's 1901 cash offer of $20,000 to jump to the new Washington Nationals franchise in the American League. Wagner later said: "I may have lost a lot of money by it, but I feel much happier and satisfied for having stayed in Pittsburg. . . . I loved my team and associations. They meant much more to me than money." Over the century that followed, the clubs and players have changed, and so too has the business of baseball.

What Price Loyalty?

Wayne Huizenga's postseason marketing of his 1997 World Series champion Florida Marlins players ranks as the most remarkable house-cleaning in baseball history. To cut his payroll in order to sell his club, Huizenga dispersed his stars around the major leagues in exchange for low-priced junior performers and prospects. Of his nine-man championship starting lineup, only three remained in Marlins teal by the end of the 1998 season—shortstop Edgar Renteria, second baseman Craig Counsell, and star hurler Livan Hernandez. Counsell had scored the winning run in the seventh game of the 1997 World Series, knocked in by Renteria. Renteria, who had become eligible for salary arbitration following the 1998 season, was then traded by Florida to St. Louis, and Counsell was released on June 11, 1999. Hernandez, named the Most Valuable Player of the 1997 World Series, was traded to the San Francisco Giants on July 24, 1999. All the big names of the World Series championship year were now gone—Moises Alou, Bobby Bonilla, Kevin Brown, Jeff Conine, Charles Johnson, Al Leiter, Robb Nen, Gary Sheffield, and Devon White—over $60,000,000 in payroll costs. (After the Hernandez trade, one wag on ESPN commented that the only one left from the 1997 championship team was the bat boy.) This unprecedented display of disloyalty to the fans of southern Florida apparently made good business sense in the short run for a man who had made his first millions in waste disposal.

A Single Team: The 1998 World Champions

Baseball players are members of a team that wins or loses games. Modern clubs are assembled through a combination of the amateur draft, trades, and free agent signings. Let us consider how one club was assembled in one last look at the remarkable 1998 New York Yankees.

The Yankees' World Series roster of twenty-five players consisted of eight free agents, thirteen players acquired by trade, and four drafted players. Five of the eight free agents were nondrafted free agents who had signed their first professional contract with the Yankees and thus were similar in status to those acquired through the amateur draft. The 1998 starting lineup included the following:

First base: Tino Martinez, acquired in a trade with Seattle for Sterling Hitchcock in 1995, as the replacement for the retired fan favorite Don Mattingly.

Second base: Chuck Knoblauch, acquired in a trade with Minnesota for minor league prospects plus $3,000,000 in cash on December 7, 1997.

Shortstop: Derek Jeter, drafted as the sixth pick overall in the first round of the amateur draft in June 1992.

Third base: Scott Brosius, the 1998 World Series MVP, acquired in a trade with Oakland for pitcher Kenny Rogers and cash consideration on February 6, 1998.

Left field: Tim Raines, acquired in a trade with the Chicago White Sox for a minor league pitcher on January 23, 1996. (The Yankees also used three other players in left field: Chad Curtis, Ricky Ledee, and Shane Spencer. Curtis was acquired by trade; Ledee and Spencer were Yankees draft choices.)

Center field: Bernie Williams, acquired as a nondrafted free agent in 1985.

Right field: Paul O'Neill, acquired in a trade with Cincinnati for outfielder Roberto Kelly on November 3, 1992.

Catcher: Joe Girardi, acquired in a trade with Colorado for two minor league pitchers on November 20, 1995. (Jorge Posada, signed as a nondrafted free agent in 1991, platooned behind the plate to catch David Wells and Orlando Hernandez, while Girardi caught David Cone and Andy Pettitte.)

Starting pitchers: David Wells, signed as a free agent on December 19, 1996; David Cone, acquired in a trade with Toronto for three minor league pitchers on July 28, 1996; Andy Pettitte, drafted in the twenty-eighth round of the amateur draft in June 1990; and Orlando Hernandez, signed as a nondrafted free agent on March 7, 1998, after his fabled raft escape from Cuba.

Closer: Mariano Rivera, signed as a nondrafted free agent on February 17, 1990.

The Yankees squad was typical of that of other major league clubs, except for the fact, of course, that it was so remarkably successful. Most everyday players were acquired by trade, an occasional star was signed through free agency, and a few were developed through the club's farm system.

Achieving Loyalty

How then should the game enhance player loyalty and stability? Like much else in the business of baseball, loyalty is a matter of economics. In almost every situation, a club owner can keep a free agent by paying him enough money, although it might not make good business sense to do so. Randy Johnson may have wanted to play close to his home in Arizona when he signed with the Diamondbacks, but had the Astros offered to double the salary the Arizona club would provide, the star pitcher might have waited a few years before returning home. Will owners pay for loyalty? Only if they think it will pay off in attendance and team success, which in turn increase the gate and the value of the franchise.

A useful measure of the importance of player loyalty is the marketplace. Would fans pay a surcharge to attend games if they were assured that the same players would appear on the diamond year after year? If loyalty is commercially valuable, who should bear the price? Should the player be expected to accept a lower salary to stay with a club, and, if so, why?

The Yankees followed their 1998 record performance with a dedicated effort to re-sign virtually all the club's players eligible for free agency. Observers thought that George Steinbrenner had learned that loyalty was a two-way street. If he was loyal to his players and paid them at competitive salaries, they would remain loyal to the Yankees. In February 1999, however, just as his pitchers and catchers were set to report to the Yankees' spring training complex in Tampa, Steinbrenner stunned New York fans by trading their beloved starter David Wells to the Toronto Blue Jays in exchange for arguably the game's finest hurler, Roger Clemens, the five-time winner of the Cy Young Award. (I learned of the trade while hearing the salary arbitration dispute between John Hudek and the Cincinnati Reds. Reds general manager Jim Bowden's beeper went off and a broad smile came over his face. I inquired as to the message, and he reported the Clemens trade. Bowden was thrilled because he had feared that Clemens would anchor the Houston Astros' pitching staff—a club in the same division as Bowden's Reds.)

No one was prouder to be a Yankee than David Wells, who once took the mound wearing a cap actually worn by Babe Ruth. His free spirit had enchanted the New York crowd, and his 1998 perfect game had displayed a virtuosity on the mound that matched his uniquely effusive style. The trade made perfect business and baseball sense, but it reinforced the basic power relationships that still control the game, despite free agency. Players play where owners want them to play.

McGwire and Sosa's Class Act

The other important variable in the movement of players is the disparity in the clubs' financial resources. Clubs like Pittsburgh and Montreal supply players to clubs like the Yankees and the Braves. That, of course, is what always has happened in baseball, long before free agency, when the financially strapped clubs, such as the Kansas City Athletics, served as virtual farm teams for the affluent clubs, such as the Yankees.

A perfect example of player movement motivated by a club's financial concerns was the Oakland A's' midseason trade of Mark McGwire to the St. Louis Cardinals in 1997. The A's knew they would not be able to re-sign their first baseman, whose contract was set to expire at the end of that campaign. The St. Louis club thought it could sign McGwire, and it did.

Mark McGwire's Olympian home run performance in 1998 will long be remembered by fans of the national game. His legend will forever be intertwined with that of his good-natured friend Sammy Sosa, who grew up selling fruit and shining shoes in San Pedro de Macoris in the Dominican Republic in order to support his widowed mother. The pure joy Sosa receives from playing baseball exhilarated the nation: "This is fun," he would say, and it was. Sosa, spreading kisses and tapping his heart, reminded us that this is the greatest game of all.

Sammy Sosa's sixty-six home runs in 1998 made him one of only four major leaguers ever to hit sixty or more homers in a season. In the 1999 repeat of their home run derby, McGwire bested Sosa once again, sixty-five to sixty-three. Could this possibly be an annual event?

McGwire and Sosa—two greats of the modern game, flawed like all their predecessors, but men of our times. Their money pitch was simple: to entertain the fans, which they did with distinction, quality, and class.

TEN

It is not the honor you take with you, but the heritage you leave behind.

BRANCH RICKEY

Conclusion

Baseball's "money pitch" has produced player salaries far higher than Marvin Miller, then executive director of the players association, could ever have imagined in the late 1960s, when he began to forge a genuine trade union out of a fraternal organization. The free market Miller achieved drove free agent salaries to astronomical levels, triggering, in turn, an increase in salary arbitration awards. The union has negotiated minimum guaranteed salaries that are now twenty times what they were in the late 1960s. Even players bound to a single club by the remaining vestige of the reserve system have used negotiation tactics to increase their salaries.

Has this dramatic change in salary levels been good for the game? If this were the union's only "heritage," as Branch Rickey might have said, then it would be subject to legitimate criticism. It certainly has been good for the young men who have been the direct beneficiaries of the new salary system. Owners have rarely suffered in the process, of course. Their franchises have increased in value, although some continue to claim their annual accounts are bathed in red ink. The fans think they have paid some of the freight in terms of increasing ticket prices, although television contracts and other sponsorships have picked up a substantial portion of the higher personnel costs.

Baseball's players union has a much more laudable heritage to leave behind, however, for it has provided the owners' cartel with its first genuine competition. As a countervailing power, the union has worked to improve the terms and conditions of employment for all ballplayers, not just a favored few. It can monitor arbitrary club conduct toward players and seek remedies through arbitration. Through use of its economic power, it can insure that the profits of the game are shared more equitably among those who provided the entertainment.

What the players association cannot do is serve as the fiduciary for the public in protecting the national pastime. It is not elected by its members to serve the public's interest, and it would breach its legal "duty of fair representation" if it were to sacrifice player interests for fan concerns. The club owners claim they represent the traditions of the game. If so, then it is their responsibility to make sure the national pastime provides the kind of entertainment the American public wants and deserves.

An Idyll Respite

Baseball is a substantial entertainment business, increasingly directed to meet the programming needs of global television. At the same time, the game has retained its unique status as an American idyll where spectators come to spend a few pleasant hours diverted from everyday cares. It is difficult to walk the line between being a pastoral pastime and a multibillion-dollar enterprise, but despite its occasional stumbles, baseball has endured and prospered.

The American public's concern with the money paid the entertainers on the diamond (but not on the stage or screen) is based on the essential baseball myth—that with quick hands and good reflexes any of us might have made it to the Big Show. Few of us think we could record a hit song or star in an Academy Award–winning film. More than that, most men who play the game fit within a prevailing myth—they are humble, hard-working "Joes" just like us. Since we do not earn $10,000,000 a year, why should they?

Baseball's "money pitch" and the modern rules of the economic game explain how its players have become wealthy. Like gold miners who reach the mother lode, the players struck it rich, but, unlike prospectors, almost everyone who played at the major league level or owned a major league franchise has shared in the wealth. The story of baseball's money pitch is a story of good fortune, good timing, and great leadership, all revolving around men who play a child's game; it is a story that is uniquely American.

How then do you measure a player's success at this game? Is it based on the amount of money he has earned? The records he has accumulated? The hard work he has put into his career? I would suggest that you measure a player's success by the amount of pleasure he has had from playing the game at the highest level and the amount of pleasure he has brought to us, the fans, who have watched his performance. For many fans, baseball remains America's sport, a source of great contentment and satisfaction.

Notes

Chapter 1

Harold Seymour's classic *Baseball: The Early Years* (1960) remains the standard text on baseball's creation and adolescence. Seymour's work was a critical source for my first book, *Legal Bases: Baseball and the Law* (1998). Chapter 1 of *Legal Bases* focuses on the activities of John Montgomery Ward as well as the formation of the first baseball players' union and the ill-fated Players League. Leonard Koppett's *Concise History of Major League Baseball* (1998) is also a very readable history of the national pastime.

For additional information on the life and times of A. G. Spalding, I recommend Peter Levine's *A. G. Spalding and the Rise of Baseball* (1985). Spalding's own *America's National Game* (1911; reprinted by the University of Nebraska Press, 1992) presents a less objective perspective. Employing the learned and fluid style one has come to expect from a great scholar of constitutional law, Professor Ted White offers a valuable analysis of baseball's golden era in *Creating the National Pastime: Baseball Transforms Itself (1903–1953)* (1996).

Chapter 2

The modern rules for setting player salaries are established by the collective bargaining agreement negotiated by the club owners and the players union. The agreement is available from Major League Baseball and the Major League Baseball Players Association at their offices in New York City. Player salaries are published annually in *USA Today*. Overall, Murray Chass's column in the *New York Times* remains the premier source for information about the business of baseball.

Chapter 3

The literature on both economics and Babe Ruth is vast. I found Steven E. Landsburg's *The Armchair Economist: Economics and Everyday Life* (1993) particularly lucid. The definitive compendium on economics is Richard G. Lipsey, Paul N. Courant, Douglas D. Purvis, and Peter O. Steiner, *Microeconomics* (10th ed.; 1993). Creamer's *Babe: The Legend Comes to Life* (1974) is a noteworthy retelling of the familiar story of the scamp from Baltimore who changed the national game.

The bibles of game theory remain Howard Raiffa's *The Art and Science of Negotiation* (1982) and Thomas C. Schelling's *The Strategy of Conflict* (1960). The more recent *Game Theory and the Law* (1994), by Douglas G. Baird, Robert H. Gertner, and Randal C. Picker, applies the latest game-theoretical models to the study of law.

Chapter 4

Honus Wagner's remarkable baseball career is well chronicled by Dennis DeValeria and Jeanne Burke DeValeria in *Honus Wager: A Biography* (1998). Data on baseball players and club owners were derived from a variety of sources, including the *New York Times, Boston Globe, Forbes Magazine*, and *USA Today*. A particularly useful new source of information on the business side of sports is *Street & Smith's SportsBusiness Journal*, first published in 1998.

Gerald W. Scully's econometric work, *The Business of Major League Baseball* (1989), provides a fine example of data analysis. Player fringe benefits discussed in this chapter are detailed in baseball's collective bargaining agreement.

Chapter 5

The characters of Roy Hobbs and Pop Fisher are the creation of one of America's great modern authors, Bernard Malamud, in his first novel, *The Natural* (1952). Raiffa's *The Art and Science of Negotiation* (1982) and Schelling's *The Strategy of Conflict* (1960) are the best sources for understanding traditional negotiation strategy. *Getting to Yes: Negotiating Agreement Without Giving In* (1981) by Roger Fisher and William Ury is essential reading for anyone interested in substituting principled for positional bargaining. David Lax and James Sebenius present a thorough account of their theories in *The Manager as Negotiator: Bargaining for Cooperation and Competitive Gain* (1986). The saga of Mo Vaughan and the Red Sox was chronicled almost daily in the sports pages of the *Boston Globe*.

Chapter 6

Al Stump tells the life story of the Georgia Peach in *Cobb: A Biography* (1994). The book should be required reading for any student of baseball history. In fact, it may be baseball's best biography, capturing the exaltation and desolation of one of baseball's most contemptible characters.

Chapter 7

The procedures for salary arbitration are detailed in baseball's collective bargaining agreement. I discussed the process in Chapter 4 of *Legal Bases* (1998) and presented my analysis of it, in particular why certain disputes were not resolved before hearing, at a 1999 sports law symposium held at the University of Chicago Law School.

Chapter 8

The early days of free agency are well described in John Helyar's *Lords of the Realm* (1994). The 1998 soap opera involving the Yankees and Bernie Williams was reported in the *New York Times* by Murray Chass.

Chapter 9

Harvard law professor Paul C. Weiler discusses the implications of shocking on-field and off-field misbehavior by ballplayers in *Leveling the Playing Field* (2000). Weiler is the nation's premier sports law academic, and his latest work contains an abundance of valuable insights into the sports business.

Bibliography

Abrams, Roger I. *Legal Bases: Baseball and the Law.* Philadelphia: Temple University Press, 1998.

Adelman, Melvin L. *A Sporting Time: New York City and the Rise of Modern Athletics, 1820–1870.* Chicago: University of Illinois Press, 1986.

Alexander, Charles C. *Rogers Hornsby: A Biography.* New York: Henry Holt and Company, 1995.

Baird, Douglas G., Robert H. Gertner, and Randal C. Picker. *Game Theory and the Law.* Cambridge, Mass.: Harvard University Press, 1994.

Brasch, Rudolph. *How Did Sports Begin?* New York: David McKay Company, 1970.

Creamer, Robert W. *Babe: The Legend Comes to Life.* New York: Simon & Schuster, 1974.

Davis, Morton D. *Game Theory: A Nontechnical Introduction.* Mineola, N.Y.: Dover Publications, Inc., 1970.

Derks, Scott. *The Value of a Dollar: 1860–1989.* Detroit: Gale Research, 1994.

DeValeria, Dennis, and Jeanne Burke DeValeria. *Honus Wagner: A Biography.* Pittsburgh: University of Pittsburgh Press, 1998.

Dworkin, James B. *Owners Versus Players: Baseball and Collective Bargaining.* Boston: Auburn House Publishing Company, 1981.

Enright, Jim. *Trade Him!: 100 Years of Baseball's Greatest Deals.* Chicago: Follett Publishing Co., 1976.

Fisher, Roger, and William Ury. *Getting to Yes: Negotiating Agreement Without Giving In.* New York: Penguin Books, 1981.

Gorman, Jerry, and Kirk Calhoun. *The Name of the Game: The Business of Sports.* New York: John Wiley & Sons, Inc., 1994.

Gorn, Elliott, and Warren Goldstein. *A Brief History of American Sports.* New York: Hill and Wang, 1993.

Harris, H. A. *Greek Athletes and Athletics*. Westport, Conn.: Greenwood Press, 1964.

Helyar, John. *Lords of the Realm: The Real History of Baseball*. New York: Ballantine Books, 1994.

James, Bill. *The Bill James Baseball Abstract 1988*. New York: Ballantine Books, 1988.

————. *The Bill James Historical Baseball Abstract*. New York: Villard Books, 1986.

Jennings, Kenneth M. *Swings and Misses: Moribund Labor Relations in Professional Baseball*. Westport, Conn.: Praeger Publishers, 1997.

Kirsch, George B. *The Creation of American Team Sports: Baseball and Cricket, 1838–72*. Chicago: University of Illinois Press, 1989.

Koppett, Leonard. *Koppett's Concise History of Major League Baseball*. Philadelphia: Temple University Press, 1998.

Landsburg, Steven E. *The Armchair Economist*. New York: Free Press, 1993.

Lax, David A., and James K. Sebenius. *The Manager as Negotiator: Bargaining for Cooperation and Competitive Gain*. New York: Free Press, 1986.

Leifer, Eric M. *Making the Majors: The Transformation of Team Sports in America*. Cambridge, Mass.: Harvard University Press, 1995.

Levine, Peter. *A. G. Spalding and the Rise of Baseball: The Promise of American Sport*. New York: Oxford University Press, 1985.

Lieb, Frederick G. *The Baseball Story*. New York: G. P. Putnam's Sons, 1950.

Lipsey, Richard G., Paul N. Courant, Douglas D. Purvis, and Peter O. Steiner. *Microeconomics*. 10th Edition. New York: HarperCollins College Publishers, Inc., 1993.

Malamud, Bernard. *The Natural*. New York: Avon Books, 1952.

Markham, Jesse W., and Paul V. Teplitz. *Baseball Economics and Public Policy*. Lexington, Mass.: Lexington Books, 1981.

McCormick, Mark H. *What They Don't Teach You at Harvard Business School: Notes from a Street-Smart Executive*. New York: Bantam Books, 1984.

Monteleone, John J. *Branch Rickey's Little Blue Book*. New York: Macmillan Publishing Co., 1995.

Morris, Desmond. *The Soccer Tribe*. London: Jonathan Cape, 1981.

Polinsky, A. Mitchell. *An Introduction to Law and Economics*. Boston: Little, Brown and Company, 1983.

Pope, S. W. *The New American Sports History*. Chicago: University of Illinois Press, 1997

Raiffa, Howard. *The Art and Science of Negotiation*. Cambridge, Mass.: Harvard University Press, 1982.

―――. *Decision Analysis: Introductory Lectures on Choice Under Uncertainty*. Reading, Mass.: Addison-Wesley Publishing Company, 1968.

Riess, Steven A. *City Games: The Evolution of American Urban Society and the Rise of Sports*. Urbana: University of Illinois Press, 1989.

Sands, Jack, and Peter Gammons. *Coming Apart at the Seams*. New York: Macmillan Publishing Co., 1993.

Schelling, Thomas C. *The Strategy of Conflict*. New York: Oxford University Press, 1960.

Scully, Gerald W. *Advances in the Economics of Sport*. Greenwich, Conn.: JAI Press, 1992.

―――. *The Business of Major League Baseball*. Chicago: University of Chicago Press, 1989.

―――. *The Market Structure of Sports*. Chicago: University of Chicago Press, 1995.

Seymour, Harold. *Baseball: The Early Years*. New York: Oxford University Press, 1960.

―――. *Baseball: The Golden Age*. New York: Oxford University Press, 1971.

―――. *Baseball: The People's Game*. New York: Oxford University Press, 1990.

Skolnik, Richard C. *Baseball and the Pursuit of Innocence: A Fresh Look at the Old Ball Game*. College Station, Tex.: Texas A & M Press, 1994.

Sommers, Paul M. *Diamonds Are Forever: The Business of Baseball*. Washington, D.C.: The Brookings Institution, 1992.

Spalding, Albert Goodwill. *America's National Game*. Lincoln: University of Nebraska Press, 1992

Stump, Al. *Cobb: A Biography*. Chapel Hill, N.C.: Algonquin Books, 1994.

Ury, William. *Getting Past No: Negotiating with Difficult People*. New York: Bantam Books, 1991.

Voight, David Quentin. *American Baseball: From the Gentleman's Sport to the Commissioner System*. University Park: Pennsylvania State University Press, 1983.

Ward, Geoffrey C., and Ken Burns. *Baseball: An Illustrated History*. New York: Alfred A. Knopf, 1994.

Weiler, Paul C. *Leveling the Playing Field*. Cambridge, Mass: Harvard University Press, 2000.

White, G. Edward. *Creating the National Pastime: Baseball Transforms Itself (1903–1953)*. Princeton: Princeton University Press, 1996.

Index